MUSIC THERAPY
for the DEVELOPMENTALLY
DISABLED

Edith Hillman Boxill, C.M.T.

Adjunct Assistant Professor
New York University

Director of Music Therapy
Manhattan Developmental Services

pro·ed

8700 Shoal Creek Boulevard
Austin, Texas 78757

Printed in the United States of America

Library of Congress Cataloging in Publication Data

Boxill, Edith Hillman.
Music therapy for the developmentally disabled.

Includes index.
Bibliography: p. 247
1. Music therapy. 2. Developmentally disabled.
I. Title.
ML3920.B59   1985   615.8'5154   84-15752
ISBN 0-89079-190-2
(formerly 0-89443-555-8)

pro·ed
8700 Shoal Creek Boulevard
Austin, Texas 78757

5   6   7   8   9   10   97   96

Music must serve a purpose; it must
be a part of something larger than
itself, a part of humanity . . .

Pablo Casals

This book is dedicated, with
love and respect,
to

my daughter Emily, her husband Robert, and
their sons Stephen and Jason

my son Paul, his wife Adrienne, and
their daughter Jesse and son Ben

and our aunt Gene

Table of Contents

Foreword

The large, brightly colored room is alive with the sounds of music making. Some of the clients are absorbed in instrument playing, others singing, and one client is animatedly moving to the rhythm of the piano improvisation. The music therapist is sensitively and creatively changing and adapting the music to the responses of the clients as they emerge.

It is in this room at Manhattan Developmental Center, working with hundreds of developmentally disabled people, that Edith Hillman Boxill has developed her theory and approach to music therapy. I have been fortunate over the last ten years to be a frequent observer/participant in these sessions and to have met many of the clients whose lives have been so deeply affected by her work. For me, there is no truer test of an effective approach to music therapy than this. It is from the rich soil of practical experience that this book has grown. It is her long-term experience in music therapy with the developmentally disabled that gives Professor Boxill's book a breadth that is rare in the field.

Professor Boxill has always been committed to sharing her wealth of knowledge generously over the years to develop the profession of music therapy and to further the understanding of the value of this work for the developmentally disabled among our own professionals as well as other mental health professionals. Furthermore, she has devoted a great deal of time to supervising and training music therapy students from the New York University graduate program. *Music Therapy for the Developmentally Disabled* is a natural outgrowth of Professor Boxill's work and reflects her experience and ability to communicate clearly her ideas and feelings about music therapy. Now this very valuable work can be explored by an even wider group of people.

Music Therapy for the Developmentally Disabled is an extensive and useful resource for music therapists and music therapy students, offering a vast amount of very practical and specific information about program planning, assessment, and treatment process. It is not just a "how to" book. Its real strength lies in the fact that the practical suggestions for treatment are accompanied by a strong theoretical rationale as well as process-oriented examples of the application of strategies and techniques. There is tremendous need for a book that offers this type of comprehensive approach to music therapy treatment.

Throughout the book we never lose sight of Professor Boxill's deep appreciation for the uniqueness of each individual or of her understanding of music therapy as a creative process that is always changing and unfolding—a process of aliveness and discovery. *Music Therapy for the Developmentally Disabled* is an inspiration as well as a valuable reference and resource.

Barbara Hesser, C.M.T.
Professor of Music Therapy
New York University

Preface and Opening Notes

As a music therapy practitioner who, for the past ten years, has specialized in the treatment of developmentally disabled persons and as a professor of music therapy at a large university, I have been keenly aware of the necessity for a text that is not only instructional but also serves as a reference and resource for the practice of music therapy with clients so identified. Therefore, at the urging of colleagues, students, and administrators of agencies for the developmentally disabled, I set about assembling much of the material contained in this volume. The catalyst for bringing it to fruition, however, was Mr. R. Curtis Whitesel, the late Editorial Director of Rehabilitation of Aspen Systems Corporation. His invitation to write this book was expressed in these perceptive words: "With growing interest in mental retardation and, more particularly, music therapy, we feel that a solid practitioner's reference/handbook would be a most important contribution to your field."

Music Therapy for the Developmentally Disabled presents an innovative approach to music therapy for persons in the five categories of developmental disabilities—mental retardation, autism, cerebral palsy, epilepsy, and other neurological impairment—with the main concentration on subcategories of mental retardation. The term *developmental disability* denotes a severe chronic disability, the onset of which is usually at birth, that is attributable to a mental or physical impairment or a combination of both resulting in substantial limitations in self-care, receptive and expressive language, learning, mobility, self-direction, and capacity for independent living and reflecting the person's need for a combination of generic care, interdisciplinary treatment, or other services of lifelong duration.

The primary audience of this book is the music therapist and the student training for a career in music therapy. It will also be useful to a broader audience—namely, special educators, music therapy faculties, music educators, administrators of mental health and health facilities, allied professionals, and, not least, parents.

The context of my approach to treatment is *A Continuum of Awareness,* the creative process of using music functionally as a tool of consciousness to awaken, heighten, and expand awareness of self, others, and the environment as a pathway to intrinsic learning and ultimately to active participation. This context evolved organically from my direct experience of the basic need of developmentally disabled persons to develop a positive sense of self in order to function on higher levels. Rooted in humanistic psychology, the approach affirms the dignity and worth of the human being and embraces the fundamental assumption that an individual's potentialities form a unique pattern for that particular person. The overall aim of the book is, therefore, to provide the music therapist with a foundation for the practice of music therapy and resources and methods through which to empower clients to develop a self and realize their humanness as fully as possible, regardless of existing disabilities.

Although the subject matter of this book is the treatment of developmentally disabled persons, the context of *A Continuum of Awareness* is applicable to the full spectrum of clients encompassed in the field of music therapy. This has been borne out by my experience and that of therapists I have trained in this approach. A context of this kind gives the therapist a solid foundation for treatment and broad scope within which to work. I conceive of this context as providing a heuristic way of practicing therapy that can inspire in the therapist *an empathic humanness as a coexperiencer in the continuum of life.* Music therapy colleagues who have examined the manuscript for this book while it was in preparation or have been introduced to this context through my training, lectures, and presentations, recognize its universality as a framework for treatment.

Chapter 1 is an overview of the field of music therapy that includes an account of its historical beginnings as a profession and the academic and clinical training required for certification by the two main national organizations (American Association for Music Therapy and National Association for Music Therapy). It defines music therapy and lists the many kinds of settings in which it is practiced and the client populations served. The diversity of client populations served by the profession is highlighted in four vignettes of treatment.

The rationale for using music therapy as a primary treatment modality for persons who are developmentally disabled is given in Chapter 2. It is predicated on the nature and power of music as it is used therapeutically and the reasons for its special significance for this population.

The subject of Chapter 3 is music therapy assessment and treatment planning based on a holistic picture of the client. The practitioner is supplied with information needed to design a comprehensive assessment form geared to this client population: tests most commonly administered to determine the existence and extent of problematic conditions and symptomatology; the various approaches to assessment presently used in this specialized area of the field; normal and abnormal development; and musical characteristics of persons with developmental disabilities. A model music therapy assessment form with guidelines for its administration and an individualized treatment plan are appended to the chapter.

In Chapter 4, the context of my approach to music therapy—*A Continuum of Awareness*—and the theoretical bases of the approach are delineated. Explanations of three main music therapy strategies devised to stimulate and develop awareness are interwoven with experiential illustrations of their application.

The nature of treatment as process within the context of *A Continuum of Awareness* is the topic of Chapter 5. The client–therapist relationship, group and individual process, treatment strategies and techniques, music therapy methodology, and therapeutic uses of the components of music are explicated.

Chapter 6 comprises process-oriented descriptions of treatment that demonstrate how growth and development are brought about through the application of specific music therapy strategies and techniques. It gives instructive pointers on the how's, what's, and why's of actual practice with a cross-section of the clients encountered in this population. Each account is preceded by an outline that serves as a guide to the overall treatment program. Music is provided for a number of these descriptions.

Chapter 7 offers resources that will assist the music therapist in carrying out the process of therapy. It consists of designs for therapeutic music activities that are built on music found particularly suitable for this population. A list of music books and a selected discography are included.

Since music therapists are often responsible for establishing a music therapy program as an integral component of the overall treatment program of an institution, Chapter 8 is devoted to this aspect of our work. Because of the increasing importance of transdisciplinary approaches to treatment, especially with the severely and profoundly retarded and multiply handicapped, a brief overview of this approach is provided that includes a look at how music therapy reinforces other disciplines by direct, hands-on cotherapy with speech therapists, special educators, physical therapists, occupational therapists, and other creative arts therapists (dance, art, and drama).

Music therapy is applicable to developmentally disabled persons of all ages, from the lowest to the highest functioning. Yet there are many common misconceptions about its nature and practice. Inasmuch as an important aspect of our responsibilities as music therapists is to impart information about this therapy to a variety of professionals and lay persons, I should like to dispel some of these common misconceptions.

We often hear such questions as: Is musical aptitude a requisite for being a candidate for music therapy? Does a person who is musically talented derive more benefit from music therapy than one who is not musical? Is it necessary to be able to play a musical instrument in order to receive music therapy? Then there is the half-question/half-statement: You do have to like music to be in music therapy, don't you? None of these questions are pertinent. Neither musicality nor an interest in music is a *requisite* for receiving this treatment, for as the book demonstrates, the nature of this therapy is such that it benefits most people regardless of their mental, psychological, or physical condition. Unless there is clarification of the erroneous thinking implicit in these questions and other misconceptions, serious misunderstandings about the therapeutic purposes of the discipline and the kinds of benefits that it provides could prevent many persons who are in the greatest need of this treatment from receiving it. Additionally, referrals for treatment might not be made unless it is fully comprehended that the goals set for the individual by the interdisciplinary treatment team (of which the music therapist is a member) are worked on in the music therapy setting through the modality of music.

A prevalent misconception stems from the vernacular use of the term *therapeutic*. A remark such as "I was listening to music and it made me feel *so good*—it was so therapeutic!" can cause misunderstanding as to what service through music involves. To be sure, the "curative" nature of music is fundamental to our work and music *can* lift a person's spirit. It is, however, essential to make a clear distinction between the *fortuitous* therapeutic effect of music and the *conscious* use of music as a treatment tool by a qualified music therapist trained to address the many conditions presented.

Then there is the confusion that exists between music therapy and music education. Though there may be some overlapping (teaching of the playing of instruments, for example, may meet the needs and interests of a client), the differentiation lies in the nature of the goals: the goal of music education is the attainment of music skills, whereas that of music therapy is the attainment of living skills through the modality of music. Also, training for the two disciplines differs. As will be found in Chapter 1, certification/registration for the practice of music therapy requires rigorous multidisciplinary training in musicianship, psychology, behavioral sciences, music therapy methods, and clinical experience as an intern in an approved mental health institution or special education setting, as well as theoretical background in diverse schools of psychotherapy.

A most misleading conception is with regard to the distinction between music therapy and recreation therapy. Very often, the two disciplines are perceived as one and the same, or as interchangeable. This mistaken idea originates mainly from the fact that a number of state agencies throughout the United States have not yet established an autonomous career line for music therapy. Because music therapy is still, in these instances, under the umbrella of recreation therapy, the error is perpetuated in the minds of administrators and other professionals.

To misconstrue music therapy as "fun and games" is to miss a basic premise of the discipline: that music used as a therapeutic *tool* has the power to change a person's manner of functioning. For example, a client whose attention span is described as minimal (two or three seconds at most) may sustain a rhythm instrument activity for five or more minutes as a result of the application of music therapy methods. When this kind of information is reported at a case conference, it is sometimes dismissed with the raise of an eyebrow that bespeaks skepticism or lack of understanding of the effect music can have on a person's energy level, attention, and purposeful use of energy. It is then the responsibility of the music therapist to stress the fact that, because the nature of the treatment modality is inherently enjoyable and has properties that capture attention, the very enjoyment of the musical experience stimulates and nourishes motivation to participate.

As will become manifest throughout *Music Therapy for the Developmentally Disabled,* the therapeutic tool—music—is a potent means of establishing contact, maintaining a relationship, and stimulating the motivation to learn.

Parallel with expanding concern for the betterment of and knowledge about developmentally disabled persons, music therapy for this client population has also become increasingly visible. As a result, there are university and college music therapy programs that offer course work and internships in this specialized area of the field. Since the inception of music therapy as a discipline in 1950, it has become recognized as a primary treatment modality for this client population.

There are still countless unknowns about what is possible for mentally retarded and other developmentally disabled persons to achieve. For this reason, it is most encouraging to find popularly accepted myths about ceiling mentalities and expectancies being dismissed as folklore by prominent authorities in the field of developmental disabilities. The quest continues for the realization of human potential—from its most minute to its most expanded forms. We must, therefore, look beyond the acquisition of specific skills in the conviction that more comprehensive gains and wider horizons can be reached when therapy lays the foundation for developing the person's self—a self that learns and desires to function on higher and higher levels.

Edith Hillman Boxill, C.M.T.
New York
November 1984

Acknowledgments

Special Mention

To Theo Merkle, administrative assistant to a former director of Manhattan Borough Developmental Services Office, for her invaluable contribution to the making of this book. Throughout, her broad knowledge of the field of developmental disabilities, expert editing, pertinent queries, and perceptive suggestions led to adjustments in the manuscript that added immeasurably to the clarification of the material. Indeed, her understanding of the creative process of communicating through the written word and her experience in organizing a text of this kind combined to give assistance that enabled me to bring the manuscript through its many stages. I truly thank her for the long-range commitment to this project, and hope that these words convey the extent and depth of my appreciation for her dedicated support and collaboration.

In Memoriam

To R. Curtis Whitesel, the late Editorial Director of Rehabilitation and Special Education of Aspen Systems Corporation, for inviting me to write this book and for being the original sponsoring editor. I came to anticipate an inspired mixture of serious business and just the right touch of humor that would give me much-needed balance and perspective as my involvement in our project intensified. Though contact with him was for an all too brief span of time, his impact on my life will be with me always. I felt an inexpressible loss when he was no longer here. My everlasting thanks to him for launching this book on a solid and secure footing.

With Many Thanks

To Anne Gousha, Associate Editor of Aspen Systems Corporation, for being instrumental in helping this book grow from its inception to its production. Her guidance and advice given with warmth and encouragement served me well throughout the trials, vicissitudes, and flowering of this project. My profound thanks to her for "being there" for me.

To Margaret M. Quinlin, current Editorial Director, for assuming sponsorship of this book and making it possible for it to be brought to completion. I thank her for recognizing the importance of music therapy for developmentally disabled persons and the contribution this book can make to further their betterment.

To Scott H. Ballotin, Special Projects Editor, for complex and artistic work that went into choreographing the book. Enduring thanks for his patience and fortitude, especially with regards to eleventh-hour requests; for the harmonious and comfortable give-and-take he created in response to an author's need for those crucial final touches.

To Barbara Hesser, Coordinator of the New York University Music Therapy Program, for giving of herself and her time unstintingly as consultant during the evolvement of the manuscript. The respect that I have for her deep insights about and broad knowledge of the field of music therapy as well as her experience in this specialized area, goes beyond mere words. My personal as well as professional gratitude to her.

To Dr. Eleanor Guetzloe, Coordinator of the Behavior Disorder Program of the University of South Florida, for her assistance in expediting the submission of the first draft of the manuscript and for her strong recommendation that students and professionals in allied fields could benefit immensely from it as a text in coursework.

To the many music therapy colleagues for sharing ideas with me and for expressing a need for this addition to the body of literature in our field.

To my graduate students at New York University for their opinions with regard to the practical information and theoretical foundations that would best prepare them for work with this client population.

To music therapy interns, whom I have trained, for their individualized application of the context of my approach to treatment for a wide variety of clients and patients as they have assumed the responsibility of becoming practitioners in the far corners of the world.

To Maurice D. Halifi, current director of the Manhattan Borough Developmental Services Office, for being a proponent of music therapy as a primary treatment modality. Also, my thanks to key administrators and members of the interdisciplinary team and to parents and advocates of my clients for permission to use photographs taken at actual music therapy sessions.

To Ellen Ashton, Director of Program Operations of the New York City County

Service Group, for championing the advent of music therapy at Manhattan Developmental Center and for offering me the support and assistance necessary for establishing the music therapy program in 1974.

To Bob Pecorini, Robert Beckhard, and M. Walter Neumann for their sensitive and expressive photographs that capture the essences of the client-therapist relationship and the quality of treatment process. Also, my thanks to Peggy Armstrong, staff music therapist, for her help in the production of the photographs.

To Elaine Magidson, former Director of Special Education at Manhattan Developmental Center, for reviewing the most recent revision of my assessment form.

To Ellen Gradenwitz for her cogent and valuable advice.

To Vivian Davidson, Educational Counsellor, for her many helpful hints given from the vantage point of an allied professional and dear friend.

To my beautiful family for lighting, lightening, and enlightening the way as I traveled this marvelous and arduous odyssey. We have always been able to strike the perfect chord and create the magical sense of being in tune with each other. And what's more, I thank them for their practical help, pertinent discussion, and songs and laughter. . . .

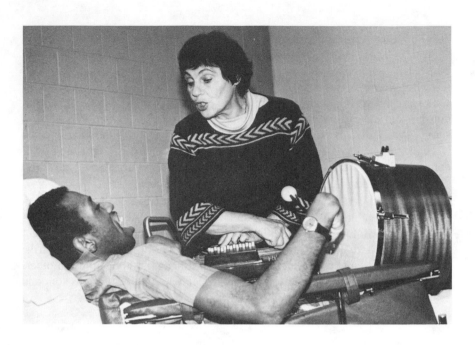

Chapter 1

Music Therapy: An Overview

Music therapy is one of the most beautiful of professions. To nourish and enhance the healthy essences of the human being through the creative, therapeutic use of music is a profoundly enriching life's work. To receive the benefits of this therapy is a profoundly enriching experience.

INTRODUCTION

Historical Perspective

Viewed historically, music as therapy is both ancient and young; its roots deep and its branches ever growing. The development of music therapy as a profession has been in process since the power of music as a mode of expression was first experienced. This power lies in its inherent nature and its congruence with human feelings, emotions, and states of being.

The concept of the power of music is found in literature ranging from that of the Egyptians and Greeks to that of the present day. Thousands of years before the advent of the profession of music therapy, the shaman or medicine man of many cultures was aware of the curative power of music and used it directly in healing. This power was also known to the healing cult of Asklepios, an actual or mythical priest-physician who was worshipped as a demigod in Greece and later as Aesculapius, the god of medicine, in Rome. In classical Greece, Pythagoras prescribed specific musical intervals and modes to promote health, and Plato linked music to the moral welfare of the nation in *Laws,* a work that contains a poetic description of music and movement as a means of restoring the being to health and harmony (Meinecke, 1948). Among the biblical tales of the restorative effects of music, we learn that David, by playing his harp, eased the afflictions of Saul.

Over the centuries, there has been a search for methods of using music for mental disorders. As milieu therapy began to be introduced into psychiatric hospitals (Jones, 1953), the seeds of a new therapy were being planted. In an attempt to bring some joy into the lives of hospitalized persons, professional musicians began to perform, conduct bands and choral groups, and encourage patients to begin or resume the study of instruments.

It was not, however, until veterans of World War II began to fill hospitals to overflowing that these same musicians became aware of the need for knowledge and understanding of the many psychopathological as well as physical conditions that plagued war victims. It was no longer possible merely to entertain or engage them in activities. It had become imperative to give service of a therapeutic nature through music. That it would mean preparation of a new and different kind to deliver such service was recognized by hospital personnel, psychiatrists, and music educators alike. The first academic program to train music therapists was developed and instituted at Michigan State University in 1944.

As the field branched out, there emerged a need to develop standards for the education and training of music therapists. As a result, in 1950—the year that marks the beginning of the profession of music therapy—a group comprising psychiatrists, professional musicians, and music educators, originating at the Menninger Clinic in Topeka, Kansas, met in New York City for the purpose of founding a national organization named the National Association for Music Therapy (NAMT).* By 1953, minimal education and clinical training requirements leading to a baccalaureate degree and registration as a music therapist were instituted in several college and university music therapy programs.

In 1971, another national organization, the American Association for Music Therapy (AAMT),* came into being. This organization was founded by music therapy practitioners, music educators, and psychiatrists to meet the needs of an expanding field and the growing diversity of client populations, especially those in large urban centers (as indicated by its original name, the Urban Federation for Music Therapists). Based in metropolitan New York, this organization approved its first music therapy program at New York University.

It is from these mythical and historical roots that the discipline of music therapy has sprung.

Academic and Clinical Training of the Music Therapist

The education of the music therapist requires multidisciplinary study including courses in musicianship, behavioral sciences, and theories of psychiatry and psychotherapy, as well as clinical experience as a music therapy intern.

---

*NAMT and AAMT are legally authorized to grant registration and certification to the music therapist as a Registered Music Therapist (R.M.T.) and a Certified Music Therapist (C.M.T.), respectively.

The approaches to curriculum planning of the NAMT and AAMT are presented in the following accounts of curricula and training programs of these two national organizations.

The approved curriculum of the NAMT leads to a baccalaureate degree in music therapy. As stated in *A Career in Music Therapy* (National Association for Music Therapy, Inc., 1975):

> Studies in music therapy, psychology, sociology, and anthropology should comprise 20 percent to 30 percent of the total degree program; studies in music, 46 percent to 50 percent; general studies, 20 percent to 25 percent; electives approximately 5 percent. Elective courses should remain the free choice of the student. . . . The professional courses deal with the theory and practice of music therapy, and are taught by instructors who are competent in their field and who have an adequate background in psychology as well.
>
> A six-month period of clinical training in a National Association for Music Therapy, Inc. approved music therapy program under the direction of a Registered Music Therapist is required in addition to the 128 semester credits of on-campus course work. This clinical training follows all academic work and generally precedes the granting of the degree. Clinical training as a degree requirement is mandatory for programs approved after fall 1979. (p. 3)

Members of the NAMT who complete an approved degree program in music therapy or its equivalent from an accredited college or university plus the six-month clinical internship are eligible to apply for registration as a Registered Music Therapist. For those wishing advanced education, a master's degree in music therapy is offered by certain universities.

The AAMT requires that each college and university design a competency-based curriculum, at either the bachelor's or master's level, that is subject to organization approval. Curricula, reflecting the educational structure and utilizing the unique resources of the institution, are based on competencies in areas considered essential to music therapy practice:

- *Music Foundations*
  music theory and history
  composition and arrangement
  performance (keyboard, guitar, voice)
  ability to play nonsymphonic instruments
  improvisation (instrumental and vocal)
  conducting choral and small instrumental ensembles
  movement to musical stimuli

- *Clinical Foundations*
  understanding of exceptionality and terminology
  dynamics of therapy
  the therapeutic relationship

- *Music Therapy*
  foundations and principles
  client assessment
  treatment planning
  therapy implementation
  therapy evaluation
  interdisciplinary collaboration
  supervision and administration
  discharge from therapy
  communication about therapy

These competencies are delineated further in "Essential Competencies for the Practice of Music Therapy" (Bruscia, Hesser, & Boxill, 1981).

Pre-internship field training is required in order to gain diverse field experience prior to the internship. This phase of training introduces and orients the student to a variety of client populations, institutional settings, treatment approaches, and music therapy methods, while defining the role of a music therapist in various clinical environments. The internship (a minimum of 900 academic hours) is the culminating experience in the student's program and is considered a crucial period in the training process. The AAMT requires that

1. students complete the internship while in academic residence and prior to the granting of the degree,
2. students receive continued supervision from academic faculty as well as from qualified clinicians at the internship site, and
3. academic institutions select clinical agencies for internship placement which meet criteria acceptable to AAMT and place interns according to individual needs. (American Association for Music Therapy, 1982, p. 4)

AAMT regards the academic institution as having primary responsibility for the internship program and grants certification/registration as a Certified Music Therapist to individuals who meet the competency-based requirements adopted by the organization.

THE PRACTICE OF MUSIC THERAPY

Music Therapy Defined

Music—a universal human phenomenon—is structured tonal sound moving in time and space. From its origins in the primitive imitation of nature's sounds—songs of birds, calls of animals, and waves of the ocean—music has evolved into organized forms that have varied in style and idiom from century to century and culture to culture. "Sound is an ordinary natural phenomenon: Music on the other hand is the result of man's conscious development of sound into an art and science" (Rowley, 1978, p. 9). The basic elements of music—designated throughout this book as the components—are rhythm, melody, harmony, pitch, tempo, dynamics, timbre, and, referentially, the text of song (included as a component because of its fundamental importance to music therapy). These components embody qualities and attributes that have an impact singly, in different combinations, and as a gestalt (Clendenin, 1965).

Therapy, from the Greek *therapeia,* is fundamentally the rendering of a health-giving service. When the term *therapy* is applied to the treatment of mental, psychological, and behavioral disorders, it becomes interchangeable with the term *psychotherapy* and covers a variety of modern therapeutic and psychotherapeutic approaches (Binder, Binder, & Rimland, 1976). Music therapy can be considered a psychotherapeutic process inasmuch as it is "a form of treatment . . . in which a trained person deliberately establishes a professional relationship with the object of removing, modifying, or retarding existing symptoms, of mediating disturbed patterns of behavior, and of promoting positive personality growth and development" (Wolberg, 1954, p. 8). As the approach to music therapy in this text demonstrates, the methods, theories, and techniques of modern therapies and psychotherapies are adapted and incorporated into the practice.

Music therapy is an amalgam of music and therapy. When music, as an agent of change, is used to establish a therapeutic relationship, to nurture a person's growth and development, to assist in self-actualization, the process is music therapy. In this process, music is consciously used for the enhancement of living, being, and becoming. Broadly defined, music therapy is the use of music as a therapeutic tool for the restoration, maintenance, and improvement of psychological, mental, and physiological health and for the habilitation, rehabilitation, and maintenance of behavioral, developmental, physical, and social skills—all within the context of a client–therapist relationship. A nonverbal treatment modality that is applicable to both the verbal and nonverbal person, it serves those of a wide age range and with a wide diversity of disorders. It can be a diagnostic aid (Nordoff & Robbins, 1971, 1977) and can reinforce other treatment modalities.

Fundamental reasons for the efficacy of using music as a therapeutic agent are as follows:

- It is a cross-cultural mode of expression.
- Its nonverbal nature makes it a universal means of communication.
- As a sound stimulus it is unique in its power to penetrate the mind and body directly, whatever the individual's level of intelligence or condition. As such, it stimulates the senses, evokes feelings and emotions, elicits physiological and mental responses, and energizes the mind and body.
- Its intrinsic structure and qualities have the potential for self-organization of the individual and organization of the group.
- It influences musical and nonmusical behavior.
- It facilitates learning and the acquisition of skills.
- It is an eminently functional, adaptable, and aesthetic modality applicable to all client populations.

The overall goals of treatment through the therapeutic use of music are (a) to effect personal change, (b) to facilitate interpersonal relations, (c) to nourish growth and development, (d) to contribute to the attainment of self-actualization, and (e) to assist the individual's entry into society.

Music therapy is both an art and a science. Art and science are acts of discovery, imagination, and inspiration that give rise, on one hand, to symbolic and aesthetic expression and, on the other, to verifiable and investigative expression. "Both . . . give a fresh world view, reslice the universe in a different way, and both are human creations" (Gerard, 1958, p. 1).

As an art, music therapy has two aspects: First, the medium of therapy, music, is an art form; second, the process of therapy becomes an art as the medium is shaped by the music therapist. The talented therapist, who is fully engaged with the client and who applies clinical skills creatively in dealing with the whole person, is practicing the art of music therapy.

The science of music therapy also has two aspects to be considered. First, in looking at the scientific application of established methods, the therapist experiments, explores, investigates, and discovers what works or does not work, what the efficacy of a particular technique is, and whether or not it has broad application. Further questions are asked, such as: Why does this strategy work or not work? When does it work or not work? What variables cause it to work or not work? What effect does the practitioner, as the instrument of the therapeutic relationship, have on the results? Is the music suitable? Is it applied in a purposeful way? In examining and evaluating therapeutic outcomes, the data offer guidelines for theory, practice, and research. Conversely, research supplies guidelines that the music therapist applies to practice.

Gaston (1968), one of the founders of music therapy, stated that the therapeutic use of music is a means of influencing human behavior and closely related music therapy to behavioral sciences. This relationship is most fitting as music therapy concerns itself with the effects of the functional use of music on human behavior (Disereus, 1926).

Music therapy is rooted in participation, in actively making music, whether repeating a rhythmic pattern on a drum or playing a Bach fugue, singing isolated words of a song or performing a Verdi aria, blowing one note on a flutophone or weaving a Glück melody on a flute. To understand the immediacy of the multisensory effect of music on the organism is to understand the fundamental meaning and beauty of this mode of treatment (Alvin, 1966). In the very act of making music and responding to musical stimuli, a person experiences instantaneous psychological and physiological sensations on many levels. The concrete reality of sensing auditorially, visually, tactually, kinesthetically, and emotionally brings the person into the present and has immediate results (Anderson, 1977). Because of mental, physical, or psychological dysfunction, however, experiencing is sometimes on a subliminal, or unconscious, level. Through music therapy strategies and techniques, the therapist aims to bring this experiencing to consciousness, to open up lines of communication, in the broadest sense, by awakening, heightening, and expanding awareness (Boxill, 1981).

The dynamic process is a continuum of therapeutically oriented musical experiences flexibly and creatively generated to attain long-term goals and short-term objectives. Those goals and objectives are part of a music therapy treatment plan formulated by the music therapist in consultation with other professional staff or an interdisciplinary treatment team. The plan is based on findings of music therapy assessment in such areas as awareness of self, others, and the environment; general characteristics; motor, communication, cognitive, affective, and social domains; creativity and self-expression; and specific musical behaviors. Methodology is based in three categories of music—composed music, clinically improvised music, and adapted music—and in three modes of therapeutic music activities—singing/chanting, instrument playing, and music-movement.

The province of the music therapist is knowledge of a special kind: a profound understanding of the influence of music on a person's total being. This understanding is deepened through the study of the aesthetics and psychology of music as well as the theoretical foundations of the discipline. And, although it is basic to understand the power of music, being able to communicate that power is vital. Apart from professional training, it is this capacity that makes the difference between practicing creative music therapy and therapy that is perfunctory.

Settings and Client Populations

From the initial programs, which were limited to psychiatric units for veterans or to general hospitals serving adults only, the practice of this treatment modality has grown to encompass a variety of settings with diverse client populations. The following list indicates that variety:

- psychiatric centers and hospitals for children, adolescents, and adults with disorders ranging from emotional disturbance to severe psychosis; hospital outpatient centers for psychiatric patients; treatment programs in community rehabilitation centers and halfway houses for posthospitalized psychiatric patients;
- general hospitals for acute care patients;
- specialty hospitals for acute care patients, including the physically handicapped;
- nursing and day-care centers for geriatric patients;
- developmental centers, hostels, group homes, and intermediate care facilities for persons with developmental disabilities;
- special public and private school, after-school programs for exceptional children, including the severely emotionally disturbed;
- community and private clinics for people with psychosocial problems, including troubled adolescents; and
- clinical treatment centers and halfway houses for alcohol and drug abusers.

Professionals in such disciplines as psychiatry, medicine, and nursing in a variety of treatment settings have corroborated the findings of music therapists that the therapeutic use of music can motivate people in ways that other therapies often cannot. And there is widespread acceptance that music therapy has evolved into a treatment modality that is suitable and effective for almost all dysfunctions—psychological, physiological, developmental, psychosocial—and for all ages, as demonstrated by the preceding list. Because the therapeutic agent, music, bridges the gap between people of different cultures, different ages, and different mental and physical conditions, the music therapy process is a leveler, an organizer, a unifier. The four vignettes presented here illustrate these points. They offer a kaleidoscopic view of treatment in a number of different kinds of settings. The first deals with a developmentally disabled young man who is a resident in a developmental center; the second, with a group of preadolescents drawn from a special education class of a day treatment center for emotionally disturbed children; the third, with a child in a private school for exceptional children; and the fourth, with a young woman in a psychiatric hospital.

Vignette 1

Toby, a resident in a developmental center, was a young man 25 years old at the time of our therapy sessions. Multiply handicapped, he was on his back in a "cripple cart.'' Diagnosis: moderate mental retardation; quadriplegia. When I first saw him he appeared to be immobile, incapable of moving his limbs. His head was the only part of his body he could move, and that in a limited, sideways fashion. He stared intently at me, his lips forming words that were inaudible. Toby sensed I had come to him to make music, and he vibrated with excitement. As I leaned over him, I saw that his mouth was quivering. When I sang, ''Hello, Toby, yes indeed, yes indeed, yes indeed. Hello, Toby, yes indeed, yes indeed, my darling,'' his quivering smile burst into O-shaped silent laughter. He attempted to sing with me, mouthing, with the beginning traces of phonation, ''Yes indeed, yes indeed, yes indeed.'' I repeated ''Hello, Toby'' slowly, very deliberately articulating, ''Y-e-s i-n-d-e-e-d, y-e-ss i-n-d-e-e-d, y-e-s i-n-d-e-e-d, my d-a-r-l-i-n-g.'' Intensely, Toby followed my lip movements as he attempted to sing with me.

Later in the session, when I sang, ''Sing'' (Raposo, 1971), Toby matched some of the words and tones immediately. Perhaps it was a tune that was familiar to him. He became very excited, and when I finished singing the song he attempted to sing it on his own, as if asking me to repeat it with him. It became Our Contact Song (see Chapter 4).

Once this contact was established, I sang this song repeatedly, seeking ways to have Toby participate in as physical a manner as possible. Perhaps the musical stimulation of a song he loved could motivate him to transcend his bodily limitations. Using a hand-over-hand technique, I slipped a drum mallet into his right hand, which was his preferred hand. His eyes gave me the signal that he was very pleased with what I was doing, his hand moving ever so perceptibly to grasp the mallet. I then placed a timpani drum (the legs of which had been removed) on the cart, maneuvering it within his reach. Toby became more and more excited. I sang, accompanying myself on the Autoharp®, while a music therapy intern guided Toby's right hand toward the drumhead. A tenuous, unsteady beat floated from the drum. I caught it and merged my singing and playing with it. His fingers tightened their grasp on the mallet, and his arm began to move spastically but more firmly. My delight at bringing him out of his isolation and providing him with a means of contact reached a peak when he began to articulate the words of the song audibly and tonally. I leaned over, singing and playing in synchrony with him. Toby's face lit up in ecstasy. Our relationship started on this note and contained the joyous, health-producing ingredients that are a therapist's dream.

Vignette 2

The music therapy room was set up for the arrival of six preadolescents who were in a special education class of a day treatment center for emotionally disturbed children. Chairs were arranged in a semicircle near the piano. Conga drums, a timpani drum, bongos, a large cymbal on a stand, a metallophone, clavés, a pair of maracas, a tambourine, and a marimba were all within reach.

Three of these young people had histories of violent acting-out behavior. One suffered from school phobia; another was diagnosed as having a schizoid personality and another, as having unsocialized aggressive reaction of childhood. The music therapist, knowing the need for structure and positive outlets that would redirect their disruptive behavior, hostility, or withdrawal, immediately matched the expressed and unexpressed intensity that pervaded the group by engaging them in vigorous hand clapping to familiar rock music. The uproar that had prevailed as they entered the room was quickly and nonverbally dealt with by focusing their energy on a stimulating music activity that reached them on many levels. The entire group, aggressive or withdrawn, experienced a common connection with the music and the therapist who ''spoke their language'' and was thereby able to gain their trust.

Once the scattered group of individuals became unified, instruments were distributed with the therapist's assurance that there would be an opportunity to exchange or take turns on the various instruments. There was also a firm but kindly reminder that the instruments were to be handled with care and played appropriately.

The musical stimuli and instruments provided both a socially acceptable channel for negative feelings and release from withdrawal. In creating therapeutically purposeful music activities suitable for their age, condition, and individual as well as collective interests, the therapist was able to direct their behaviors and feelings into positive, creative expression.

It was many months into therapy when the session just described took place—many months of exploration and discovery, of peaks and valleys.

Vignette 3

At the time of my relationship with her, Madeline was 7 years old. She was diagnosed as having withdrawing reaction of childhood/overanxious reaction of childhood. Upon admission to a school for exceptional children, she was described as having a symbiotic relationship with her mother, who infantilized her. The description indicated that she spoke in monosyllables, had poor motor coordination, did not engage in spontaneous play, was extremely inhibited, and had marked variability in functioning.

In our initial sessions Madeline's hands flew to cover her ears every time the dynamic level of the music or my voice intensified. When I played or sang softly, she smiled and shyly whispered, ''I like that. That's pretty. You sing nice.'' Her sessions were cloaked in a kind of mistiness. She seemed to be confluent with the environment. When she moved to music, she seemed to fade into the corners of the room. I wondered about her inability to tolerate sound that exceeded a moderate level of intensity. A report of her early childhood mentioned elective mutism. Was there any correlation?

As she grew to trust me, I experimented with different dynamic levels, seeking to discover the key to this extreme sensitivity, which was isolating her from peers as well as adults. At one session I thought she might be ready to accept an increase in the volume of my singing and instrumental accompaniment. Instantaneously, she clamped her hands over her ears. Her face was engulfed in anguish. "Don't scream! Don't scream! My mother screams at me all the time!" Then she pounded on a drum with all the strength she could muster. After this outburst, her body crumpled as if deflated. She was completely spent.

Over a period of time, with cautious yet deliberate changes in dynamics and kinds of music, our sessions took on a new dimension. A world of sound began to open up to Madeline. It became fun to pound on the drum and make loud sounds. She could make soft or loud sounds on the xylophone, whichever she felt like doing. She even asked for "that loud song." Dropping passive-aggressive, fearful behaviors, she began to be assertive and direct. Her speech and entire bodily expression revealed a high-spirited little girl who was beginning to come out of hiding and play with the other children she had previously considered "too noisy." That no longer bothered Madeline as it had before she experienced music therapy.

Vignette 4

Highly intelligent, boyish, Helene was 18 years old at the start of treatment. Diagnosis: anorexia nervosa and borderline personality disorder. Symptoms of anorexia nervosa developed over a period of two years, resulting in two psychiatric hospitalizations. As her condition worsened, she exhibited increasing signs of self-destructive behavior with classic anorectic and bulimic episodes. After she graduated from high school, her work history was sporadic. As the symptoms became intolerable, she was unable to sustain work and was hospitalized. Typical of the syndrome, she experienced extreme swings from hyperactivity to lethargy, hostility to amiability, aggression to passivity.

When she became completely resistant to verbal psychotherapy, threatening to flee from the hospital, the psychiatrist recommended one-to-one music therapy sessions as a possible means of reaching her and staving off a situation fraught with disaster. Having witnessed the benefits of music therapy in this psychiatric hospital, the staff made the referral.

At first, her oppositional behavior carried over to the music therapist. She threw up a wall to protect herself from any intrusion into her familiar, hopeless, frantic world. "No one is going to make me do anything or feel any way!" she would spit out defiantly.

After several brief, exploratory music therapy encounters, a discovery was made. Helene could strum a few chords on the guitar to accompany herself while singing. This was a possible path to establishing rapport and building a relationship, and, indeed, it happened. She began to relax her impenetrable stance and allow the therapist to share musical experiences that fed her emotionally and broke through her alienation and terror.

It was not a smooth path that therapist and patient were treading together. Helene constantly manifested erratic behavior. She had to be right. She had to play without making mistakes. She had to be perfect. "Why am I always wrong? Why do I always spoil everything? I'm a mess!" she would spew out. And herein lay the challenge: to free her from the obsession in which she was trapped, to liberate her from the vicious cycle of rigid expectations and intense disappointments that consumed her bodily, mentally, and emotionally.

With the therapist's acceptance of her, Helene was gradually able to receive support from this gentle guidance and nonjudgmental attitude. Specific music therapy strategies and techniques were used to encourage freewheeling, free-from-failure musical improvisations on the guitar and percussion instruments, as well as vocally. Helene responded to the warm, safe environment that the therapist created. The music therapist addressed her strengths, her need for freedom within the structure of musical forms, and her cry for release from the tensions of having to be "good" and "right" and "perfect" instead of being "bad" and "wrong" and "nothing" (in her distorted opinion of herself). In doing so, the therapist helped Helene to gain a measure of emotional stability and a feeling of self-worth. The swings of mood diminished in severity as her sense of being capable of gratifying her hungers in a pleasurable and socially acceptable way became more reliable.

And when she played and sang for other patients on the unit, it was all right with her if she struck a wrong chord on the guitar. What of it! She was having a great time, and the others loved it!

CONCLUSION

Since its beginnings as an ancillary therapy in psychiatric and veterans' hospitals (Ludwig, 1977), music therapy has come of age as an autonomous treatment modality. Increasingly, it is regarded as an integral component of institutional, community, and private treatment programs. Indeed, the branches of the profession have spread worldwide. In the three decades since its establishment as a discipline, college and university training programs have increased considerably, and music therapy programs have been introduced in health care institutions in such divergent areas of the world as the Philippines and India. As a result, national music therapy organizations have been formed in many countries. International conferences also highlight the growth of the profession. In 1979 music therapists from many countries met in Europe to share knowledge and concerns about the profession. In 1981, music therapy was represented at an international conference held at the United Nations in support of the International Year of Disabled Persons. And in 1982, an international symposium in New York ushered in a new phase in the growth of the profession. Two important trends have been emerging in the field: the inclusion of music therapy as an integral part of allied mental health and health professional organizations (for example, as a Special Interest Group of the American Association on Mental Deficiency), and cooperation among countries with formal music therapy organizations (23 at this writing) regarding the formation of a World Federation of Music Therapy.

REFERENCES

Alvin, J. *Music Therapy*. London: John Baker Publishers, 1966.

American Association for Music Therapy, Inc. *Brochure*. New York: Author, 1982.

Anderson, W. Introduction. In W. Anderson (Ed.), *Therapy and the arts: Tools of consciousness*. New York: Harper Colophon Books, 1977.

Binder, V., Binder, A., & Rimland, B. (Eds.). *Modern therapies*. Englewood Cliffs, N.J.: Prentice-Hall, 1976.

Boxill, E.H. A continuum of awareness: Music therapy with the developmentally handicapped. *Music Therapy*, 1981, *1*(1), 17–23.

Bruscia, K., Hesser, B., & Boxill, E.H. Essential competencies for the practice of music therapy. *Music Therapy*, 1981, *1*(1), 43–49.

Clendenin, W.R. *Music: History and theory*. Garden City, N.Y.: Doubleday & Company, 1965.

Disereus, C.M. *A psychology of music: The influence of music on behavior*. Princeton, N.J.: Princeton University Press, 1926.

Gaston, E.T. (Ed.). *Music in therapy*. New York: Macmillan, 1968.

Gerard, R.W. Education and the imagination. In I. Kaufman (Ed.), *Education and the imagination in science and art*. Ann Arbor, Mich.: University of Michigan, 1958.

Jones, M. *The therapeutic community*. New York: Basic Books, 1953.

Ludwig, A.J. Music therapy. In P.J. Valletutti & F. Christoplos (Eds.), *Interdisciplinary approaches to human services*. Baltimore: University Park Press, 1977.

Meinecke, B. Music and medicine. In D. Schullian & M. Schoen (Eds.), *Music and medicine*. New York: Henry Schuman, 1948.

National Association for Music Therapy, Inc. *A career in music therapy*. Lawrence, Kans.: Author, 1975. (Brochure)

Nordoff, P., & Robbins, C. *Music therapy in special education*. New York: John Day, 1971.

Nordoff, P., & Robbins, C. *Creative music therapy* (audiocassette included). New York: John Day, 1977.

Raposo, J. Sing. In J. Raposo and J. Moss, *The sesame street songbook*. New York: Simon & Schuster, 1971.

Rowley, G. (Ed.). *The book of music*. Englewood Cliffs, N.J.: Prentice-Hall, 1978.

Wolberg, L.R. *The technique of psychotherapy*. New York: Grune & Stratton, 1954.

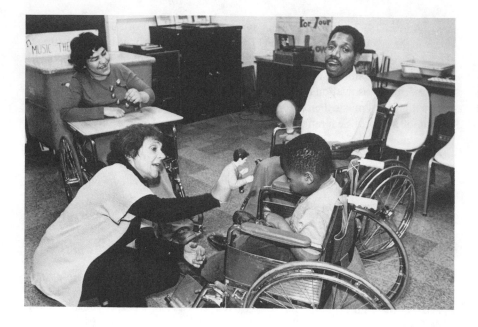

Chapter 2

Music Therapy As a Primary Treatment Modality for the Developmentally Disabled

Music can be and is almost an immediate *revelation, requiring little interpretative effort on the part of the . . . listener.*

Sound waves can more deeply penetrate our subconscious—can more profoundly affect our emotions—than any other impressions Man's ultimate leap . . . is through music.

Yehudi Menuhin (1972, p. 10)

INTRODUCTION

As a primary treatment modality (Boxill, 1981, 1982), music therapy deals with the full range of disorders presented by the developmentally disabled. It is a means of opening new channels to the furthest reaches of personal development and humanness, of opening paths for expression and learning in the broadest sense for persons who are limited in their ability to relate to themselves, others, and the environment because of mental and physical disorders usually originating at birth. Inasmuch as the therapeutic tool—music—offers a nonverbal means of making contact, this treatment modality is of vital significance to persons who are inaccessible, in varying degrees, through the spoken word because of subaverage intellectual functioning and deficits in communication skills. As an agent of therapy, music has the power to contact people on multidimensional organismic levels, wide applicability for the acquisition of living skills, and normalizing effects that make the modality particularly efficacious for developmentally dis- abled individuals, who are usually isolated from the ordinary stream of life. The humanistic approach to music therapy espoused in this text gives full attention to the holistic person. This approach encompasses a broad spectrum of musical experiences that are designed to enhance all domains of functioning—motoric, communicative, cognitive, affective, and social—always with a view to nurturing the human being as an entity, as a whole that is greater than its parts.

RATIONALE

The rationale for using music therapy as a primary treatment modality for developmentally disabled persons follows. Used as a therapeutic tool, music:

- effects direct contact on a psychobiological basis with people who often are otherwise unreachable
- serves to establish, maintain, and strengthen the client–therapist relationship in ways that are uniquely attributable to the power of this tool
- facilitates expression in people who either are nonverbal or have deficits in communication skills
- provides the opportunity for experiences that open the way for, and motivate, learning in all domains of functioning
- creates the opportunity for positive, successful, and pleasurable social experiences not otherwise available to them
- develops awareness of self, others, and the environment that improves functioning on all levels, enhances well-being, and fosters independent living

A fundamental consideration of music therapy, as a primary treatment modality for this client population, is its scope in relation to the psychosocial, mental, physical, and emotional dysfunctions presented by the developmentally disabled (Boxill, 1981, 1982). Those dysfunctions include conspicuous lack of awareness of self, others, and the environment; major deficits in the capacity for communication in the broadest sense; critical neurodevelopmental deficits in motoric functioning; underdevelopment of cognitive skills; and extreme limitations and deficits in social skills. All these are often compounded by an overlay of affective disturbance (Menolascino, 1965, 1969). Communication and motoric deficits constitute the two largest groups of associated dysfunctions. They seriously affect all domains of functioning by restricting a person's response to and interaction with the environment.

How does the process of music therapy bring to light aspects of personality, interests, and capabilities that may otherwise go undetected? What is the uniqueness of the medium used clinically that can motivate the unaware person into active participation and interaction, impel the nonverbal person to attempt to utter words, help the neurologically impaired person to direct energy purposively, and inspire the multiply handicapped person to move with a modicum of grace?

When the interdisciplinary nature of music, as it is used in music therapy, is fully comprehended, the dimensions of the therapy come into focus. Treatment deals with improving motor skills (physical, occupational, and recreation therapies); cognitive skills (special education); affective states and adjustment (psychology); and social skills (all disciplines). This interdisciplinary application of music makes the therapy uncommonly appropriate for these clients because it supplements and reinforces other therapies and disciplines while implementing its own program.

Whatever the client's handicapping condition or level of retardation, musical and nonmusical skills are developed through involvement and participation in therapeutic music activities—singing/chanting, instrument playing, and music-movement. Expressing oneself and communicating by these means are nurturing and pleasurable experiences that generate feelings of success and well-being. In turn, these feelings of success and well-being are the motivating force for intrinsic learning, the nature of which brings about transformation and change (see Chapter 4). Because singing is rarely a spontaneous behavior of the mentally retarded at any age, treatment that is song oriented is especially valuable. For those who cannot or do not sing spontaneously, the act of singing stimulates inner sensations that awaken bodily, emotional, and mental awareness; it is a path to speech, comprehension, and mind body integration. Instrument playing provides tangible sensory stimulation auditorially, visually, and tactually. This kind of sensorimotor experience, even on the most elementary levels, yields instantaneous feedback that activates awareness of self and, in varying degrees, an awareness of *doing*. In music-movement, bodily and emotional awareness stimulate clients kinesthetically. By tapping the full sensorium or by stimulating the five senses, either singly or in combination, the mind–body becomes an expressive instrument that remembers movements through deep muscle sense (proprioception). This process of preparing the person, through internal and external excitation of the senses, helps the individual to focus attention and thus become more receptive to and capable of learning. More often than is commonly known, a person who is hampered by a disorder will transcend the disabling condition and become a harmoniously functioning whole when participating in therapeutic music activities. Even if this phenomenological synthesis is momentary, it can have a lasting effect. Once a person has experienced kinesthetic awareness, bodily memory is retrievable and can lead to intentional action through the application of specific music therapy strategies and techniques (see Chapter 5).

In approaching the human being holistically, the music therapist explores responses to music on various levels of human experience. Remarkable changes have occurred: Intelligible speech has emerged for the first time through singing song phrases and the words of songs. Coordination has improved through music-movement activities that concentrate on learning rhythmic musical patterns. Maladaptively used energies have been redirected into purposeful and productive activity through playing instruments. Memory has been stimulated by the design of specific therapeutic music activities that use repetition inherent in the structure of music. All these gains are made possible through the development of a sense of self that unfolds through relating to musical stimuli. The paradigm for the approach to this process is the cyclical nature of awakening, heightening, and expanding awareness of self, others, and the environment within the context of *A Continuum of Awareness* (see Chapter 4). In cultivating this emerging self, music therapy actively engages individuals in their own growth, development, and behavioral change. The overall aim is to transfer musical and nonmusical skills to other aspects of the client's life and to bring the person from isolation into active and normalizing participation in the external world.

Now let us look at some reasons why music has the power to contact the organism directly on psychobiological bases (Sperry, 1971), to facilitate self-expression, and to develop awareness of self, others, and the environment in persons who are developmentally disabled.

PSYCHOBIOLOGICAL BASES

As both a physiological ''language'' (Hudson, 1978) and a psychological ''language'' (Lundin, 1967), music has a direct sensory effect upon the human organism. It is an agent of arousal and plays on the sentient organism in immediate and instantaneous ways, sending vibratory and auditory messages that can be apprehended at autonomic levels, messages that do not require encoding or decoding to be beneficial. Incoming impulses such as musical sound have a direct effect on, and are filtered through, the thalamus, the chief center for transmission of sensory impulses to the cerebral cortex. The thalamus is the part of the brain that is the seat of emotions, sensations, and feelings. Many signaling systems of brain and body converge in the thalamus, resulting in instantaneous pooling of influences that stimulate the organism to react and act (Calder, 1970). Weigl (1959) tells us:

> Effects of sound are not limited to conscious perception. The elements of sound—rhythm, pitch, and intensity—mediated by the thalamus, affect the functioning of the autonomic nervous system. Thereby, even when conscious perception through the involvement of the cortex does not take place, feelings can be aroused and [people] can be reached, whereas on an intellectual level they may be inaccessible. (p. 676)

Of critical importance is the fact that music can be experienced on many organismic levels that do not involve conscious mental processes. Even in someone whose sense of self may be only a dim awareness, and in whom there appears to be little interest in the environment, music can stimulate emotions and activity that propel the person into the external world. Music contacts the human being on primordial to intricate physiological levels, on basic to dynamic psychological levels, and on simple to complicated cerebral levels. This modality has thus been found, particularly at the low range of the continuum of functioning, to be the only means of bridging the gap between the person and the immediate environment; it is a most effective means of bringing the person into present reality.

Music has acoustical properties that permeate the environment and surround the person totally. When used with therapeutic intention by the therapist, it becomes the dominant stimulus in the environment and evokes bodily and emotional sensations that generate cycles of awareness and give meaning and purpose to actions (see Chapter 4). Although subjective responses to music cannot be anticipated, we do know that the vibratory qualities of music can effect immediacy of contact physiologically as well as psychologically, causing highly individual responses. We also know that structured musical sound has great power as an aesthetic means of sensory stimulation, and that its congruence with human feelings and emotions (Langer, 1942) makes it an integrative force, both intrapersonally and interpersonally.

Once contact is made through musical sound, perception begins to develop. Authorities in brain research and mind–body studies tell us that perception, the beginning of mental activity, is "sensation plus the way experiences, learning, and motivations alter the information directed by the senses" (Brown, 1975, p. 43); and, further, that if increased attention improves learning, then agents which have effects on arousal and attention have effects *directly* on learning (Rose, 1973).

Music used functionally not only activates and energizes a person; it also organizes the body and mind into a *unit of action*. The most elementary musical behavior—for example, the tinkling of a bell—stimulated and supported by aesthetic, structured musical stimuli provided by the therapist, gives immediate feedback that brings the person into present experiencing and lays the foundation for an awareness of self. The rhythmic patterns and pulsation of music support— actually hold together—bodily movement that might otherwise be uncontrolled, random, or uncoordinated. The cohesion and unity generated by active involvement in therapeutic music activities are not only integrative for the individual but also galvanize a group, bringing people from alienation and isolation into an enlivened world that breaks through these barriers. The intrinsic structure of music becomes a source of internal and external organization. Whatever the style, idiom, ethnic origin, harmonic texture, or mode, structured musical sound reaches and penetrates the human organism in ways that can lead to purposeful action and can bring a person from disorder to order, from fragmentation to integration, from unaware experiencing to aware experiencing.

With music as a catalyst, perception and expressivity occur in new and enlarged ways, with new and enlarged meanings. Projected by the therapist vocally and instrumentally as a clear foreground in the environment, music sets off cycles of awareness (see Chapter 4) and thus provides a focus. Its tempo changes can influence the distractible child whose behaviors are haphazard and purposeless to direct energy to a structured musical activity. Its dynamics can arouse the hypoactive, profoundly retarded person from a state of lethargy into self-initiated action. Its melodic line can bring the autistic person into contact with other human beings who are the intimate source of the music, particularly through the human singing voice. Its rhythmic drive can bring scattered individuals to wholeness and the cooperative experience of making music together.

CONCLUSION

Concurrent with the increase in knowledge about the mentally retarded and other developmentally disabled persons, music therapy has branched out as a specialized area of treatment for this client population. It has kept pace with trends in new and better services that are being explored and implemented. A primary treatment modality, it has become an integral component of institutional services.

Pioneers in music therapy, such as Alvin and the team of Nordoff and Robbins, who worked mainly with the developmentally disabled, attest to the importance of music as a treatment tool for this population. Alvin (1966) observes:

> There is . . . agreement that music is good for these children and that they respond well to music. . . . If this is so, could we not use music at a deeper and more effective level in order to help specifically towards the mental, emotional, and social maturation of handicapped children in need of integrating and enriching experiences at their level? Further-more, can we not find a relationship between their response to certain musical experiences and their mental, physical, or emotional state? . . . We may also ask how musical experiences can be adapted to any kind or degree of handicap. (p. 2)

Nordoff and Robbins (1971) describe the efficacy of music therapy with handicapped children:

> Therapy that lies in music can have a far-reaching effect upon the development of children who bear handicaps of mental impairment, emotional disturbance or physical disability. . . . That the cultural inheritance of music is endowed with countless gifts for every human being is common knowledge, but for these children . . . the "gifts" that music holds are so important that they demand our special considera-tion. (p. 15)

That music has impact on people with all gradations of retardation and handi-capping conditions is undeniable. As a nonverbal means of contact and one of humanity's oldest and most natural resources for self-expression and communication, it has become a potent therapeutic tool. Consequently, this primary modality of treatment can be a cogent vehicle for affecting developmentally disabled persons' attitudes toward themselves and, in turn, for influencing the attitudes of the general public and professionals toward them and the contributions they can make to society.

Music therapy is normalizing, it is socializing, it is humanizing. In a word, it is music therapy for living.

REFERENCES

Alvin, J. *Music therapy*. New York: Humanities Press, 1966.

Boxill, E.H. *Music therapy as a primary treatment modality for the developmentally disabled*. Paper presented at the 105th annual meeting of the American Association on Mental Deficiency, Detroit, Michigan, May 1981.

Boxill, E.H. Music therapy: A primary treatment modality for the developmentally disabled. In J.M. Levy, P.H. Levy, N. Liebman, T.A. Dern, R. Rae, & T.-R. Ames (Eds.), *From the 60s into the 80s: An international assessment of attitudes and services for the developmentally disabled—papers from a conference organized by the Young Adult Institute & Workshop, Inc. in support of the International Year of Disabled Persons, April 6–10, 1981*. New York: Young Adult Institute & Workshop, Inc., 1982.

Brown, A.L. The development of memory: Knowing, knowing about knowing, and knowing how to know. In H.W. Reese (Ed.), *Advances in child development and behavior* (Vol. 10). New York: Academic Press, 1975.

Calder, N. *The mind of man*. New York: Viking Press, 1970.

Hudson, W.C. Music: A physiological language. *Journal of Music Therapy*, 1978, *10*, 137–140.

Langer, S.K. *Philosophy in a new key*. New York: Mentor Books, 1942.

Lundin, R.W. *An objective psychology of music* (2nd ed.). New York: Ronald Press, 1967.

Menolascino, F.J. Emotional disturbance and mental retardation. *American Journal of Mental Deficiency*, 1965, *70*, 248–256.

Menolascino, F.J. Emotional disturbances in mentally retarded children. *American Journal of Psychiatry*, 1969, *126*, 168–176.

Menuhin, Y. *Theme and variations*. New York: Stein and Day, 1972.

Nordoff, P., and Robbins, C. *Therapy in music for handicapped children*. New York: St Martin's Press, 1971.

Rose, S. *The conscious brain*. New York: Alfred A. Knopf, 1973.

Sperry, R. The great cerebral commissure. In N.R. Chalmers, R. Crawley, & S.P.R. Rose (Eds.), *The biological bases of behavior*. London: Harper and Row Ltd., 1971.

Weigl, V. Functional music. A therapeutic tool in working with the mentally retarded. *American Journal of Mental Deficiency*, 1959, *63*, 672–678.

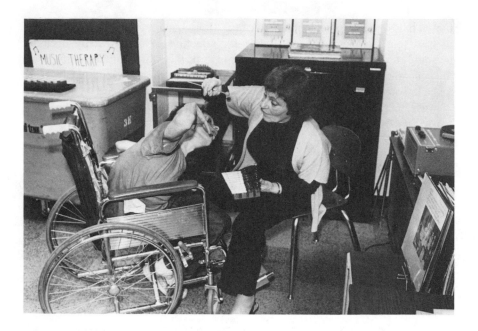

Chapter 3

Assessment and Treatment Planning

Concern for man himself and his fate must always form the chief interest of all our technical endeavors. . . . Never forget this in the midst of your diagrams and equations.

Albert Einstein

INTRODUCTION

Designing a Music Therapy Assessment Form

Music therapy assessment is a tool of a special kind. A treatment modality such as music therapy deals with the totality of human functioning: physical, mental, psychological, and social. Therefore, it demands extensive and highly specialized knowledge about musical and nonmusical behaviors of the complex client population identified as developmentally disabled. Though assessment procedures are addressed in music therapy literature, the area still requires continuous exploration. This chapter concerns itself with music therapy assessment specifically designed for persons who are developmentally disabled.

In designing a music therapy assessment form especially tailored to this client population, one that will enable the therapist to begin to know an individual holistically and to understand deviations from the norm, investigation of the following is essential: (a) the tests most commonly administered to determine the existence and extent of problematic conditions and symptomatology; (b) the various approaches to assessment presently used in the field; (c) normal and abnormal development in adaptive, motoric, communicative, cognitive, affective, and social functioning; and (d) musical characteristics attributed to developmental and maturational stages. Recognizing that assessment is at the core of the practice of music therapy, Bruscia, Hesser, and Boxill (1981) stipulate that the qualified therapist must have the ability to:

23

- identify the client's primary assessment needs in music therapy
- select, design, and implement effective methods for assessing the client's assets and problems through music
- select, design, and implement effective methods for assessing the client's musical preferences and level of musical functioning or development
- observe and record the client's responses to assessment accurately
- determine the reliability and validity of the assessment data collected
- interpret and utilize the assessment findings of other disciplines
- identify the client's therapeutic needs through analysis and interpretation of the assessment data (pp. 46–47)

Inasmuch as this client population presents both common problems and diverse conditions, music therapy assessment, which involves assessment of musical as well as nonmusical behaviors, is comprehensive in scope. Administered by means of music therapy methodology, it examines significant aspects of functioning relative to musical responses and music-related activities, is concerned with the influence of music on the person, and reveals aspects of an individual that may not surface in other situations. A prerequisite for music therapy treatment planning, it provides a unique contribution to the total service of the client. The success of therapeutic intervention is directly related to the quality of a holistic assessment. Such assessment entails identifying (a) developmental skills, (b) deficits and discrepancies in functioning, (c) lags in developmental milestones, (d) adaptive behaviors, (e) behavioral problems, (f) emotional states and disorders, (g) pathology (mental, physical, psychological), and (h) strengths, interests, and abilities (musical and nonmusical).

At the same time as investigation is conducted through music and music activities, information is garnered from four main sources: (a) direct observation of the individual, (b) the developmental history of the individual, (c) written and verbal reports from members of a treatment team, including representative tests (see Table 3–1); and (d) discussions with the family. Although music therapy assessment forms or approaches may vary, the initial process is best extended over a period of weeks. The rationale for this lies in the fact that music therapy assessments are most often task-oriented procedures (in the Piagetian sense) rather than testing procedures.

Some Approaches to Music Therapy Assessment

The literature contains discussions and models for music therapy assessment of developmentally disabled persons (Bitcon, 1976; Cohen, Averbach, & Katz, 1978; Cohen & Gericke, 1972; Rider, 1981; Wasserman, Plutchil, Deutsch, & Taketomo, 1973).

Table 3–1 Representative Tests Used in Identifying Persons with Developmental Disabilities

Test	Age range	Subject of test
Bayley's Scale of Development, 1969	2–30 months	Global intelligence
Bender–Gestalt Test, 1970	4 years and over	Visual motor
Cattell Infant Intelligence	3–30 months	Global intelligence
Frostig Developmental Test of Visual Perception, 1966	4–10 years	Visual perception
Gesell Developmental Schedules (GDS), 1949	4 weeks– 6 years	Global intelligence
Goodenough–Harris Drawing Test, 1963	3–15 years	Nonverbal intelligence, body image, personality
Illinois Test of Psycholinguistics (ITPA), 1968	2–10 years	Mental processing
Merrill–Palmer Scale of Mental Tests, 1931	24–36 months	Global intelligence
Motor-Free Visual Perception Test (MVPT), 1972	4–8 years	Visual perception
Peabody Picture Vocabulary Test (PPVT), 1970	2½–18 years	Verbal intelligence (receptive language)
Purdue Perceptual Motor Survey, 1966	4–10 years	Motor development
Stanford–Binet Intelligence Scale, 1973	2 years and over	Global intelligence
Vineland Social Maturity Scale (VSMS), 1965	infant–adult	Social competence
Wechsler Intelligence Scale for Children (WISC), 1949	5–15 years	Global intelligence
Wechsler Preschool and Primary Scale of Intelligence (WPPSI), 1967	4–6½–years	Global intelligence
Wide Range Achievement Test (WRAT), 1965	K–college	Word recognition, spelling, arithmetic

Source: Adapted from Nocera, S. *Reaching the special learner through music.* Morristown, N.J.: Silver-Burdett Co., 1979.

In the words of Cohen et al. (1978):

A music therapy assessment of the developmentally disabled client incorporates all significant aspects of a person's functioning relative to musical response and music-related activity. . . . It considers the dimensions of primary musical influence whether the client is a participant or observer, whether for developmental growth/normalization, or as therapeutic intervention uniquely applicable in the specific skill and functioning level of the client. (p. 98)

These authors emphasize that the nature of the assessment should be such as to include a wide range of functioning levels and disabilities.

According to Cohen and Gericke (1972), music therapy assessment for the developmentally delayed is concerned with:

- determining the extent to which music and musical stimuli influence the developmentally disabled person's behavior
- identifying nonmusical behaviors and deficits that are revealed through the assessment instrument
- covering a wide range of functioning levels and disabilities
- incorporating significant aspects of human functioning relative to musical responses and music-related activities
- findings that are documented and recorded through skillfully administered assessment
- presenting findings and recommendations to appropriate treatment team members
- integrating findings with other data treatment plans with a view to determining overall programming
- devising a music therapy program on a one-to-one basis or within a group setting

Wasserman et al. (1973) assess musical aptitudes and social behaviors of developmentally disabled people by observing their response in a rhythm group, a singing group, and a vocal dynamics group. They look for:

1. *Individual Participation*
   - willingness to participate
   - level of participation
2. *Rhythmic Responses*
   - ability to imitate rhythmic pattern played by the therapist
   - ability to imitate changes in rhythm
   - ability to imitate changes of tempo
   - ability to initiate rhythmic patterns
   - ability to maintain rhythmic pulse

3. *Use of Instruments*
   - choice of instrument
   - ability to use instrument
   - ability to use different kinds of instruments: percussive (drums), shaking (maracas), scraping (guiro), plucking (strings), blowing (song flute)

Bitcon (1976) is concerned with:

1. *Measurement of Attention Span*
   - makes eye contact with leaders
   - makes eye contact with peers
2. *Measurement of Retention*
   - stays within circle during routine
   - recognizes other members of the group
3. *Awareness of Self and Others*
   - verbalizes own name during chant
   - names other members in the group
   - responds to own name
   - recognizes body parts
4. *Attitudes*
   - participates in activity
   - initiates activity
   - volunteers to lead activity

For a thorough assessment of the cognitive functioning level of the mentally retarded child through musical perception, Rider (1981) uses Piaget's cognitive schemata.

In investigative studies using the methodology of musical improvisation, Nordoff and Robbins (1971, 1977)* found responses in the form of drum beating to be rich in their yield of information about a disabled or handicapped child's pathological, mental, emotional, and physical condition. The categories of responses they offer can guide assessment and contribute to diagnosis. Compulsive drum beating, for example, may be symptomatic of a lack of contact with self and the environment. Chaotic drum beating may reveal a lack of integration. In characterizing unstable rhythmic freedom in drum beating, they observe: "Here there is rhythmic freedom and perception of music but the response is marred or limited by the child losing self-control through excessive reaction to the stimulus of the music" (1971, p. 64), the cause of which may be psychological or neurological.

---

*See the Nordoff and Robbins books (1971, 1977) for a comprehensive discussion of categories of response.

Normal and Abnormal Development

To understand the information gathered in the assessment, knowledge of normal development is required (Gesell & Ilg, 1946; Mussen, 1965; Stone & Church, 1957). For instance, knowing that the neonate begins to vocalize in response to verbal or tonal sound between two and five weeks of age, one can assess the extent of a developmental lag if there has been failure to respond or to progress to other maturational sequences within a reasonable range. Therefore, this section discusses the many aspects of the human being that are assessed—adaptive behavior, the various domains of functioning, and musical characteristics of average and atypical development—and the ages at which they usually develop.

At least four broad types of influence have a role in determining developmental growth: (a) biological properties, such as genetic endowment, temperament, rate of maturation; (b) cultural group membership and variations; (c) the individual's personal experiences and relationship with others; and (d) situations and stimuli in the immediate environment. The biological, psychic, and environmental determinants are combined and interwoven—operating on, interacting with, and affecting development concurrently.

Acquired characteristics and abilities result from two basic processes that always interact: maturation and learning. *Maturation,* as defined by McCandless (1961), is "the organic process of structural changes occurring within an individual's body that are relatively independent of external environmental conditions, experiences, or practice. By maturation is meant development of the organism as a function of time, or age" (p. 118). *Learning* is generally a term that refers to changes in behavior or performance as a consequence of experience (Hilgard, 1948). The interaction between these two phenomena is directly related to developmental changes as well. To assess developmental lags, it is necessary to know the average course of maturation and development. It is thus also necessary to know that there are *critical periods* of development of certain organs or functions and that interference with normal development at such periods is likely to result in permanent deficiencies or malfunctions (Mussen, 1965). Mindful of this, the music therapist must realize that although a child may develop the age-related ability to carry a tune at the age of four, environmental conditions could arrest further maturation and development in the capacity for musical expression. The therapist who is conversant with the normal course of motoric development will be able to make an accurate assessment of deviant development and, at the very least, to recognize areas of disability and dysfunction that can be improved through the therapeutic use of music.

It must be clearly understood that the domains of functioning are inextricably interwoven. Human development proceeds simultaneously in the various domains and involves interaction between many areas of functioning. Constitutional and environmental influences affect this interaction in both normal and abnormal development. Therefore, in viewing delayed or arrested development or psychosocial dysfunction, it is of utmost importance to be aware that behaviors become maladaptive when communication and emotions are seriously disturbed. It is also necessary to be alert to the fact that cognitive, social, and physical development can be extremely uneven, resulting in marked discrepancies between functioning levels in these different domains.

A developmentally disabled person is described as having failed to progress at a normal rate if he or she does not acquire:

- motor skills, such as gross and fine body movements, coordination, and balance
- adaptive skills, such as the problem-solving abilities and manipulative skills necessary to interact effectively with the environment
- communication skills, such as the capacity to express oneself verbally or nonverbally
- cognitive skills, such as the ability to recognize numbers, colors, and words
- social skills, such as the abilities required to interact with others and to use leisure time productively

Thoughtful scrutiny of the environment and responses to it, as well as full attention to the importance of individual differences in growth and development, are necessary for an encompassing appraisal of a person's functioning. The age-related behavioral expectancies cited in Table 3–2 provide some measure of guidance regarding delayed functioning levels.

Adaptive Behavior

The complex sphere of adaptive behavior is influenced by a combination of factors—biological, psychological, and sociocultural (Garrard & Richmond, 1965). The conceptual scheme outlined next serves as a foundation for a comprehensive view of a person:

1. *Biological*
   - perception
   - motor disorders
   - sensory disorders (visual, auditory, tactual, kinesthetic)
   - language pathways
   - somatic handicaps
2. *Psychological*
   - sensory deprivation
   - adaptational patterns

Table 3–2 Adaptive Behaviors of Mentally Retarded Persons

Degree	1 to 5 years	6 to 20 years	21 and over
Mild	Is capable of communication, social, and self-help skills; some delay in sensorimotor functioning	Is capable of limited academic skills, good self-help skills, social, and communication skills	Can acquire adequate social and vocational skills for minimal independent living
Moderate	Develops communication skills (including speech), fair motor skills, some self-help skills, and social awareness	Is capable of rudimentary academic, communication, and social skills, and fair self-help skills	Is capable of unskilled work in sheltered workshop
Severe	Has little or no communication skills and poor motor development	Is capable of rudimentary nonacademic, social, and communication skills and limited self-help skills	May be capable of simple tasks in sheltered workshop, home, or institutional setting
Profound	Has no speech or communication skills and little or no capacity for psychomotor functioning	Has some motor skills and minimal or no self-help skills; speech for communicative purposes does not develop	Has some motor skills and minimal or no self-help skills; speech for communicative purposes does not develop

Sources: Adapted from Gardner, W.I. *Learning and behavior characteristics of exceptional children and youth: A humanistic behavioral approach.* Boston: Allyn & Bacon, 1977; Sloan, W., & Birch, H. A rationale for degree of retardation. *American Journal of Mental Deficiency* 1955, *60,* 258–264.

- conflict and anxiety
- self-concept
3. *Sociocultural*
   - familial history
   - cultural group

Grossman (1977) defines adaptive behavior as the degree to, or effectiveness with which an individual meets the standards of personal independence and social responsibility expected for members of his or her age and cultural group. This definition allows for variance between aspects of the environment and responses to it as well as the importance of individual differences in growth and development.

The instrument most often used to rate adaptive behavior is the American Association on Mental Deficiency (AAMD) Adaptive Behavior Scale (ABS) (Nihira, Foster, Shellhaas, & Leland, 1974). It represents the widest variety of behavioral domains among current published instruments and is divided into two parts. Part I measures domains in self-care and socialization, such as:

- independent functioning
- physical development
- economic activity
- numbers and terms
- domestic activity
- vocational activities
- self-direction
- responsibility
- socialization

Part II rates interpersonal and intrapersonal maladaptations, such as:

- violent and destructive behavior
- antisocial behavior
- rebellious behavior
- untrustworthy behavior
- withdrawal
- stereotyped behavior and odd mannerisms
- inappropriate interpersonal manners
- unacceptable vocal habits
- unacceptable or eccentric habits
- self-abusive behavior

- hyperactive tendencies
- sexually aberrant behavior
- psychological disturbances
- use of medications

The use of medications "is not a behavioral domain, but does provide information about a person's adaptation to the world" (Nihira et al., 1974, p. 7).

Motor Domain

A delay in motor development is frequently the first apparent sign of a developmental problem. Even if there is no organicity, severe environmental and sensory deprivation can interfere significantly with development. Since much of music therapy deals with musical behaviors that require expressive use of the body, motor development is of major concern to the music therapist who specializes in working with clients whose physical disabilities and dysfunctions are conspicuously prevalent. It is essential to be knowledgeable about the natural course of motoric development and maturation so as to be able to identify developmental stages and recognize motor problems and their resultant interference with the acquisition of skills. Emphasis on this area of functioning is growing in light of research and empirical studies (Barsch, 1967; Cratty & Martin, 1969) indicating that improvement of physical skills leads to enhancement of emotional well-being and increased ability to learn. To skip rhythmically to music and climb on a jungle gym are joyous experiences often denied the developmentally disabled child.

Motor development proceeds in a proximodistal or outward direction, the central parts of the body maturing earlier and becoming functional before those toward the periphery. Thus, an infant exhibits arm movements before moving the wrists, hands, and fingers. In locomotion, the upper arm and upper leg are brought under voluntary control before the forearm, foreleg, hands, and feet. Another trend is from general to specific activities. Most of an infant's earliest motor behaviors are undifferentiated movements of the whole body or large segments of it. Diffuse movements are gradually replaced by differentiated and controlled actions.

The cephalocaudal (head to toe) maturational process of the nervous system emerges toward the end of the first year. As this maturation takes place, many new functions and skills are manifested. Balance and fine motor skills improve in the normal course of neurological maturation, which continues through the teenage years as outlined in Table 3–3.

Deviations from normal motor development occur for many reasons. There may be a delay because of a specific defect that interferes with the acquisition of age-related motor skills, or the rate of progress through sequences of motor abilities may be slower than expected for a certain age. Johnston (1976) wrote:

Table 3–3 Motor Behaviors from Infancy to 12 Years

Age	Neuromotor maturation	Sample skills
0–3 months	Head	Holds head in erect position
3–6 months	Upper torso and arms	Sits, reaches, creeps, waves arms
6–9 months	Lower trunk and legs	Crawls, pulls to stand
9–12 months	Integration of legs	Ambulates
1–2 years	Increase in interaction between motor system and other brain functions	Develops stair skills: ascent and descent by creeping, then marking time (two feet on each step)
3 years	Increase in capacity for conscious control of movement	Jumps forward with both feet leaving ground at same time
		Runs forward and walks backward without stumbling for short distances
4 years	Improvement of body equilibrium	Descends stairs alternating legs
5 years	Neuromotor system well advanced in development	Hops on one foot two or three times
6–7 years	Continued change and enhancement of coordination (gross and fine motor) and eye–hand coordination	Skips alternating legs in rhythmic manner, ties shoelaces
7–12 years and up	Advancement in motor control, coordination, balance, and strength	Engages in sports, games of skill, and creative and social dancing

The proper understanding of the [person] with abnormal development requires assessment as to whether the problem rests with *rate,* as seen in normal familial patterns and mental retardation, with *defective patterns* interfering with skill progression . . . or with both components, slow rate and defective patterns, as seen in mental retardation with cerebral palsy. (pp. 48–49)

Communication Domain

One of the common denominators for people with developmental disabilities is a lack of communication skills in the broadest sense—from gestures to facial expressions to vocalizations to tactual cues to oral language. Investigators and clinicians are now turning their attention to the use of forms of nonspeech and nonverbal communication that transmit meaning from one individual to another. Fristoe and Lloyd (1979) observe that "the need for a nonspeech communication system occurs when spoken communication is inadequate due to . . . personal factors such as physical constraints (cerebral palsy, deafness, dysarthria) and . . . cognitive and intellectual constraints (severe mental retardation, aphasia, oral apraxia)" (p. 402).

For the music therapist whose modality offers myriad means of expression and communication, assessment of the person's condition and potential for various means of communication, both nonverbal and verbal, is vital. As an example, when Ricki, who had been tested as having a severe hearing problem and not being responsive to the spoken word, sang the musical phrase "day by day" and clapped a steady beat in her third assessment session, new possibilities for developing communicative skills opened up.

In the normal developmental pattern of speech and language acquisition, the earliest manifestation is largely a motor function that follows a definite sequence strongly suggesting a maturational progression (see Table 3–4). Through the use of musical stimuli, the music therapist can use as a guideline the broad areas of receptive and expressive language that Hedrick, Prather, and Tobin (1975) offer in a sequenced inventory of communication development. Assessing communication abilities of normal and retarded children who are functioning between the ages of four months and four years, they offer a series of tests that are outlined below:

1. *Receptive Scale*
   - awareness: observable responses such as turning to or looking toward source of sound
   - discrimination: observable response such as responding differentially to sounds being presented
   - understanding: observable responses and actions that relate to sound stimulus
2. *Expressive Scale*
   - motor response: points to, touches, or manipulates object when requested to identify it
   - vocal response: responds by uttering sound(s) not classified as belonging to the linguistic code of child's community
   - verbal response: responds by uttering sound(s) classified as belonging to the linguistic code of child's community
3. *Receptive and Expressive Scale*
   - imitating behaviors: repeats motor or speech event
   - initiating behaviors: motor and speech behaviors that occur without previous verbal event
   - responding behaviors: utterances, excluding imitation, that follow verbal antecedent events

It is essential that the music therapist be acquainted with causes of communication disorders, such as:

Table 3–4 Normal Developmental Pattern of Language Development

Approximate age	Type of expression	Characteristics
0–6 weeks	Cooing and babbling	Nondescriptive sounds; spontaneous utterances: ma-ma-ma-ma, da-da-da-da
2–9 months	Lallation echolalia	Gives evidence of hearing: During lalling phase, child is likely to imitate gestures and facial expressions, as well as sounds
10 months	Jargon/vocalizations (Note: not all children go through jargon stage)	Change in vocalizations: Child begins to pick up lilt and inflections of adult speech and incorporates them in lalling behavior
		Vocalizations are not rhythmic; have intonations and ring of real speech
8–12 months	First words	

- developmental lags
- maturational lags
- organic deficits and anomalies
- severe restriction of sensory input
- sensory impairment
- sensory deprivation
- perceptual-motor disturbance
- maladaptive behaviors
- emotional disorders
- functional retardation
- inadequate vocal apparatus
- impairment of interpersonal relations

Cognitive Domain

For cognitive development, according to Tanguay (1980, p. 84), "there exists only one comprehensive model, that of Swiss psychologist Jean Piaget. Piaget's model is especially relevant to clinical work."*

---

*For a detailed account of Piaget's theory, see *The Origins of Intelligence in Children* (Piaget, 1952) and *The Developmental Psychology of Jean Piaget* (Flavell, 1963).

Piaget describes cognitive development as taking place in two main periods (Richmond, 1970), the functions of which are quantitatively and qualitatively different: (1) the period of sensorimotor operations, which is divided into six stages; and (2) the period of the development of conceptual intelligence, which is divided into three stages. Table 3–5 provides the Piagetian constructs of cognitive development.

It was Inhelder (1968) who first suggested the applicability of Piaget's theory of cognitive development to people who are retarded. He found that although retarded children may follow the same order of stages, though at a slower rate than average children, those who are severely retarded may cease to develop while still in the sensorimotor or early operational stage. And those who are moderately or mildly retarded may only reach the earlier stages of concrete operation. This means that their capacity for abstract thinking may never develop.

Table 3–5 Piagetian Constructs of Cognitive Development

Age	Period	Schemata/operations
Birth to 2 years:	Sensorimotor intelligence (six stages):	
0–2 months	Stage 1	Reflexive behavior
2–4 months	Stage 2	Repetitive behavior
4–8 months	Stage 3	Intentional adaptation
8–12 months	Stage 4	Intentional activity; more complex memory stores
12–18 months	Stage 5	Systematic variation of behaviors; exploratory and experimental activity
1½–2 years	Stage 6	Beginnings of internal thought processes; simple problem solving
2–12 years and up:	Conceptual intelligence (three stages):	
2 years to 6 or 7 years	Stage 1—Preoperational thought	Beginnings of conceptualization and representational thoughts and images
6 or 7 years to 12 years	Stage 2—Concrete operational thought	Understanding of how objects and events relate to each other
12 years and up	Stage 3—Formal operational thought	Ability to use symbols and deal with abstract as well as concrete reality

Extending Inhelder's research, Woodward (1979) indicated that Piaget's sensorimotor period is especially relevant to the assessment of people with developmental disabilities. And Kahn (1979) makes the interesting and original observation that mannerisms and seemingly strange behaviors are "to be expected of severely and profoundly retarded individuals, who are functioning within the sensorimotor period, and should not be viewed as bizarre. Quite the contrary, these behaviors should be viewed as possibly indicating the stage at which an individual is functioning cognitively" (p. 274).

Affective Domain

Normal affective development involves human relationships—starting with parents, peers, and adults other than family and gradually expanding to wider social horizons. The foundation of emotional strength and self-worth is rooted in what Erik Erikson (1963) calls *basic trust* and the subsequent acquisition of *autonomy* and *socialization*. With disturbances in development, for whatever reason, the ability and often the opportunity to form such relationships are not available. Mistrust in the early years results in emotional responses that may be limited in range from distress to apathy.

In actuality, the person with mental retardation is subject to the same kinds of emotional stress, frustration, anxiety, and conflict as the normal person. Because of the inability to express these emotions and feelings in acceptable or sublimated ways, the disturbance often dominates the person's existence and compounds psychosocial dysfunctioning. Living with failure breeds vulnerability, inadequacy, and hostility. Though descriptive phrases such as "low self-esteem," "lack of motivation to learn," "overwhelming sense of failure," and "fearful and low in energy" appear frequently in clinical reports of developmentally disabled people, the affective states implied in these descriptions are often neglected or ignored. As a result, emotional disorders and disturbances are prevalent. Yet, as Szymanski (1980) points out, "A common mistake committed . . . is focusing excessively on diagnosing the retardation and neglecting . . . mental disorder" (p. 76).

One of the difficulties now being addressed is "differentiating the symptoms of major affective disorders from environmentally produced symptomatology or organic illness" (Rivinus, 1980, p. 208). It has been found that the incidence of affective disorder of the manic, depressive, and bipolar type occurs as frequently in persons with mental retardation as in the general population (Reid, 1972).

In the music therapy assessment process, one looks for musical behaviors that are indicative of psychological conditions. In the first stage of assessment, emotions, feelings, and moods—sometimes mood swings—are visible even to the least discerning eye. Clinical improvisations in various musical moods, idioms, and styles are used to evoke responses that are clues to the person's personality structure as well as the here-and-now person. These responses are raw material for the music therapist. Much information about the person's emotional makeup is revealed in how he or she moves or does not move, relates or does not relate to the music or an instrument, sings or does not sing, and, most of all, interacts or does not interact with the therapist.

The hyperactive child serves as a graphic illustration of these points. Though the condition may be organic, emotionally induced symptoms stem from anxiety, emotional instability, feelings of helplessness and failure, fears, and a poor self-image. In coping with fear and attempting to allay anxiety, the child generates excessive motor activity. A cycle is set in motion, and the child is caught in a whirlwind. Even in the assessment process the therapist seeks ways to make contact through musical improvisation that either reflects the child's behaviors or effects changes in them. Assessment and the therapeutic process overlap and intertwine on a continuum.

Social Domain

The construct of social intelligence, or a person's ability to understand and deal effectively with social and interpersonal events, has many implications for social skills and adaptive behavior that offer direction for music therapy group work. Both Doll (1965), in measuring a person's social quotient, and Gesell and Ilg (1946), in measuring the developmental quotient, concur that social competency is an age-related developmental attribute. The broad view in Table 3–6 of the

Table 3–6 Social Behaviors from Infancy to Adolescence

Age	Psychosocial development
Infancy	Interactions progress steadily from initial indifference toward other partner to social interest and cooperative play; development of basic trust
6–8 months	Generally ignores partner
9–13 months	Some attention given to partner
14–18 months	Attention to partner increases considerably
Toddler and nursery school years	Social adjustment markedly accelerated; development of autonomy
1–3 years	Rudimentary forms of social interaction; parallel play
4–6 years	Social interaction with peers and adults; associative or cooperative play; initiation of activities
School and adolescent years	Socialization progresses; identity is defined
6–11 years	Increased peer relationships; sexual identification; development of sense of industry
12–18 years	Social and sexual maturation; identity formation

progression of social behavior over a span from infancy to 18 years is intended to alert the music therapist to the need to make a study of social and psychosocial development.

As in emotional or affective development, interpersonal relationships are the fundamental issue in social development as well. The development of a child's interpersonal behavior is of critical importance. During the first year or 18 months of life, three basic phases of attachment take the form of (a) indiscriminate or diffuse attachment; (b) single or specific attachment; and (c) multiple attachments. These phases are directly related to parent–child relationships. From the ages of two to four movement occurs away from adults and toward other children as objects of attachment or dependency. Interaction with peers increases as egocentrism lessens. By the time they reach school age, children have developed a sense of group; relationships with peers take on a qualitative change.

In the course of normal development and acquisition of social behaviors, Waite (1972) tells us that the individual:

- develops the ability to take turns
- develops the ability to share
- develops the ability to cooperate
- develops awareness of self
- develops awareness of others
- develops awareness of immediate environment
- identifies main parts of body
- acquires linguistic skills
- acquires self-help skills
- acquires home-help skills
- participates in group activities
- develops the ability to participate as a team member
- accepts social responsibilities within the home
- accepts social responsibilities outside the home
- converses to exchange information or convey desires
- uses concepts of time (tomorrow, yesterday) with understanding
- uses a calendar (day, week, year)
- selects leisure time activities

Because of individual differences in the attainment of social maturity and independent functioning, deviant or atypical development of the individual must be assessed in light of constitutional (endogenous) and environmental (exogenous) variables relative to the normative societal framework.

Musical Characteristics

Because musical *abilities* appear to be largely innate, there is at any given age an enormous range (Bentley, 1975). In order to assist the therapist in assessment of atypical development, in this section we will look at some of the musical *characteristics* that have developmental implications, keeping in mind the fact that musical abilities or aptitudes are to be distinguished from musical characteristics.

The development of musical expression is usually investigated by observation. It is often correlated with the normal stages the child moves through in acquiring speech. The music psychologist Révész (1954) gives us a broad glimpse of age-related musical characteristics, offering a developmental progression that indicates characteristic utterances of children at various stages. Révész recounts that by the end of the first year of life, the child begins to imitate pitch. In the second and third years—the first period of speech development—children may begin to sing their own melody fragments, which are usually related to movement. In fact, movement and speech sounds are inseparable at this age, and a strong rhythmic sense begins to emerge. During this period, words gradually acquire a connection to the melody, replacing babble songs. Three- and four-year-olds develop the ability to run, jump, and gallop *in time* to music.

In one of the studies that deals with musical characteristics of children, Zimmerman (1971) informs us that, with regard to the perception of musical sounds, there are findings that loudness discrimination develops at an early age and can be studied experimentally through discrimination tasks of varying intensities of sound. It is helpful for the music therapist-assessor to have age-related guidelines, such as the fact that a four-year-old child manifests *awareness* of relative volume of musical sound and that the five- or six-year-old readily *discriminates* between changes in volume. As might be anticipated, the development of auditory perception and the ability to reproduce melodies do indeed increase in the maturational process, particularly in an environment that stimulates sensitivity and natural ability.

Also, the greatest improvement in tonal memory occurs between the ages of eight and nine. In investigating vocal development of the young child, Zimmerman finds that the first songs learned range from C' to F' or from D' to G'. These should be followed by songs in the range of C' to A', with the final range including the pitches from C' to E''.*

Petzold (1963) finds that development of a sense of tonality between the ages of six and seven is concurrent with rhythmic discrimination, and that although vocal development is dependent on maturation, musical experiences further the ability to sing with accuracy.

---

*The middle register of the voice is indicated as follows: C' to F', D' to G', and D' to A'; E'' refers to the upper register.

When assessing auditory perception and vocal range, it is important to be aware of the singing range of the developmentally disabled person. It has been found that the singing range of the mentally retarded person is lower (sometimes by as much as four half steps or two whole tones) than that of nonretarded peers, and that it has been positively and significantly correlated to intellectual functioning levels as well as adaptive behaviors.

In a study of musical characteristics of mildly and moderately retarded children, Bruscia (1981) attributes many of the perceptual deficits of this client population to attentional problems. Because the ability to discriminate between foreground and background is lacking or minimal, extraneous stimuli in the environment easily distract the child from attending to the musical stimuli provided. First of all, it is necessary to determine whether there is organic impairment affecting perceptual-motor functions. As Bruscia (1981) reports:

> For example, some children have specific learning disabilities (e.g., auditory perceptual impairment due to brain damage or motor apraxia) which may interfere grossly with music perception tasks, and particularly those requiring auditory figure-ground discrimination, auditory sequencing, and motor planning. (p. 103)

ADMINISTRATION OF THE ASSESSMENT

A Model Assessment Form

Appendix 3-A, the Music Therapy Assessment Form (Boxill, 1983), is applicable to persons of all ages and with diverse conditions. It can be used with equal success by both the experienced and inexperienced therapist. A music therapy assessment is best administered over a period of weeks. For this reason, the therapist arranges to see clients on a one-to-one basis and in a group setting, in order to explore the person's musical and nonmusical behaviors both individually and in relation to others. In administering the assessment form, the therapist uses improvised or composed music (vocal and instrumental) for singing, chanting, instrument playing, and music-movement activities. Where specific songs are indicated in the guidelines (Appendix 3-B), they are intended to serve as suggestions only. It is assumed that the trained, qualified therapist administering this form has a repertoire of suitable music available and is competent in clinical improvisation. The author invites a heuristic attitude toward the use of the form as well as the guidelines offered for administering it.

Because music therapy assessment is administered over a period of time, it enables the therapist to become acquainted with the person with whom a therapeutic relationship is about to begin. And because assessment is the initial encounter with the client, it is crucial to the client–therapist relationship. The therapist enters the assessment process viewing the client as a total human being, observing and recording every fine detail that contributes to a portrait on which to base a treatment plan. Before beginning the actual assessment or consulting any client records, however, it is essential that the therapist observe the client in as many settings and situations as possible in order to avoid prejudgments (conscious or unconscious). By not only identifying problems but also noting strengths that can bolster the client's opportunity to become as full a human being as possible, the therapist uses the process of assessment to discover facets of the person that may have heretofore lain dormant. With this attitude, the therapist sets the continuum of the music therapy experience into motion for the individual.

The realization that latent strengths and capabilities may emerge is a compelling aspect of the assessment process. A person's individuality or originality may burst forth during a response to musical stimuli, as was the case for 29-year-old Teddy. During the first assessment session, Teddy hissed and spat at the therapist. At the second session, he continued to express resistance in the same manner. Suddenly, upon hearing a dance rhythm that the therapist was playing on the piano, he picked up a drum mallet. With a grin on his face, he started to beat a timpani drum in a vigorous, steady beat related to the therapist's musical improvisation. After a few minutes of this energizing activity, he stood up and danced around the room, his entire body animated (except for his left arm, which was inert because of paresis), his feet moving in an original interpretation of the music.

When a person is involved in music activities and is responding to musical stimuli, dimensions of the various domains of functioning are uncovered in musical as well as nonmusical behaviors. For example, a problem may be uncovered during the assessment encounter by the tapping of rhythm sticks that is invariably the same, no matter what tempo or dynamic changes the therapist improvises. This stereotypic tapping could be the manifestation of a motor deficit, an auditory deficit, a perceptual-motor deficit, emotional disturbance, or an unawareness of the immediate environment. Another example is a person whose fine motor skills are minimal but who is motivated by energetic music to make an attempt—and eventually succeed—at plucking the strings of a guitar in a steady, rhythmic pattern. Ambiguities and discrepancies in cognitive functioning are especially obvious in the person who cannot comprehend a simple verbal directive, yet sits down at the piano and plays a somewhat garbled but still recognizable version of Chopin's "Minute Waltz."

TREATMENT PLANNING

Once problem areas and strengths have been identified through a holistic assessment of the client, an individualized treatment plan is formulated. Treatment planning involves (a) formulating long-term goals and short-term objectives, (b) determining the appropriateness of individual or group therapy or both, and (c) determining procedures for writing individual and group therapy session reports, monthly progress reports, and annual evaluations. The existence of an interdisciplinary treatment team at an institution mandates that long-term music therapy goals—designed to achieve developmentally appropriate skills, adaptive behavior, and higher functioning levels—be determined in conjunction with the team and be incorporated into the client's overall treatment plan (the order of priority determined by the team) as well as the music therapy treatment plan.

With respect to goal writing, terminology differs from therapy to therapy and from one orientation to another. In this text, the term *goal* is used to designate a broad statement of the direction therapy will take, while an *objective* is a specific means toward that end. The distinction between goals and objectives is their degree of specificity and the time element involved in their attainment. Short-term objectives are the means or methods by which long-term goals are attained. They are designed to help the person reach long-term goals in ways and through processes that tap his or her own resources, build upon the healthy parts of the individual, call forth areas of growth, and reflect the changes that take place. Some long-term goals are achieved through a progression of developmental steps, such as work on acquiring the skill to skip. This skill requires the building of abilities through a developmental sequence of prerequisite motoric skills: (a) hopping on one foot, (b) hopping on the other foot, (c) adding a short step between each hop, and (d) alternating feet rhythmically. The final action of skipping, however, is best evoked by the power of "skipping" music. When the movements become coordinated and are experienced kinesthetically, the power of the rhythmic pattern of the music can propel the person into the desired action. Also, the spirit or quality of the music can generate physical expression that might otherwise be laborious or unattainable.

Music therapy goals and objectives are congruent with the treatment goals of other disciplines. They are written on an individualized basis, in accordance with the initial and yearly music therapy assessment, and are interwoven in numerous ways into the process of developing awareness of self, others, and the environment within the context of *A Continuum of Awareness* (see Chapter 4). Examples of long-term music therapy goals follow:

- to increase attending behavior
- to increase adaptive behavior
- to improve self-image and body awareness
- to increase communication skills
- to increase cognitive skills

- to increase the ability to use energy purposefully
- to improve gross motor skills
- to improve fine motor skills
- to improve perceptual-motor skills
- to improve auditory perception
- to increase visual perception
- to reduce maladaptive (stereotypic, compulsive, self-abusive, assaultive, disruptive, perseverative, impulsive) behaviors
- to increase interaction with peers, interpersonal contact, and socialization
- to increase independence and self-direction
- to stimulate creativity and imagination
- to enhance affective adjustment

Table 3–7 offers some long-term goals and several short-term objectives for each as they would be formulated in a music therapy treatment plan.

It is important to note that once clients have been assessed and groups set up, group goals are formulated. These goals are based on the needs inherent in group therapy, such as group cohesion and socialization, and on the predominant needs of the group as an entity. Whether the group is homogeneous or heterogeneous with respect to age and level of functioning, there will always be common problems that can be addressed. For instance, if all the members have problems in focusing their energies, a group goal would be to increase attending behavior. If members of the group lack a cognitive skill that is being dealt with in special education, a group goal would be to reinforce that skill. Because clients have problems in common, group goals and individual goals are being met simultaneously. In other words, the individual and group goals are interwoven into the fabric of the session.

The discrepancies and disparities in functioning within the same person and the nature of the disabilities that this client population presents make it unfeasible to specify an exact date for the attainment of goals and objectives. It would be unfortunate, indeed inadvisable, to set limits on a person's potential or put a timetable on a person's progress. At the same time, the therapist must ensure that clients achieve experiences of success and a sense of gratification by setting goals and objectives that they can reasonably attain. As clients manifest more and more relatedness to musical stimuli in the three modes of therapeutic music activities (see Chapter 5) and show signs of being capable of going beyond the ''reasonable'' attainment of a goal, the therapist must be ready to follow their lead and set higher goals.

Knowledge of normal and abnormal development is a requisite for evaluating progress, just as it is for making an assessment. Evaluation of progress can be

Table 3–7 Long-Term Goals and Short-Term Objectives

Long-term goals	Short-term objectives
To increase attending behavior	Hold up hands when the therapist, modeling action, sings "Hands"
	Clap hands together imitatively when the therapist models and sings "Clap hands"
	Sing last word of song phrase (the therapist waits for client to fill in word)
	Play (rhythm instrument), taking turns
	Play (rhythm instrument) for duration of music/song
To improve nonlocomotor gross motor skills	Raise arms/turn around/bend up and down/swing arms to music
To improve locomotor skills	Walk slowly/quickly to music/drumbeat
	Run/hop/jump/skip to music/drumbeat
To increase fine motor skills	Grasp drum mallet when offered by the therapist
	Pick up and use drum mallet appropriately to music
	Grasp and hold handbell
	Sign: "Start," "Stop," and "Wait"
	Finger play as indicated in song/chant
	Pantomime buttoning shirt as indicated in song
To improve perceptual-motor skills	Manipulate a single resonator bell and mallet to music
	Beat a drum/xylophone with a mallet
	Tap rhythm sticks/clavés together/clash hand cymbals together
	Beat a melodic rhythm on drum
To reduce rapid, stereotypic arm waving	Clap hands/move arms/shake handbell/beat drum slowly to musical stimuli
	Chant/sing (if the client is verbal) rhythmic word pattern: "Clap hands slowly/beat drum slowly," etc.
To develop impulse control	Count 1-2-3 and sign "Start/Play"
	Stop playing rhythm instrument, singing, or moving when the therapist sings, "And now we're going to stop," using sign for "Stop"
	Sign "Stop/Wait" (sing/chant word, also, when possible)
	Take turn playing rhythm instruments
To improve auditory perception	Track direction of sound stimulus
	Select and imitate same instrument the therapist is using (e.g., handbell)
	Imitate simple rhythmic patterns on drum
	Play (rhythm instrument) slowly/quickly to change in tempo, loudly/softly in response to change in dynamics

made in terms of an increase in the ability to manifest a skill or perform a task and in terms of a decrease or increase in certain behaviors, namely:

- developmental skills attained
- other skills attained
- need for less verbal and/or gestural prompts or assistance to perform a task
- the quality of performance of a task
- increase in the spontaneous performance of a task
- increase in the independent performance of a task
- increase in a desired behavior
- decrease in a maladaptive behavior
- improvement in motivation to learn and function at a higher level
- transfer of a skill to daily life
- shifts and leaps in functioning that come from improvements in well-being

A Model Treatment Plan

The Music Therapy Treatment Plan (Appendix 3-C) includes the following forms:

1. *Long-Term Goals and Short-Term Objectives:* This form is used to list long-term goals and short-term objectives. It includes, among other data, the current level of functioning relative to each goal, the date of the establishment of the goal or objective, and the date the goal or objective is attained.
2. *Individual Session Report:* This form is used to give a process-oriented description of each individual session and to list music and nonmusic materials used.
3. *Group Session Report:* This form is used to give a process-oriented description of each group session and to list music and nonmusic materials used.
4. *Monthly Progress Report:* Based on the Individual and Group Session Reports, this form is used to summarize the progress made by the client during the preceding month with regard to response to the treatment plan and changes in short-term objectives.
5. *Annual Evaluation:* Based on the Monthly Progress Reports and the Music Therapy Assessment, which is given annually, this form is used to summarize the progress made by the client during the preceding year and to make recommendations to the interdisciplinary treatment team for the continuation of, or change in, treatment.

In addition to the preceding forms, the therapist may find it useful to prepare and keep handy a personal data card (a sample appears in Appendix 3-D) containing pertinent information on the client.

CONCLUSION

The quality of the assessment is directly related to the formulation of an appropriate and realistic treatment plan and, hence, to the success of the therapeutic intervention. Because treatment is long-range—in fact, it may continue throughout the person's lifetime—yearly assessment is essential to evaluating progress in all areas of development. Although wide and varied discrepancies in the development of a person with developmental disabilities may be bewildering, particularly to neophytes in the field of music therapy, these very discrepancies should warn against falling prey to the self-fulfilling prophecy (often referred to as the "Pygmalion effect") that imposes preconceived limits on what is possible or not possible. Human beings are subject to countless internal influences as well as external ones. When motivated by the power of a therapeutic tool such as music to reach out beyond all prediction, they may be capable of much more than we are yet able to envision or assess. How a person makes music—which is inherent in the assessment process—can bring to the surface qualities, capacities, energy, spirit, and joy that have never before been experienced or expressed. It can reveal aspects of a client that provide a new perspective on how to approach overall treatment team planning and how to effect changes in the person.

REFERENCES

Barsch, R. *Achieving perceptual-motor efficiency.* Seattle: Special Child Publications, 1967.

Bentley, A. *Musical ability in children and its measurement.* London: Harrap, 1975.

Bitcon, C.H. *Alike and different: The clinical and educational use of Orff-Schulwerk.* Santa Ana, Calif.: Rosha Press, 1976.

Boxill, E.H. *Music therapy assessment form.* New York: Author, 1983.

Bruscia, K.E. The musical characteristics of mildly and moderately retarded children. In L.H. Kearns, M.T. Ditson, & B.G. Roehner (Eds.), *Readings: Developing arts programs for handicapped students.* Harrisburg, Pa.: Arts in Special Education Project of Pennsylvania, 1981.

Bruscia, K.E., Hesser, B., & Boxill, E.H. Essential competencies for the practice of music therapy. *Music Therapy,* 1981, *1*(1), 43–49.

Cohen, G., Averbach, J., & Katz, E. Music therapy assessment of the developmentally disabled. *Journal of Music Therapy,* 1978, *15*, 88–99.

Cohen, G., & Gericke, O.L. Music therapy assessment: Prime requisite for determining patient objectives. *Journal of Music Therapy,* 1972, *9*, 161–189.

Cratty, B.J., & Martin, Sister M. *Perceptual-motor efficiency in children.* Philadelphia: Lea & Febiger, 1969.

Doll, E.A. *Social maturity scale*. Circle Pines, Minn.: American Guidance Service, 1965.

Erikson, E.J. *Childhood and society*. New York: W.W. Norton, 1963.

Flavell, J.H. *The developmental psychology of Jean Piaget*. New York: Van Nostrand Reinhold, 1963.

Fristoe, M., & Lloyd, L.L. Nonspeech communication. In N.R. Ellis (Ed.), *Handbook of mental deficiency: Psychological theory and research* (2nd ed.). Hillsdale, N.J.: Lawrence Erlbaum Associates, 1979.

Garrard, S.D., & Richmond, J.B. Diagnosis in mental retardation and mental retardation without biological manifestations. In C.H. Carter (Ed.), *Medical aspects of mental retardation*. Springfield, Ill.: Charles C Thomas, 1965.

Gesell, A., & Ilg, F.L. *The child from five to ten*. New York: Harper Brothers, 1946.

Grossman, H.J. (Ed.). *Manual on terminology and classification in mental retardation*. Washington, D.C.: American Association on Mental Deficiency, 1977.

Hedrick, D.L., Prather, E.M., & Tobin, A.R. *Sequenced inventory of communication development*. Seattle: University of Washington Press, 1975.

Hilgard, E.R. *Theories of learning*. New York: Appleton-Century-Crofts, 1948.

Inhelder, B. *The diagnosis of reasoning in the mentally retarded*. New York: John Day, 1968.

Johnston, R.B. Motor function: Normal development and cerebral palsy. In R.B. Johnston & P.R. Magrab (Eds.), *Developmental disorders: Assessment, treatment, education*. Baltimore: University Park Press, 1976.

Kahn, J.V. Applications of Piagetian literature to severely and profoundly mentally retarded persons. *Mental Retardation*, 1979, *17*(6), 273–280.

McCandless, B.R. *Children and adolescents: Behavior and development*. New York: Holt, Rinehart & Winston, 1961.

Mussen, P.H. *The psychological development of the child*. Englewood Cliffs, N.J.: Prentice-Hall, 1965.

Nihira, K., Foster, R., Shellhaas, M., & Leland, H. *AAMD Adaptive Behavior Scale*. Washington, D.C.: American Association on Mental Deficiency, 1974.

Nordoff, P., & Robbins, C. *Therapy in music for handicapped children*. New York: St Martin's Press, 1971.

Nordoff, P., & Robbins, C. *Creative music therapy*. New York: John Day, 1977.

Petzold, R.G. Auditory perception of music sounds by children in the first six grades. *Journal of Research in Music Education*, 1963, *11*, 21–54.

Piaget, J. *The origins of intelligence in children*. New York: International Universities Press, 1952.

Reid, A.H. Psychoses in adult mental defectives: Manic depressive psychosis. *British Journal of Psychiatry*, 1972, *120*, 205–212.

Révész, G. *Introduction to the psychology of music*. Norman, Okla.: University of Oklahoma Press, 1954.

Richmond, P.G. *An introduction to Piaget*. New York: Basic Books, 1970.

Rider, M.S. The assessment of cognitive functioning level through musical perception. *Journal of Music Therapy*, 1981, *18*(3), 110–119.

Rivinus, T.M. Psychopharmacology and the mentally retarded patient. In L.S. Szymanski & P.E. Tanguay (Eds.), *Emotional disorders of mentally retarded persons: Assessment, treatment, and consultation*. Baltimore: University Park Press, 1980.

Stone, L.J., & Church, J. *Childhood and adolescence* (2nd ed.). New York: Random House, 1957.

Szymanski, L.S. Psychiatric diagnosis of retarded persons. In L.S. Szymanski & P.E. Tanguay (Eds.), *Emotional disorders of mentally retarded persons: Assessment, treatment, and consultation.* Baltimore: University Park Press, 1980.

Tanguay, P.E. Cognitive development: Neuropsychological basis and clinical assessment. In L.S. Szymanski & P.E. Tanguay (Eds.), *Emotional disorders of mentally retarded persons: Assessment, treatment, and consultation.* Baltimore: University Park Press, 1980.

Waite, K.B. *The trainable mentally retarded child.* Springfield, Ill.: Charles C Thomas, 1972.

Wasserman, N., Plutchil, R., Deutsch, R., & Taketomo, Y. A music therapy evaluation scale and its clinical application to mentally retarded adult patients. *Music Therapy Journal,* 1973, *10,* 64–77.

Woodward, W.M. Piaget's theory and study of mental retardation. In N.R. Ellis (Ed.), *Handbook of mental deficiency: Psychological theory and research.* Hillsdale, N.J.: Lawrence Erlbaum Associates, 1979.

Zimmerman, M. *Musical characteristics of children.* Washington, D.C.: Music Educators National Conference, 1971.

Music Therapy Assessment

Name of Client: _____ Date of Birth: _____ Date(s) of Assessment: _____

Directions:
1. Administer through the use of music and musical stimuli (vocal and instrumental), music activities, and music materials.
2. Administer over a period of two to three consecutive weeks.
3. Check all areas that are applicable.

A. **Diagnosis (DSM–III):** _____
   _____

B. **Developmental History:** _____
   _____
   _____

C. **Family History:** _____
   _____
   _____

D. **Standardized Test Information:**

Test Name:	Date Given:	Age of Client:	Score:
_____	_____	_____	_____
_____	_____	_____	_____
_____	_____	_____	_____
_____	_____	_____	_____

E. **Developmental Disability:**
   1. Mental Retardation   _____   4. Neurological Impairment   _____
   2. Cerebral Palsy   _____   5. Epilepsy   _____
   3. Autism   _____

   _____

F. **General Characteristics:**
1. *Observable Behaviors:*

   a. Cooperative _____
   b. Resistive _____
   c. Stereotypic _____
   d. Perseverative _____
   e. Compulsive _____
   f. Impulsive _____
   g. Ritualistic _____
   h. Assertive _____

   i. Withdrawn _____
   j. Hyperactive _____
   k. Hypoactive _____
   l. Abusive _____
   m. Self-abusive _____
   n. Self-stimulative _____
   o. Other_____

2. *Physical Handicap(s) and Condition(s):*

   a. Extremities:
      Right arm _____
      Left arm _____
      Right leg _____
      Left leg _____
   b. Auditory impairment:
      Deaf _____
      Loss in right ear _____
      Loss in left ear _____
      Loss in both ears _____
      Wears hearing aid _____

   c. Visual impairment:
      Blind _____
      Strabismus _____
      Astigmatism _____
      Nystagmus _____
      Wears glasses _____
   d. Seizures:
      Grand mal _____
      Petit mal _____
      Psychomotor _____
      Other_____

3. *Handedness:*

   a. Right _____
   b. Left _____
   c. Mixed dominance _____

4. *Eye Contact:*

   a. Good _____
   b. Fair _____
   c. None _____

5. *Attention Span:*

   a. Sustains musical activity
      for length of music _____
   b. Sustains musical activity
      for major part of music _____
   c. Sustains musical activity
      for short periods of
      music _____
   d. Sustains sporadically _____
   e. Distractible _____
   f. Does not attend _____
   g. Starts and stops in response
      to music _____

6. *Mannerisms:*

   a. Grimaces _____
   b. Tics _____
   c. Hand movements _____
   d. Finger configurations _____
   e. Arm movements _____
   f. Head movements _____
   g. Idiosyncratic sounds,
      vocalizations, utterances _____

7. *Gait:*

   a. Steady _____
   b. Awkward _____
   c. Rigid _____
   d. Shuffling _____
   e. Waddling _____

8. *Posture:*

   a. Good _____
   b. Fair _____
   c. Poor _____

G. **Motor Domain:**

1. *Gross Motor*:

   a. Locomotor skills:

Walks	_____
Runs	_____
Jumps	_____
Hops	_____
Gallops	_____
Skips	_____

   b. Nonlocomotor skills:

Bends torso up and down	_____
Swings arms up and down	_____
Stretches arms up	_____
Swings arms back and forth	_____
Rolls to one side and the other	_____
Rolls over	_____
Turns around	_____

   c. Dynamic balance:

Controlled	_____
Uncontrolled	_____

   d. Static balance:

Stable	_____
Unstable	_____

   e. Appropriate use of body:

	Imita-tively	Inde-pend-ently
Claps hands	_____	_____
Stamps feet	_____	_____
Raises arms	_____	_____
Swings arms	_____	_____
Bends knees	_____	_____

2. *Fine Motor:*

   a. Fingers:

Opens and shuts	_____
Moves fingers separately	_____
Counts with fingers	_____

   b. Grasp:

Palmar	_____
Pincer	_____

   c. Eye–hand coordination:

	Imita-tively	Inde-pend-ently
Shakes handbells	_____	_____
Taps rhythm sticks together	_____	_____
Clashes hand cymbals together	_____	_____
Strikes single tone bell with mallet	_____	_____
Strikes xylophone bars with mallet	_____	_____
Beats drum with mallet	_____	_____

3. *Perceptual–Motor Functions*:

   a. Types of drum beating:

Steady	_____
Rhythmic	_____
Stereotypic	_____
Perseverative	_____
Disordered	_____
Compulsive	_____
Chaotic	_____
Uncontrolled	_____
Evasive	_____

   b. Types of strumming on Autoharp®:

Related to musical stimuli	_____
Steady	_____
Changes in tempo	_____
Changes in dynamics	_____
Confined to area of strings	_____
Erratic	_____
Random	_____
Spillover	_____

4. *Psychomotor Skills:*
   a. Uses appropriate
      movements in action
      songs   _____
   b. Movements are related to
      musical stimuli   _____

   c. Moves rhythmically in
      response to pulse of
      music   _____

H. Communication Domain:

1. *Speech and Vocal Characteristics:*
   a. Expressive:
      Single words   _____
      Word phrases   _____
      Sentences   _____
      Echolalic   _____
      Perseverative   _____
      Idiosyncratic   _____
      Nonverbal   _____
   b. Receptive:
      Comprehends words of
         song   _____
      Executes appropriate
         actions to words of
         song   _____
      Dramatizes words of song
         or musical story   _____
      Follows verbal directives _____
   c. Articulation:
      Intelligible   _____
      Fairly intelligible   _____
      Unintelligible   _____
   d. Phonation:
      Respiration adequate for
         sound production   _____
      Range of pitch:
         High   _____
         Medium   _____
         Low   _____
      Range of volume:
         Audible   _____
         Moderately audible   _____
         Inaudible   _____
      Aphonia (hysterical/
         functional)   _____

   e. Tonal quality of voice:
      Clear   _____
      Muffled   _____
      Harsh   _____
      Nasal   _____
      Hypernasal   _____
      Breathy   _____
      Raspy   _____
      Resonant   _____
      Shallow   _____
   f. Prosody:
      Inflection   _____
      Cadence   _____
      Monotone   _____
   g. Rate:
      Fast   _____
      Moderate   _____
      Slow   _____
      Belabored   _____
   h. Organic condition:
      Dysarthria   _____
      Dyslalia   _____
      Aphasia   _____

2. *Other Communication Skills:*
   a. Purposeful gestures/body
      language   _____
   b. Purposeful gestures
      accompanied by
      vocalizations   _____

   c. Sign language   _____
   d. Manual language   _____
   e. Vocalizations   _____

I. **Cognitive Domain:**

1. *Comprehension*:
   a. Demonstrates understanding of words of song _____
   b. Demonstrates understanding of and sings: _____
      Articles of clothing _____
      Colors _____
      Numbers _____
      Days of week _____
      Months _____
      Objects in environment _____

2. *Body Awareness*:
   Identifies in response to song by singing or pointing to:
   a. Eyes _____
   b. Ears _____
   c. Head _____
   d. Face _____
   e. Neck _____
   f. Nose _____
   g. Mouth _____
   h. Tongue _____
   i. Hands _____
   j. Fingers _____
   k. Thumb _____
   l. Arms _____
   m. Legs _____
   n. Feet _____
   o. Knees _____
   p. Hips _____
   q. Shoulders _____
   r. Chest _____
   s. Stomach _____
   t. Back _____
   u. Elbows _____
   v. Wrists _____

3. *Laterality and Directionality:*
   Moves in response to words of song:
   a. Left _____
   b. Right _____
   c. Forward _____
   d. Backward _____
   e. Up _____
   f. Down _____

4. *Visual Perception*:
   a. Indicates recognition of visual aids used within musical framework:
      Flash cards with environmental objects _____
      Flash cards with numbers _____
      Pictures of animals _____
      Pictures of vehicles of transportation _____
      Colors _____
      Puppets _____
   b. Indicates recognition of and names rhythm instruments:
      Drum _____
      Bells _____
      Rhythm sticks _____
      Maracas _____
      Xylophone _____

5. *Auditory Perception*:
   a. Gross changes in dynamics:
      Loud _____
      Soft _____
   b. Gross changes in tempo:
      Fast _____
      Slow _____
   c. Gross changes in pitch (vocally):
      High _____
      Low _____
   d. Discriminates between different instrumental sounds:
      Drums and bells _____
      Bells and cymbals _____
   e. Imitates serial drumbeats:
      1 _____
      1–2 _____
      1–2–3 _____
      1–2–3–4 _____

f. Imitates chanted/sung
   syllables:
   La-la-la   _____
   Ba-ba-ba   _____
   Da-da-da   _____
   Ma-ma-ma   _____
   Ha-ha-ha   _____

g. Imitates musical intervals:
   Descending third, fifth,
   octave   _____
   Ascending third, fifth,
   octave   _____

J. Affective Domain:

1. *Facial Expression*:
   a. Alert   _____
   b. Pleasant   _____
   c. Fixed   _____
   d. Tense   _____
   e. Hostile   _____
   f. Anxious   _____
   g. Depressed   _____

3. *Appropriate Emotional
   Responses*:
   a. Usually   _____
   b. Sometimes   _____
   c. Rarely   _____

2. *Range of Affect*:
   a. Broad   _____
   b. Restricted   _____
   c. Labile   _____
   d. Blunted   _____
   e. Flat   _____

4. *Emotional Responses to
   Musical Stimuli and Text of
   Song:*
   a. Related to music   _____
   b. Unrelated to music   _____
   c. No visible response   _____

K. Social Domain:

1. *Awareness of Self, Others, and Environment*:
   a. Recognizes when sung/
      chanted:
      Own name   _____
      Names of others _____

   b. Sings/chants:
      Own name   _____
      Names of others _____

2. *Interaction:*
   a. With adults:
      Good   _____
      Fair   _____
      Poor   _____
      None   _____

   b. With peers:
      Good   _____
      Fair   _____
      Poor   _____
      None   _____

3. *Participates in Group Music Activities*:
   a. Group singing   _____
   b. Rhythm instrument
      playing   _____
   c. Action songs   _____
   d. Music circle games   _____
   e. Group movement   _____
   f. Group dramatizations to
      music   _____

   g. Creative movement/
      dancing   _____
   h. Social dancing   _____
   i. Initiates activity   _____
   j. Willing to lead activity   _____
   k. Volunteers to lead activity _____
   l. Sustains activity for
      length of music   _____

L. **Specific Musical Behaviors:**

1. *Vocal:*
   a. Sings on pitch _____
   b. Carries a tune _____
   c. Sings song(s) of own choice _____
   d. Sings isolated words in tonality of song _____
   e. Sings phrases of song _____
   f. Sings phrases in tonality of song _____
   g. Sings melodic line in tonality of song _____
   h. Sings words and melody of entire song _____
   i. Chants isolated words of song _____
   j. Chants word phrases of songs _____
   k. Chants words of entire song _____

2. *Percussion Instruments (Drums, Clavés, Temple Blocks):*
   a. Plays rhythmic pattern of instrumental music _____
   b. Plays rhythmic patterns of songs _____
   c. Changes rhythmic patterns in response to music _____
   d. Uses instruments expressively _____

3. *Melodic Percussive Instruments (Piano, Xylophone, Resonator, or Tone Bells):*
   a. Plays melodic phrases _____
   b. Plays melody _____
   c. Uses instruments expressively _____

M. **Major Problem Area(s) of Adaptive Behavior:**

1. Motor Functions _____
2. Communicative Skills _____
3. Cognitive Skills _____
4. Affective State _____
5. Social Adjustment _____

N. **General Comments:**

1. Any musical behaviors that appear to be characteristic of a particular disability: _____

_____

_____

2. Any musical behaviors that are significant: _____

_____

_____

3. Any significant differences in behaviors in response to musical stimuli from those reported in other sources or observed in other settings: _____

_____

_____

O. **Present Medication:**

Medication:	Dosage:	Schedule of Administration:
_____	_____	_____
_____	_____	_____
_____	_____	_____
_____	_____	_____

P. **Current Service Information:**

1. Special Education	_____	6. Psychological Services	_____
2. Speech Therapy	_____	7. Recreational Therapy	_____
3. Medical Services	_____	8. Social Services	_____
4. Occupational Therapy	_____	9. Art Therapy	_____
5. Physical Therapy	_____	10. Dance Therapy	_____

Q. **Recommendation Regarding Type of Session:**
   1. Individual   _____
   2. Group   _____
   3. Both   _____

Music Therapist-Assessor: _____

Guidelines for Administering Music Therapy Assessment

A. Diagnosis

B. Developmental History

C. Family History

D. Standardized Test Information

E. Developmental Disability. Information from medical charts and psychological evaluation reports.

F. General Characteristics
   1. *Observable Behaviors* (a through o): Direct observation and behaviors as they emerge through responses to music and music activities.
   2. *Physical Handicap(s) and Condition(s)* (a through e): Direct observation and medical charts.
   3. *Handedness* (a through c): Hold a mallet at midline of the seated client. While chanting or singing, extend the mallet toward the client. If the individual accepts the mallet, repeat this action several times in order to determine right or left preference or mixed dominance. Then place a timpani drum close to the client. Play rhythmic music, composed or improvised, while chanting or singing:

      (Name of client) is beating the drum.

      Repeat four or five times, noting whether or not one hand is used consistently or if there is occasional shifting or constant shifting of hands.
   4. *Eye Contact* (a through c): Direct observation. Note the client's behavior when sitting directly in front of him or her while singing or playing a musical instrument (Autoharp® or guitar).

5. *Attention Span* (a through g): Over a period of weeks, observe the client's ability to sustain musical activities, such as playing a rhythm instrument in response to music, participating in an action song, or starting and stopping in response to music.
6. *Mannerisms* (a through g): Direct observation and responses to musical stimuli. Note if music activates, diminishes, or interrupts behaviors.
7. *Gait* (a through e): Direct observation. Also, note if influence of music effects any changes.
8. *Posture* (a through c): Direct observation. Also, note if there are any postural changes during music-movement activities.

G. Motor Domain
   1. *Gross Motor:*
      a. Locomotor skills: Improvise instrumental and vocal music or use adaptations of composed music designed to evoke specific motoric responses indicated by improvised words (sung or chanted) such as:

> (Name of client) is walking, walking,
> (Name of client) is walking, walking,
> (Name of client) is walking, walking,
> Walking around the room.

   Repeat the same procedure for other locomotor functions, leading the client into various activities through the nature of the musical stimuli and the improvised words. Use the drum for a variety of appropriate rhythmic patterns, improvising words that indicate actions. Suggested song: "Going to Boston."*
      b. Nonlocomotor skills: Improvise instrumental and vocal music that indicate the nonlocomotor movements listed.
      c. Dynamic balance: Improvise instrumental and vocal music that is expressive of various kinds of activities executed in space.
      d. Static balance: Observe client's ability to maintain posture and balance while performing the nonlocomotor activities listed above.
      e. Appropriate use of body: Improvise instrumental and vocal music that is expressive of the various kinds of activities listed. For imitative skills, the therapist models the movements while singing/chanting. For independent skills, the therapist sings action words to an instrumental accompaniment (piano, guitar, Autoharp®, Casiotone®, Omnichord®).
   2. *Fine Motor:*
      a. Fingers: Improvise song to elicit finger movements.

---

*Langstaff, N., & Langstaff, J. (Compilers). "Going to Boston." *Jim along, Josie*. New York: Harcourt Brace Jovanovich, 1970.

   b. Grasp: Improvise music to facilitate grasping of rhythm band instruments.

   c. Eye–hand coordination: Once these functions are determined, offer the following instruments in order of difficulty of manipulation: handbells, rhythm sticks, tone bell(s), or xylophone with mallet. The client is encouraged to play each instrument in response to improvised music that reflects (mirrors) or matches what he or she is doing. Record the client's ability to manipulate these instruments imitatively or independently.

3. *Perceptual-Motor Functions* (a and b): Types of drumbeating are determined by responses elicited through musical improvisations in various tempi, dynamic levels, rhythmic patterns, and musical idioms. Follow the same process with the Autoharp®.

4. *Psychomotor Skills* (a through d): This area is observed and noted throughout the assessment process. For appropriate movements in an action song, use music such as "Little Betty Martin,"* substituting the person's name throughout.

> Verse A:
> (Name of client), tiptoe, tiptoe,
> (Name of client), tiptoe fine,
> (Name of client), tiptoe, tiptoe,
> (Name of client), tiptoe fine.
>
> Verse B:
> Swing and swing and swing your arms,
> Swing and swing and swing your arms,
> Swing and swing and swing your arms,
> Swing and swing and swing your arms.
>
> Verse A (repeat).
>
> Verses C, D, E, etc.

Other psychomotor activities/movements, such as turning around, jumping, hopping, are explored.

H. Communication Domain

1. *Speech and Vocal Characteristics* (a through g): Vocal characteristics are explored throughout the assessment process, as are expressive and receptive speech. Articulation, phonation, tonal quality, and rate are evinced through areas explored in the section on the cognitive domain (sung syllables, intervals, and words of song).

---

*Langstaff, N., & Langstaff, J. (Compilers). "Little Betty Martin." *Jim along, Josie*. New York· Harcourt Brace Jovanovich, 1970.

    h. Organic condition: Information from medical charts and direct observation.

  2. *Other Communication Skills* (a through e): This area is explored throughout the assessment process.

I. Cognitive Domain

  1. *Comprehension* (a and b): Sing/chant words of improvised or composed/folk song eliciting the client's response to colors, numbers, articles of clothing, days of the week, objects in the environment, etc. Repeat many times for changes of words and word phrases to be filled in by the client. Adjust tempo and content to the client's level of functioning. For severely mentally retarded or multiply handicapped persons, sing/chant very slowly, deliberately articulating and emphasizing words; and wait for the client's responses to fill in the words. Suggested song: "Mary Wore a Red Dress"* (see the section on visual perception).

  2. *Body Awareness* (a through v): Improvise the words of a song/chant that instructs the client to point to parts of the body.

  3. *Laterality and Directionality* (a through f): Improvise songs/chants or use composed songs with action words that are designed to elicit motoric responses to "Left," "Right," "Forward," "Backward," "Up," and "Down."

  4. *Visual Perception* (a and b): Improvise vocal music with appropriate words for object, number, or color recognition. Also, use a song that is suitable for these activities, such as "Mary Wore a Red Dress." The song could be improvised as follows:

> (Name of client) is wearing a (color) shirt, oh yes!
> (Name of client) is wearing a (color) shirt, oh yes!
> (Name of client) is wearing a (color) shirt, oh yes!
> All day long.

  5. *Auditory Perception* (a through g):
    a. Gross changes in dynamics: Improvise music on the piano that is loud and soft to evoke client responses on the drum.
    b. Gross changes in tempo: Improvise music on the piano that is fast and slow to evoke client responses on the drum.
    c. Gross changes in pitch (vocally): Instruct the client to imitate vocal sounds modeled.
    d. Discriminates between different instrumental sounds: Use sets of instruments, one of which the therapist plays (not visible to the client).

---

*Langstaff, N., & Langstaff, J. (Compilers). "Mary Wore a Red Dress." *Jim along, Josie.* New York: Harcourt Brace Jovanovich, 1970.

Place the other on a table in front of the client. Ask him or her to play the instrument heard.

e. Imitates serial drumbeats: Sit opposite the client. Both client and therapist have a drum mallet. Sing/chant:

> Beat the drum one time (beat),
> Beat the drum two times (beat, beat),
> Beat the drum three times (beat, beat, beat),
> Beat the drum four times (beat, beat, beat, beat).

This is repeated several times to determine comprehension and perception.

f. Imitates chanted/sung syllables: Therapist chants or sings syllables within the tonal range of C' to G', exaggerating (at discretion of therapist) tongue movements in order to determine client's level of perception and ability to produce speech sounds.

g. Imitates musical intervals: Therapist sings descending third, fifth, octave, and ascending third, fifth, octave within the C' to C" range in order to determine client's ability to perceive and reproduce musical tones in relation to the musical stimuli.

J. Affective Domain

Direct observation of the client's general demeanor, musical responses, and emotional responses throughout the assessment process. Also, responses to instrumental and vocal improvisations of varying moods, idioms, styles, and musical components. The meaning of lyrics of songs and how they affect the client are important areas to explore with the more highly functioning person. Select suitable songs.

K. Social Domain

This area is explored throughout the assessment process.

1. *Awareness of Self, Others, and Environment* (a and b): Sing and play the song about either you and the client or, in a group setting, about all the people in the room; also, about objects and areas in the room. Record the client's awareness that is evinced by signs of recognition—facially, gesturally, or by singing of own name and others' names with your name. Suggested song: "The People in The Room Today" (adapted from "The People in Your Neighborhood."*

2. *Interaction* (a and b): In one-to-one interplay with the therapist, use a set of hand cymbals. Chant/sing while modeling movement:

---

*Moss, J. The people in your neighborhood. In J. Raposo & J. Moss, *The sesame street song book.* New York: Simon & Schuster.

When (client) and (therapist) clash cymbals together,
When (client) and (therapist) clash cymbals together,
I want to be in that number,
When we clash our cymbals together.

Suggested song: "When the Saints Go Marching In."*

3. *Participates in Group Music Activities* (a through l): Group participation is assessed through rhythm band activities, music-movement activities, action songs/games, dramatizations, and social dances. Select suitable music for these diverse activities.

L. Specific Musical Behaviors
These behaviors are explored and noted throughout the assessment process as well as in this section. Ask direct questions, such as, "Do you have a song that you would like to sing?" Or play and sing a song that might be familiar or is simple musically and textually. Clients' responses are indicative of their degree of musical sensibility, experience, and expressive abilities.

M. Major Problem Area(s) of Adaptive Behavior

N. General Comments

O. Present Medication

P. Current Service Information

Q. Recommendations Regarding Type of Session: Self-explanatory.

---

*Cromwel Music. When the saints go marching in. *50 fabulous favorites*. New York: Author, 1962.

Appendix 3-C

Music Therapy Treatment Plan

Long-Term Goals and Short-Term Objectives

Date: _____

Client: _____

Date of Birth: _____ Date of Admission: _____

Diagnosis: _____

Current Medication(s): _____

_____

Therapy Session:

Starting date: _____ Frequency: _____ Length: _____

Type: Group _____ Individual _____ Both _____

Long-Term Goal 1: _____

Date established: _____ Date attained: _____

Current Level of Functioning Relative to Goal:	Short-Term Objectives:	Date Established:	Date Attained:

Long-Term Goal 2: _____
Date established: _____ Date attained: _____

Current Level of Functioning Relative to Goal:	Short-Term Objectives:	Date Established:	Date Attained:

Long-Term Goal 3: _____
Date established: _____ Date attained: _____

Current Level of Functioning Relative to Goal:	Short-Term Objectives:	Date Established:	Date Attained:

Long-Term Goal 4: _____

Date established: _____ Date attained: _____

Current Level of Functioning Relative to Goal:	Short-Term Objectives:	Date Established:	Date Attained:

Music Therapist: _____

Director of Music Therapy: _____

Individual Session Report

Date: _____

Session #: _____

Client: _____

Assistant: _____

Description of Session (include therapeutic music activities and purposes for using them, long-term goals and short-term objectives worked on, strategies and techniques used, client's response, quality of participation, interaction with the therapist, and significant events):

Music Materials Used:

Nonmusic Materials Used:

Music Therapist: _____

Group Session Report

Date: _____
Session #: _____

Clients: _____
_____

Assistant(s): _____

Description of Session (include therapeutic music activities and purposes for using them, strategies and techniques used, clients' responses, quality of participation, interaction with peers, interaction with the therapist, significant events, and group goals worked on):

Music Materials Used:

Nonmusic Materials Used:

Music Therapist: _____

Monthly Progress Report

Date: _____

Client: _____

Response to Treatment Plan (specify any developmental growth or significant changes in the client's behavior, functioning, and progress in attainment of long-term goals and short-term objectives):

Changes in Long-Term Goals:

Updates of Short-Term Objectives:

Music Therapist: _____

Annual Evaluation

Period of Evaluation: _____ to _____

Client: _____

Date of Birth: _____ Date of Admission: _____

Diagnosis: _____

Summary of Significant Changes in the Client as a Result of Treatment (based on Monthly Progress Reports and the Annual Assessment):

Recommendations to the Interdisciplinary Treatment Team Regarding the Continuation of or Change in Treatment:

Music Therapist: _____

Director of Music Therapy: _____

Date: _____

Appendix 3-D

Client Personal Data Card

Client: _____   Date of Birth: _____

Date of Admission: _____   Photo Consent: Yes_____ No_____

Client Coordinator: _____   Social Worker: _____

Diagnosis: _____

Current Medication(s): _____
_____

Family History: _____
_____
_____

Developmental History: _____
_____
_____

Psychological Tests Administered (Most Recent), Dates Administered, and Scores:
_____
_____

Parent(s) or Guardian(s):

Name(s): _____

Address(es): _____

Telephone(s): _____

Other Services Provided: _____
_____

Chapter 4

The Context for Treatment: A Continuum of Awareness*

The experientialist sees that in the center of life is the means of communication . . . namely, awareness.

Frederick S. Perls (1974, p. 64)

INTRODUCTION

The Context for Treatment

The context of my approach to music therapy for people who are developmentally disabled is *A Continuum of Awareness,* the creative process of using music functionally as a tool of consciousness to awaken, heighten, and expand awareness of self, others, and the environment. Originating with Frederick S. Perls and applied to therapy, the term *continuum of awareness,* as he defines it, is being aware of what is going on—being in touch with the here and now from moment to moment (1974). Establishing a trusting client-therapist relationship is fundamental to this approach; engaging the client in active participation is key. The process, one of intrinsic learning that leads to action, places emphasis on self-motivation, intrapersonal and interpersonal integration, and autonomy. This context evolved organically from my direct experience of the critical need of developmentally disabled persons to develop a basic awareness of self.

Rooted in modern humanistic ("third force") psychologies,** the approach

---

*This chapter is a revision of an article entitled, "A Continuum of Awareness: Music Therapy with the Developmentally Handicapped," which appeared in *Music Therapy*, Vol. 1, No. 1, Summer, 1981. Used by permission.

**Modern humanistic psychologies are concerned with topics such as love, creativity, self, growth, the organism, basic need gratification, self-actualization, higher values, being, becoming, spontaneity, play, humor, affection, naturalness, warmth, autonomy, responsibility, meaning, transcendental experience, peak experience, courage, and related concepts (Severin, 1965).

affirms the dignity and worth of the human being and embraces the fundamental assumption that an individual's potentialities form a unique pattern for that particular person. Underlying this approach are psychotherapeutic theories of Perls (1966, 1974, 1977a, 1977b, 1978), Rogers (1951, 1959, 1961, 1964, 1965), and Maslow (1954, 1962, 1972, 1976, 1977) holding that the ultimate therapeutic objective is the development of the self. These theories deal with such concepts as (a) self-regulation of healthy needs and wants, which leads the person into experiencing awareness and cultivates means of communication in the broadest sense; (b) intrinsic learning, which leads the person toward participation in the external world and affords personal fulfillment and wholeness; and (c) human relationships, which lead a person on the path to becoming a developed self. Therapy that is humanistically oriented embraces the human being holistically.

What is referred to as the "self theory" had its origin in the work of William James (1981) and has had a resurgence in contemporary theorizing (Allport, 1955; Erikson, 1963; Maslow, 1976; Moustakas, 1974; Perls, 1974; Rogers, 1961; Zinker, 1978). James defined the self (the "empirical me"), in its most general sense, as the sum total of all that constitutes a person—body, attitudes, traits, abilities, needs, and wants. Variously defined by modern humanistic psychologists, the self can be considered the central core within each individual that is the deep source of growth, as a person's attitudes and feelings about himself or herself, or as a group of psychological processes that govern behavior and adjustment. Critical to the development of the self is relationship with others. Indeed, a human being cannot be understood as a participating self if relationship with others is omitted or not experienced (Sullivan, 1953).

Cycle of Awareness

The theoretical basis for using music as a tool of consciousness or awareness is the cycle of awareness-excitement-contact, hereafter referred to as the cycle of awareness (Zinker, 1978). Based on the satisfaction of needs and wants that shift from one figural need or want to another, this psychophysiological cycle of self-regulation—the homeostatic process by which the organism interacts with its environment psychologically as well as physiologically (Perls, 1974)—begins with sensations. When sensations are experienced, they set into motion the cycle of awareness, the process by which a figure or foreground (in the figure-ground relationship) develops. Awareness leads to the mobilization of energy, which leads to contact in the psychological and/or physiological sense, then to a satisfactory fulfillment of the need or want in some form of action or behavior. Once the need or want is satisfied, a shift in foreground gives impetus for a new cycle to begin. In a healthy state of existence, the cycles flow rhythmically (Zinker, 1978):

> The healthy individual is able to clearly experience and differentiate something in his foreground which interests and captivates him. . . . He

experiences the sharpness and clarity of the figure. . . . In disturbed individuals, there is confusion between figure and ground . . . there is lack of purpose and focusing. . . . The development of awareness can be likened to the emergence of a clear figure. (p. 93)

Meaning emerges from the relationship of this clear figure to the ground. The shift from one cycle to another in the healthy person moves with a natural rhythm whose accents fall in the right place in time and space for that particular individual and can bring about integration and self-awareness. Perception of self and of the immediate environment is, at these moments, a harmonious, energizing, and fulfilling experience. As individuals come to distinguish between external and internal events, and as they become psychologically differentiated from their surroundings, awareness of self and others increases. This expanding awareness is a liberating force that enables people to take responsibility for their own actions, to make their own choices.

It seems that if there is an interruption in the cycle of awareness; if perceptions are not experienced or are experienced with distortions; if there is a marked discrepancy between the sensoric and motoric systems, an imbalance between sensing and doing results. When development is impaired or interrupted for idiopathic, organic, congenital, or psychosocial reasons, awareness is seriously deficient, untapped, or limited and energies are largely maladaptive, unchanneled, or blocked. The inability to be aware of experiencing is manifest in lack of purpose and resultant misused, misdirected, unused, unoriented energy.

Intrinsic Learning

The concept of intrinsic learning* generated by the modern humanistic psychologies is especially important to understanding the development of the self. Intrinsic learning, as Maslow (1976) states, engenders "development of the fullest height . . . that the particular individual can come to. In a less technical way, it is helping the person to become the best that he is able to become" (pp. 162–163). The process of intrinsic learning and change, as it is developed through *a continuum of awareness*, is viewed in terms of ever-increasing levels of awareness of self, others, the environment and the self in relation to others and the environment. Arising from the individual's fundamental needs, this kind of learning

---

*This is distinct from the concept of extrinsic learning espoused by the behaviorist. Historically, humanism and behaviorism are two opposing points of view in psychological thinking (Watson, 1930). The essential philosophical divergence lies in the perception of the nature of the human being, one aspect of which is the difference in how learning takes place. The behaviorist deliberately eliminates the study of the inner person (self-motivation, self-perception, etc.), emphasizing behavior that is conditioned and elicited by external stimuli (Bandura, 1969). Intrinsic learning involves internalized changes in awareness rather than conditioned responses to external stimuli.

entails organic growth and the development of capacities inherent in the nature of the human being. It stimulates a sense of self that can lead to the desire for adaptive behavior and purposeful functioning. In essence, it develops and nurtures the inner being and the drive for self-expression (Ellis, 1974). As conceived in the Gestalt tradition, such learning takes the form of awareness that involves a reorganization of the field of experience (Köhler, 1929). In the healthy course of being and becoming, self-awareness and awareness of others generate intrinsic learning that progresses developmentally from sensory experiences through the physical self to symbolic forms of expression.

Implicit in the concept of awareness is the uniquely human phenomenon of consciousness of self. Explicit is the state of being aware, of being in contact with one's holistic field, of having sensory, emotional, cognitive, and energetic support of the psychobiological being. This awareness of feeling, thinking, seeing, hearing, smelling, and touching provides the psychic food that the human organism depends on for growth and development. It gives a sense of self-identity—the condition of consciousness that underlies the differentiation between self and others and gives meaning to experience. Without self-identity, the person remains on the level of unaware experiencing that has no purposeful direction or relatedness to the external world (Stevens, 1980).

The initiation of the individual into conditions of conscious awareness—the ability to direct attention, to pay attention, to focus energy—can lead to ever-increasing degrees of sensory perception, responsiveness, expressivity, and, ultimately, higher forms of functioning and full realization of the person's potential. In this process, the self-as-doer (a self who is sensing, perceiving, experiencing, doing) actively participates in his or her own growth, development, and behavioral change. The foundation of the treatment process, therefore, rests on the ability to be aware of experiencing. It is upon this foundation that intrinsic learning develops.

Concrete musical experiences and expression through singing/chanting, instrument playing, and music-movement promote functioning and learning on many levels of mind–body awareness. Numerous therapeutic music activities, music materials, and nonmusic materials are used to help the client to gain the awareness and self-control needed to acquire a skill or decrease a behavior that interferes with daily living, and to develop the ability to use, consciously and purposefully, energy that has been untapped, misdirected, or would otherwise be dissipated. Within this context, skills are not dealt with in linear fashion. Treatment focuses on improving functioning holistically in that intrinsic learning and change nurture the total being as a specific skill in any one domain is attained. Work toward attainment of goals is therefore within the horizontal, vertical, and circular dimensions of a continuum. A person's motor and language development, for example, may be at different stages yet be worked on simultaneously. Change occurs through the development of the client's self-awareness and awareness of the total environment. The consequence of this movement is an alteration in behavior, with increased flow and continuity in functioning as more and more territory is covered.

Progress in the ability to perceive, encode, assimilate, and act upon what has been perceived is relative to the person's level of functioning, physical condition, degree of motivation generated, and the creative pathways used to help the person achieve change. Exposure to musical sensory experiences activates the person internally, setting in motion the cycle of awareness that leads to external action. As the capacity to respond to musical stimuli increases and progress from simple to more complex musical experiences and activities takes place, transfer to forms of higher functioning can result. Table 4–1 traces levels of awareness and musical behaviors in response to musical stimuli. These levels can also be used as a guide for evaluating growing awareness in the same person inasmuch as they are synonymous with some of the short-term objectives set for the client.

THREE MAIN STRATEGIES

With a view to awakening, heightening, and expanding awareness in the underdeveloped person, three main strategies have been devised that are applicable to all mentally retarded and developmentally disabled persons, whatever their age or level of functioning: (a) *Reflection*—the mirroring and matching, in musical and nonmusical forms, of the here-and-now client; (b) *Identification*—the symbolic representation, in musical forms (both vocal and instrumental), of the here-and-now client and therapist; and (c) *Our Contact Song*—a composed or improvised song that serves as an affirmation of the client–therapist relationship and is the catalyst for the first reciprocal expression or two-way communication (Ruesch & Bateson, 1951) initiated by the client. As will become evident, *Reflection* and *Identification* are strategies that play an important part in the discovery of *Our Contact Song*.

The following process-oriented description of the treatment of Margarita is set within the discussion of the strategies of Reflection, Identification, and Our Contact Song.

At the time of treatment Margarita was 13½ years of age. She was a prime example of someone whose unawareness of self and others was all-pervasive, whose physical and psychic energies were caught up in a ritual of stereotypic and perseverative behaviors, whose boundaries were undefined. She functioned in the severe range of mental retardation and could be described as having autisticlike characteristics, such as lack of contact with others, no speech for communicative purposes, preoccupation with inanimate objects, the need for sameness, idiosyn-

Table 4–1 Levels of Awareness and Musical Behaviors in Response to Musical Stimuli

Vocal responses and behaviors	Instrumental responses and behaviors
Randomly moves body (arms, hands, legs) in response to sound	Randomly moves body (arms, hands, legs) in response to sound
Moves or blinks eyes in response to sound	Moves or blinks eyes in response to sound
Localizes sound with eyes	Localizes sound with eyes
Turns head toward sound	Turns head toward sound
Looks at the therapist	Looks at the therapist
Reaches out for source of sound (the therapist who is singing with or without instrumental accompaniment)	Reaches out for source of sound (instrument the therapist is demonstrating and offering to the client)
Vocalizes randomly	Reaches out to grasp instrument
Vocalizes in tonality of musical stimuli	Grasps instrument
Vocalizes melodic phrases on pitch	Holds rhythm instrument
Sings syllables on pitch in imitation of the therapist	Imitates the therapist's modeling of instrument
Sings isolated words on pitch in imitation of the therapist	Independently manipulates instrument appropriately (e.g., shakes bells and tambourine, strikes resonator bell with mallet)
Sings melodic phrases and words on pitch in imitation of the therapist	
Sings an entire song in imitation of the therapist	Plays/uses the instrument in ways that are related to musical stimuli (e.g., beats a drum in a steady pulse, starts and stops in relation to musical stimuli)
Sings syllables (e.g., la-la-la) on pitch spontaneously	
Sings isolated words on pitch spontaneously	Plays rhythmic patterns on percussion, melodic, and wind instruments
Sings melodic phrases and words of a song on pitch spontaneously	Plays melodic rhythm on percussion, melodic, and wind instruments
Sings an entire song on pitch independently	Plays melodic line on melodic instrument
	Presses chord bars in a chordal progression and strums the strings of an Autoharp®
	Plays simple chord progressions on the guitar
	Plays simple melody on song flute/ flutophone/recorder

cratic utterances, and self-stimulatory as well as self-abusive behaviors (autoeroticism and outbursts of scratching).

When I first sought her out, Margarita was standing in a ramrod position close to a wall, blankly staring into space, wrapping and unwrapping a leather belt around her left hand and arm with intense rapidity and unerring dexterity. A stream of unintelligible utterances gushed forth from time to time, interspersed with high-toned vocalizations emitted in a birdlike fashion. Her neck was extended and her head thrust upward. I stood near her, watching, listening, waiting. I chanted her name softly. I didn't exist for Margarita.

Cautiously and gently, I led her to the music therapy room. Though her body appeared to have a defiant stance, she gave no sign of awareness *or* resistance to my presence. Once in the music therapy room, I observed a startlingly beautiful girl sitting immobile in the chair I had seated her in, head bent to her chest, hands urgently wrapping and unwrapping, wrapping and unwrapping the leather belt, hands that bore evidence of self-abuse, hands that I later discovered had much to express. She then yawned and placed one hand to her right ear in a self-stimulatory gesture.

Reflection

An adaptation of Rogers' psychotherapeutic technique to the music therapy process, Reflection is instantaneous playback of vocal (verbal and nonverbal), instrumental, and bodily movement of the here-and-now person that is structured by the music therapist into musical forms. In essence, it is the therapist's acknowledgment of, and unconditional positive regard for, the client that is designed to establish contact. It is this transmutation into musical forms that is especially appropriate and important for reaching people who have deficits in communication skills.

In initial encounters with a person who is unaware of self and others, mirroring and matching what the person is doing or *not* doing in song, rhythmic chants, instrumental improvisations, and movement signify acceptance of that person. Seemingly random, purposeless sounds and behaviors are received nonjudgmentally by another. Reflecting and coexperiencing what may be the person's only threads to ''reality'' can be a key to the person's center. The therapist tunes in and vibrates on the same wavelength, stimulating sensations that can lead to awareness and eventual contact.

With the strategy of Reflection as the taking-off point for establishing a therapeutic relationship, two other main strategies are designed to maintain, affirm, and deepen the relationship, namely, Identification and Our Contact Song.

These strategies bring what is happening into the client's awareness and mobilize organismic energy (physical, mental, and emotional) for action. The therapist stays absolutely in the present, coexisting and coexperiencing with the client, avoiding interpretations that might be subjective projections or misconstrued readings of what is occurring. As will become evident, both Reflection and Identification are used in the initial stage of therapy to make contact with the person and to lead to the discovery of Our Contact Song. This discovery may take the form of many musical and emotional experiences and explorations. There are frustrations, plateaus, impasses, peak experiences. Once this two-way communication is established, treatment progresses and the process deepens through further application of these strategies. Our Contact Song can be used throughout treatment in numerous ways to serve the therapeutic relationship and attain objectives and goals.

The initial stage of therapy with Margarita began in this way:

> Margarita was receiving two half-hour sessions a week. During the first month we were together yet isolated by the barrier of her unawareness. Vocally and instrumentally, I repeatedly reflected her sounds. She would continue without any overt response to my vocalizations, placing herself in the corner of the room and emitting birdlike outpourings, her eyes looking inward. I wrapped and unwrapped with her the ever-present leather belt around and around her left arm as I sang the spiritual, "There's a Little Wheel Turnin' in My Heart" (Landeck, 1950) adapting words to identify what she was doing, incorporating her name. In essence, I was sending a message: I am with you, I see you, I hear you, I am joining you in your world. Maybe you will see me, hear me, be with me. Together, let us find healthy expression for your energy. But first we need to make contact—you, Margarita, with me.
>
> Self-involved, her head intently bent over her busy hands, she sometimes smiled as if enjoying a private joke. As the weeks went on, there seemed to be a growing sense of my presence on a subliminal level. In response to my singing to her, an occasional look was directed my way. Though fleeting, this delicate breaking through the invisible but seemingly impenetrable wall that separated us was what I had set my antennae to receive. Perhaps it was the beginnings of a trusting relationship?

Identification

Identification, often used simultaneously with Reflection, is also a dimension crucial, first of all, to awakening and then to continuously raising awareness in individuals who are unaware of their experiencing or are unable to communicate what they are experiencing. It is instantaneous feedback of the here-and-now person and what is happening in the environment in improvised words of song and rhythmic chants. Identification of who the person is, what the person is doing, who we are, and what we are doing together is designed to heighten awareness of self, others, and the environment. If the person is nonverbal, the therapist becomes the alter ego, providing meaning and focus for the experience in order to heighten the person's level of awareness. If clients are verbal or have even a modicum of speech available, they are encouraged to engage in this process by singing or chanting along with the therapist or in response to the therapist's prompts.

As we moved closer to each other, Margarita's needs and wants began to surface. At a session three weeks later, as I strummed the Autoharp® and hummed a soothing lullaby in her ear, she suddenly pushed me aside, snatched the Autoharp® (still clutching her belt in her left hand), and ran her fingers over the strings. I ran my fingers over the strings, too. She then lowered her head to the vibrating strings. I did the same. As she repeated this over and over, smiling with a look of satisfaction, we entered a new phase of therapy. I improvised a tune with a rhythmic pattern that Margarita's name evoked, singing words that identified what she was doing:

> Margarita, Margarita,
> Margarita is playing the harp.
> Margarita, Margarita,
> Margarita is playing the harp.

And what we were doing together:

> Margarita and Edi
> Are playing the harp.
> Margarita and Edi
> Are playing the harp.

Existentially, we were sharing an experience that seemed to give Margarita a sense of gratification. Her body relaxed, her fingers relinquished their twisted mannerisms, and her tensely clutched lips parted in a lovely open smile.

For the next several sessions, though I offered her other instruments—drum, xylophone, resonator bells—Margarita preferred to engulf herself in the sea of sounds and vibrations that her fingers produced by strumming the Autoharp®. Reflecting and identifying her choices, I supported her developing assertions to experience musical sounds in her own way.

It was during the following session that Margarita impulsively pushed aside the Autoharp®, flung her head back and emitted a stream of high-pitched melodic phrases interspersed with idiosyncratic utterances. At the piano, I provided a harmonic structure, reflecting her vocalizations, stopping and starting when she did, matching her changes in pitch, her line of melody, her rhythmic patterns. Margarita's eyes flickered toward me as if in surprise. Then she burst out in a sudden gale of laughter. She was beginning to throw a signal my way. I, too, laughed with delight and sang out spontaneously:

> Margarita, Margarita,
> Margarita is singing a song.
> Margarita, Margarita,
> Margarita is singing a song.

Strongly rhythmic, it had a familiar Spanish flavor. I was singing to the tune of "La Cucaracha!" Aha! Maybe I had something there. I played and sang it to Margarita once more. She seemed to have retreated into her own world. Perhaps to absorb, to assimilate?

At following sessions, we danced to this tune, we clapped its melodic rhythm, we beat the drum to its pulse. I chanted, identifying our activities, constantly singing Margarita's name in the attempt to awaken a sense of who was dancing, who was clapping. I sang my name to establish our separate identities yet weave them into an interexperience. Her responses were for the most part mechanical and uninvolved. Little energy was directed outward. I then observed that when I played the piano, she tended to notice me. I was putting clues together. I went to the piano and played and sang the song, giving it its full measure of rhythmic and dynamic vitality. Until this moment, Margarita's interaction with me had been touch-and-go, response and retreat, a spark of outer light and a return to inner "darkness." Is it darkness? How much do you know? What are you hiding? Where are you hiding? I know that you know much more than you can allow yourself to know.

Our Contact Song

Our Contact Song is the first reciprocal musical expression, the first two-way musical communication, the first overt musical indication *initiated by the client* of an awareness of the existence of another. Although the client may have responded to the therapist and the many ways that music has been molded and shaped to establish a relationship—until the client consciously initiates this give-and-take, the connection between the two people has not taken place (Ruesch, 1972).

Based on the client's interests, strengths, behaviors, and problems, this song might come to the therapist intuitively; it may be consciously chosen by the therapist or "clued in" by the client. It is a composed or improvised song that lends itself to improvisational changes and adaptations. It becomes a fountainhead for a myriad of activities and experiences, always changing and being transformed in the service of therapeutic goals. It is our "hello," our "goodbye," a return to security when the world is toppling, a reminder of the safety in our relationship, an affirmation of trust, of being and becoming, of reaching out. Because Our Contact Song provides this secure base for the person, it can be used over and over and in numerous ways. Its repetitions and variations on a theme, rather than reinforcing undesirable behaviors such as perseveration or the need for sameness, pave the way for learning new behaviors and new ways of perceiving (Boxill, 1976).

At a later session as I sat at the piano playing and singing what became Our Contact Song—"Margarita" (Boxill, 1976, side 2, band 6), Margarita dropped her belt, rushed to the piano, sat *on* me, and—with intense concentration—depressed clusters of keys with her left hand, moving from tonic to dominant, dominant to tonic, in the harmonic progression I had played on the piano and Autoharp®. Could I believe my ears? I continued to play and sing the melody. Again, she played the same clusters, following the melodic lines. Her right hand lay tightly pressed to her lap.

I hugged her. She looked up at me. We smiled at each other. Then I began to play the melody, singing her name and touching her each time I sang:

> Margarita, Margarita,
> Margarita is your name,
> Margarita, Margarita,
> Margarita is your name.

She played the clusters in rhythmic accompaniment. We were in contact with each other. We had found Our Contact Song through the piano (which I discovered to be a natural means of expression for her). A figure–ground had become clear to her and had meaning that we were sharing and experiencing together.

Our Contact Song, expressed in the form of a piano duet, became the path to a trusting relationship and many enriching experiences together. In the process of heightening and expanding Margarita's awareness, her idiosyncratic vocalizations gradually advanced to verbalizations (at first, echolalic ones), and her self-abusive behaviors gave way to purposeful use of her energetic, busy hands. With much tender nurturing, gestural demands of needs and wants transferred to making connections between words and actions—transformations all.

> Therapist: Margarita wants piano?
> Margarita: Margarita wants pi-a-no?

With that, we would walk arm in arm to the piano, approaching it with enthusiastic anticipation rather than the demanding desperation that she had exhibited in so many ways. And with more tender nurturing:

> Therapist: Margarita, what do you want?
> Margarita: Want pi-a-no, want pi-a-no.

And with more:

> Therapist: Margarita, do *you* want piano?
> Margarita: I want pi-a-no! I want pi-a-no!

CONCLUSION

The role of the therapist is to initiate the person into states of awareness on all levels (physical, mental, emotional), to assist the person to mobilize energy and inner resources, to allow time for assimilation of awakened attention and growing awareness, and to bring the person from inner action to outer action. What we look for is the emotional impact that the simplest action can have on the person's sense of self. If he or she moves a hand in a new way or makes a sound never before uttered or strikes tone bars for the first time, that person has performed a creative act. This creative act, when acknowledged and expanded upon musically, can give rise to the innate urge to push outward, to stretch, to grow.

As can be seen from the preceding description, by building a pattern of small successes, giving direct reinforcement, and identifying the client's accomplishments in ways that can be received, understood, and assimilated, the momentum for reaching objectives and goals is created.

The therapist's full engagement and involvement are essential to building a trusting relationship and to the client's movement toward higher levels of development and expression. Indeed, the client–therapist relationship is central to this approach. To create this process of awakening, heightening, and expanding awareness on a continuum, the therapist existentially participates in another's existence, striving constantly to expand awareness by being open to the holistic person—all conditions, behaviors, and responses, musical and nonmusical. For, in this phenomenological work, the therapist who is cognizant of the cyclical nature of change, as well as readiness for learning, will be able to journey through the rhythmic patterns of growth—advances and retreats—with the client, creating and experimenting in ways that will work for that individual. The therapist and the client together explore means of increasing the client's self-support and self-actualization to the greatest degree possible. They coexist, coexperience, and interexperience.

By means of clinical improvisation and adaptation of music, the therapist uses or redirects as working material the "good or bad stuff, violent or placid stuff, coloured or dun" (Ashton-Warner, 1964, p. 32) of the client—mannerisms, symptoms, behaviors, sounds, idiosyncratic vocalizations, verbalizations, feelings, emotions, moods. This acknowledgment of the person is designed to stimulate sensations that effect a shift in the client's perception of self in relation to the environment, a shift from a state of confluence to one of existing and making contact as a separate being. Until this happens, as Perls (1978) points out: "The person in whom confluence is a pathological state cannot tell what he is and he cannot tell what other people are. He does not know where he leaves off and others begin. As he is unaware of the boundary between himself and others, he cannot even make contact with himself" (p. 38).

Raising awareness involves change or transformation in the client's manner of experiencing. Intrinsic change can occur when the therapist helps the person move from a state of unaware experiencing to aware experiencing. Initially, the person may be remote, unable to be expressive, incapable of receiving or tolerating musical stimuli. From remoteness, the combined impact of the therapeutic relationship, the power of music, and the therapist's style and skill move the client toward being aware of experiencing, toward awareness and a greater ability to be self-directed. Rogers (1961) states that as the client "becomes more self-aware . . . he is at last free to change and grow in the directions natural to the human organism. . . . We know that the client shows movement on each of a number of continua. Starting from wherever he may be on each continuum . . . he moves toward the upper end" (p. 64).

What could be more appropriate, therefore, for persons whose awareness of self, others, and the environment is poorly realized than a therapy based in the process of cultivating levels of awareness that give rise to higher forms of functioning and a greater sense of self? How can a person develop intrinsically if some measure of awareness of self and others does not exist or is not activated to self-expression?

REFERENCES

Allport, G.W. *Becoming: Basic considerations for a psychology of personality*. New Haven: Yale University Press, 1955.

Ashton-Warner, S. *Teacher*. New York: Bantam Books, 1964.

Bandura, A. *Principles of behavior modification*. New York: Holt, Rinehart & Winston, 1969.

Boxill, E.H. *Developing communication with the autistic child through music therapy.* Paper presented at the meeting of the American Association for Music Therapy, New York, November 1974. (ERIC Document Reproduction Service Nos. ED 149 534 and EC 103 762)

Boxill, E.H. "Margarita" *Music adapted, composed, and improvised for music therapy with the developmentally handicapped* (side 2, band 6). New York: Folkways Records, 1976. (Record FX 6180, booklet included)

Boxill, E.H. A continuum of awareness: Music therapy with the developmentally handicapped. *Music Therapy,* 1981, *1*(1), 17–23.

Ellis, A. *Humanistic psychotherapy: The rational-emotive approach.* New York: Julian Press and McGraw-Hill Paperbacks, 1974.

Erikson, E.H. *Childhood and society* (2nd ed.). New York: Norton, 1963.

James, W. *Principles of psychology* (3 vols.). (F.H. Burkhardt, Ed.). Cambridge, Mass.: Harvard University Press, 1981.

Köhler, W. *Gestalt psychology.* New York: Liveright, 1929.

Landeck, B. (Compiler). *Songs to grow on.* New York: Edward B. Marks Music Corporation, 1950.

Maslow, A.H. *Motivation and personality.* New York: Harper & Brothers, 1954.

Maslow, A.H. Lessons from the peak-experiences. *Journal of Humanistic Psychology,* 1962, *2,* 9–18.

Maslow, A.H. Neurosis as a failure of personal growth. In W.S. Sahakian (Ed.), *Psychopathology today: Experimentation, theory and research.* Itasca, Ill.: Peacock, 1972.

Maslow, A.H. *The farther reaches of human nature.* New York: Penguin Books, 1976.

Maslow, A.H. *The creative attitude.* In W. Anderson (Ed.), *Therapy and the arts.* New York: Harper Colophon Books, 1977.

Moustakas, C.E. *The self: Explorations in personal growth.* New York: Harper Colophon Books, 1974.

Perls, F.S. Gestalt therapy and human potentialities. In H.A. Otto (Ed.), *Explorations in human potentialities.* Springfield, Ill.: Charles C Thomas, 1966.

Perls, F.S. *Gestalt therapy verbatim.* New York: Bantam Books, 1974.

Perls, F.S. Group vs. individual therapy. In J.O. Stevens (Ed.), *Gestalt is.* New York: Bantam Books, 1977. (a)

Perls, F.S. Theory and technique of personality integration. In J.O. Stevens (Ed.), *Gestalt is.* New York: Bantam Books, 1977 (b).

Perls, F.S. *The gestalt approach & eyewitness to therapy.* New York: Bantam Books, 1978.

Rogers, C.R. *Client-centered therapy: Its current practice and theory.* Boston: Houghton Mifflin, 1951.

Rogers, C.R. A theory of therapy, personality, and interpersonal relationships as developed in the client-centered framework. In S. Koch (Ed.), *Psychology: A study of a science* (Vol. 3). New York: McGraw-Hill, 1959.

Rogers, C.R. *On becoming a person.* Boston: Houghton Mifflin, 1961.

Rogers, C.R. Toward a science of the person. In T.W. Wann (Ed.), *Behaviorism and phenomenology: Contrasting bases for modern psychology.* Chicago: University of Chicago Press, 1964.

Rogers, C.R. *Client-centered therapy.* Boston: Houghton Mifflin, 1965.

Ruesch, J. *Disturbed communication: The clinical assessment of normal and pathological communicative behavior.* New York: Norton, 1972.

Ruesch, J., & Bateson, G. *Communication: The social matrix of psychiatry.* New York: Norton, 1951.

Severin, F.T. (Ed.). *Humanistic viewpoints in psychology.* New York: McGraw-Hill, 1965.

Stevens, J.O. *Awareness: Exploring, experimenting, experiencing.* New York: Bantam Books, 1980.

Sullivan, H.S. *The interpersonal theory of psychiatry* (H.S. Perry & M.L. Gawel, Eds.). New York: Norton, 1953.

Watson, J.B. *Behaviorism.* Chicago: University of Chicago Press, 1930.

Zinker, J. *Creative process in gestalt therapy.* New York: Vintage Books, 1978.

Chapter 5

Treatment As Process

Music creates order out of chaos; for rhythm imposes unanimity upon the divergent, melody imposes continuity upon the disjointed, and harmony imposes compatibility upon the incongruous.

Yehudi Menuhin (1972, p. 9)

What is needed is nothing less than a new methodology to acquire . . . knowledge concerning the highest manifestation of life—the humanness of man.

René Dubos (1980, p. xx)

INTRODUCTION

Treatment as process is an opening up and an eventual deepening of awareness through a growing capacity for adaptive musical and nonmusical behaviors; it is an opening up of pathways for developing the mind–body unity that lays the groundwork for intrinsic learning. As in other modern action therapies, the focus is on what the therapist does *with*—not *to*—the client. Experiential in nature, therapy involves clients in actively participating in processes that bring about their own behavioral change.

In a creative process of this kind, intrinsic learning and the phenomenon referred to as a breakthrough may enable a person to reach a stage of development or attain a skill in a leap rather than step by step. Essential to its success, therefore, are the facilitation and maintenance of the experiential nature of participation and of relatedness without adherence to predetermined procedure.* In discussing treatment process, Bugental (1978) points to "a continuity of experience which is ever changing. . . . It is an experience which must be allowed to unfold" (p. 2).

From its root meaning, the term *process* indicates movement, or a moving forth. It is antithetical to any concept of therapy that is based in fixed procedures. It does not abolish form but rather encompasses it. In the humanistic sense, process indicates cyclical evolvement and organic growth whether it refers to an individual, a therapy session, or the entire course of treatment. This cyclical evolvement and organic growth occur within a creative structure in which the therapist engages in a dynamic give-and-take with the client and in which the therapy session is a moment-to-moment living experience. In discussing psychotherapeutic process, Yalom (1970), asserts that "A focus upon the here-and-now process is . . . fundamental to effective therapy technique. The words here-and-now make a deceptively simple phrase out of a complex therapeutic process" (p. 109). Replete with subtleties and nuances, the moment-*to*-moment and moment-*by*-moment process requires empathic understanding of the inner organic flow in its many forms: impulses, pulsations, connections, mood changes, feeling states—energy that generates musical as well as nonmusical expression and behavior. Whatever the particular dynamic of the moment may be, the therapist coexists and interexperiences with the client. To be in process with a client, therefore, means to be in synchrony, in rhythm, with that person.

Discovery and newly acquired accomplishment occur as the therapist moves with the client into realms of functioning and experiencing that had been unknown or unstimulated or unused. Getting to the heart of this approach, Zinker (1978) states that "The sine qua non of the creative process is change: the transformation of one form into another" (p. 5). This change or transformation in the manner of experiencing develops through the shared experience of the client and the therapist. In Rogers' (1961, 1962) client-centered therapy, this process of transforming the manner of experiencing takes place as the therapist brings about a state of congruence between client and therapist.

CLIENT–THERAPIST RELATIONSHIP

It is axiomatic that a strong client–therapist relationship is essential to successful treatment. The foundation of this relationship is basic trust (Erikson, 1963). From the very moment of encounter with the client, the therapist sets about

---

*Behaviorally oriented music therapy is characterized by stepwise hierarchical actions or procedures. As does the generalist of behavior therapy, the behaviorally oriented music therapist looks to increasing and decreasing behaviors by means of reinforcements designed to alter behavior in measurable terms. According to Madsen, Madsen, and Cotter (1968), when music therapy is approached in this way, it is a method of behavioral manipulation and, therefore, falls within the purview of the behavior modification movement.

establishing a positive, trusting therapeutic relationship. Essential for establishing and building such a relationship are the respect of the therapist for the dignity and worth of the client, and the security of the client engendered by the therapist's attributes and attitudes. Whether it is a group or one-to-one setting, this mutuality between the two people is carefully and tenderly nurtured.

In music therapy, the therapist's ability to project himself or herself musically is crucial to a client–therapist relationship that taps the farther reaches of human nature (Maslow, 1976). It is this ability, together with the therapist's attributes and the power inherent in the therapeutic tool, that gives a special quality to a therapeutic relationship established through music therapy. As has been discussed in Chapter 2, the contact made through music can create a uniquely nonthreatening kind of bond and can create synchrony between client and therapist. As the living instrument of therapy, the therapist follows accepted pathways as well as searching for new ones to the individual's well-being. Some attributes of an effective therapist are endowed, others are acquired. In order to enter into a relationship with a client that will nurture the individual's growth, the therapist must:

- understand and have knowledge of the influence of music on a person
- be able to project himself or herself musically
- be able to communicate through music
- be able to select appropriate music materials and adapt them to the client's level of functioning
- have self-understanding
- have understanding of the other
- accept and acknowledge the other
- observe people and situations with acuity
- evaluate people and situations nonjudgmentally
- be empathic, flexible, and spontaneous
- be aware of and alert to his or her effect on others
- be intuitive, creative, and imaginative
- have a sense of humor
- have the capacity to grow personally and professionally

Note that patience, often considered a desirable attribute, has been deliberately omitted from this list. When the therapist is actively and fully engaged with the individual, patience is not required. What is required is the ability to be in the present, to be aware of the individual's problems and one's purpose, and to direct one's energies toward dealing with each situation that arises. It is no secret that recognizing the individual's interests, strengths, and problems and meeting his or her needs are fundamental to conducting effective therapy.

The therapist who is capable of making experiences successful will find that discipline, like patience, is not an issue. The motivation that comes of positive acknowledgment, genuine encouragement, and the use of specific music therapy techniques engenders self-control, intrinsic learning, and creative action. Ashton-Warner (1964) understood this well: "I see the mind . . . as a volcano with two vents: destructiveness and creativeness. And I see that to the extent that we widen the creative channel, we atrophy the destructive one" (p. 27).

Conditions in a therapeutic relationship that stimulate awareness, facilitate development, and release a person's energies for self-direction and independent living can be said to exist when the therapist is genuine and without facade, accepts the client with unconditional positive regard, and empathically, senses and perceives the feelings the client is experiencing.

Because response to sound and music is highly subjective and has many aspects that result from a multitude of factors, the ability to receive empathically and nonjudgmentally all possible cues—verbal and nonverbal, musical or nonmusical—that the client sends out is a basic requisite for establishing the therapeutic relationship. Observable responses may be related or unrelated to the musical stimuli; they may be specific or undifferentiated, varied or stereotypic, spontaneous or consciously initiated. Therefore, the therapist studies the total person: impulses unique to that individual, behaviors and responses characteristic of the person's condition, and variables causing moment-to-moment changes as well as changes the therapy is effecting. This means that the therapist must not only deal with identified disorders but must also be sensitive to and attentive to all behaviors and responses. He or she must be constantly alert to messages sent overtly and covertly by the other person in the therapeutic relationship. To do this, therapists must sharpen their powers of observation and intuition* and must develop the ability to translate these perceptions into action.

GROUP AND INDIVIDUAL PROCESS

The underlying tenets of the therapeutic relationship apply to both individual and group therapy.** In both settings, concern is for the individual and the relationship of that person to the therapist, yet each setting has qualities—we might say advantages—that are peculiar to the nature of the setting. Basic premises of both processes are the primacy of present, ongoing experience; the importance of active contact between client and therapist; and the accomplishment

---

*Intuition is direct awareness (without conscious attention) that emanates from the mind that is prepared, the mind that has accumulated knowledge and materials, the mind that searches, explores, and experiments. It is referred to as the *Eureka!* experience (Pearce, 1971). The prepared and trained mind can be intuitive and ready to respond to the here-and-now person.

**Core music therapy groups consist of four to six clients at most.

of the goals and objectives set for the client. Premises specific to group process are the awareness of one another as members of a group; the importance and quality of interaction between clients; the flow of interactional situations stimulated by an actively involved therapist; the group unity and cohesion achieved by a skilled therapist; the interweaving of the objectives and goals set for each person with those set for the group; and the *active* participation of each individual spontaneously or with assistance.

Competence in creating group unity and meeting individual needs must not only be highly developed in group work; knowledge and an understanding of group dynamics are also of utmost importance. In fact, there are very definite benefits that can be derived only from the group experience. The energy, unity of purpose, and communication that can be generated when a group makes music together are exciting to witness, particularly as growth in relatedness to music progresses and successful experiences inspire the motivation to learn. Through the group activity, the therapist creates and nurtures connections between clients, devising ways of making them aware of what they are doing, stimulating interplay and intercommunication both verbally and nonverbally. Transfer to affective and social domains of functioning in everyday life is an important result of this kind of group experience. Leadership qualities that have heretofore been untapped emerge. The person who demands excessive attention can be helped to respect and be sensitive to others. Often, one client will spontaneously help another. This kind of interaction is not only stimulated but *created* by the skilled therapist. If a group is not homogeneous with respect to age and level of functioning, the therapist may view this situation as an opportunity to stimulate higher functioning clients to assist those who are functioning at a lower level.

In many centers for the developmentally disabled, the major portion of music therapy treatment necessarily is done in group sessions. Therefore, the music therapist must have special clinical skills in group work directly applicable to this population. Coexperiencing and being quick to act upon needs of the moment are required—indeed, demanded—of the therapist no matter what the group's level of functioning or the kinds of conditions presented. One thing is certain: There will be maladaptive behaviors and deficits in communication. As any experienced, qualified therapist knows, working with a group, keeping it together as an entity while interweaving group goals with individual objectives, poses ongoing challenges. Therapists-in-training are very quickly awakened to these challenges when they come face to face with actual clients. A way to meet these challenges is to develop a solid foundation on which to build an approach to therapy. Finding a context that is workable, appropriate, and effective is all-important. Discovering that a solid foundation lies in the context of *A Continuum of Awareness* has made it possible to offer music therapists, interns, and students a framework for the totality of the experience. Many parts of what often seems an insoluble puzzle gradually fall into place through this approach.

The relationship in the individual therapy setting is qualitatively different from that of group therapy and places different demands on the skill of the therapist. Although both types of sessions are based on the needs, capabilities, and interests of the individuals, the one-to-one setting is a more intensive experience for both client and therapist. The complete concentration of the therapist on one individual allows for in-depth experience—as illustrated in descriptions of one-to-one therapy in Chapter 6—that is not always possible in the group setting. Although all clients would benefit from this kind of therapeutic experience, in a large facility where the number of therapists may be insufficient to serve all clients, referrals for one-to-one therapy depend on the needs of each client relative to those of others.

Within the context of a *continuum of awareness*, the therapy session is viewed as encompassing everyone and everything in the environment in which the therapy is being experienced—who the people are, what they are doing, what related or unrelated situations are occurring. By encompassing the total environment, the experiences of everyday life are simulated as closely as possible. All that happens can be grist for the mill. Although it is clear that privacy during a session is necessary and desirable, in a large center, situations that interrupt the flow of a session will occur. What might otherwise be considered a negative element, such as an interruption, distraction, or disturbance, can be incorporated into the process and translated into musical forms. Perhaps the nature of the therapy session is best understood when thought of as analogous to a family or home situation. If, for example, the telephone rings during a session, it need not throw the process off course. Rather, it can become part of it, just as it would be part of the family scene. If there is an observer in the room, by singing a song such as "The People in the Room Today" (Boxill, 1976, side 1, band 1), an adaptation of "The People in Your Neighborhood" (Moss, 1971), that person can be acknowledged musically and asked to join the group. This approach provides latitude for the therapist as well as for clients, and it eliminates constraints that the therapist may mistakenly view as necessary for keeping sessions "nice and orderly." Above all, we are talking about an environment and an attitude that can enrich the scope of awareness and aliveness—the humanness—of an individual or group.

TREATMENT STRATEGIES AND TECHNIQUES

Treatment of developmental disabilities addresses the four major problem areas presented: mental deficits, maladaptive behaviors, physical dysfunctions, and emotional disorders. In guiding the course of treatment, the therapist must always keep in mind the learning characteristics of this population: an inability to generalize; concrete thinking; limited or nonexistent ability to think in abstractions; an inability to attend or sustain attention; large disparities in long- and short-term memory; a delay in responding to and acting upon stimuli; and longer than average time needed for assimilation.

As a result, there are many instances, especially with regard to people who are profoundly retarded, in which significant change or improvement either does not occur or occurs only over extended periods. Given the nature of the dysfunctions, disorders, and impairments involved, treatment is a prolonged, often slow-moving process. With clients who have extreme organic deficits or behavioral disorders, change or improvement may not readily be discernible and may manifest itself only after a long time. At times it will appear that little or no progress is being made toward the accomplishment of a short-term objective. This, however, may very well be the period of assimilation and accommodation that Piaget designates as a condition of learning. There may be inner growth and learning that results in a shift of foreground–background (in other words, awareness) that effects a sudden change in perception and generates a new behavior.

This is one reason why the therapist must guard against having expectations of what the client should achieve and when he or she should achieve it. The mind set of expectations can reinforce the self-fulfilling prophecy of failure because it implies that the therapist expects a certain result and, if this result is not attained, either the therapist or the client has failed. By not having rigid expectations of what the client can or cannot achieve and by building a series of successful experiences toward the accomplishment of objectives and goals, the therapist is able to provide a climate in which the client *can* achieve.

A therapist is often faced with what appears to be a dilemma: Should therapy be directive or nondirective? In actual practice, it is directive at times and nondirective at others, depending on what objective or goal is being worked on, what situation prevails, and the client's level of functioning. In other words, in working toward an objective or goal, there are times when we are directive and others when we wait to see what the client will initiate or what the client's response will be without any direct intervention. Because of the nature of the conditions of this population, however, the work must be primarily directive. The therapist must constantly make decisions as to what objectives to continue or change, how best to attain a skill, when to use different levels of assistance, when to use or not use certain music, therapeutic music activities, or instruments, and so on. We look, we listen, we work with the client.

There are no formulas as to how a particular person will respond, nor are there expected emotional or motoric responses, to a particular kind of music. If a person does not respond to "happy" music as "expected," has either the person or the therapist failed? The answer is an unequivocal *no*. The error is in the expectation. The well-trained music therapist learns not to make the error of expecting another person to act in a predictable way. Rather, the therapist always works toward a therapeutic end and changes the music to serve the mood of the here-and-now person in the most beneficial way possible. On a given day, a hyperactive boy may need vibrant, rhythmic, lively music to *match* his behavior, rather than soft, lulling music that might not reach him.

In view of the characteristics of learning of this population, musical as well as nonmusical stimuli are presented at a slower than average rate; in smaller than average quantities; with frequent and exact repetitions; and with gestural, physical, and verbal assistance or prompts. Concrete, familiar, everyday materials are used and adapted to suit the needs of the client. There are several important rules of thumb. First, repeated singing of the individual's name is often necessary to awaken awareness of self, establish self-identity, and gain the person's attention. Second, verbal communication must be adjusted to the person's level of comprehension (for example, one word may have meaning, whereas a string of words may be meaningless and cause confusion and frustration). Third, because the therapist's attitude is often epitomized by the way directives are given, it is best, whenever possible, to give verbal directives in positive terms ("We're playing instruments now" rather than "Don't do that") and to redirect behaviors nonverbally or gesturally.

The following is a selection of music therapy strategies and techniques that can be applied to work with clients of every age and level of functioning:

- Reflection/matching/mirroring
- Identification
- Our Contact Song
- unmatching (i.e., use of improvised or adapted vocal or instrumental music that is purposefully opposite or different from the person's behavior or affective state)
- use of music that is familiar to or has meaning for the person or group
- use of the components of music singly and in combination for many therapeutic purposes (e.g., emotional, motoric, behavioral, perceptual)
- exact repetition of rhythmic patterns, words of a song, and musical phrases for auditory perception and memory
- exact repetition of music for emotional security
- lining-out singing (i.e., filling in isolated words, last word, or words of musical phrases, etc.) for nonechoic vocabulary
- call-and-response singing for auditory perception, sound imitation, echoic vocabulary
- antiphonal (musical imitation) use of instruments and singing
- humming for relaxation
- matching tonal register of client to create synchrony and contact with the client
- onomatopoeic and action words sung or chanted with appropriate movements for motoric, cognitive, or communication skills
- selection and use of instruments for specific therapeutic purposes

- translating a person's leads and cues (e.g., movements, sounds, interests expressed, ideas) into musical forms
- pacing and tempo adjustments of activities and musical stimuli in response to needs and conditions of the individual and the group
- sequential movements to songs (adaptation of Orff-Schulwerk method for specific motoric activities/skills)
- exaggerated and expressive modeling of bodily movements while singing or playing an instrument in order to convey the mood, quality, and rhythmic patterns of the music and evoke client responses
- nonverbal musical dialogue (on drums, etc.)
- use of syllables and nonverbal sounds (vocalizations) to stimulate communication skills
- exaggerated enunciation and articulation of words of song to facilitate or stimulate speech; stressing and accenting words and syllables to stimulate natural inflections and cadences in speech
- use of the structure and form of a song (e.g., repeated verse, choruses and refrains, rondo form) for memory, recall, retention, word retrieval
- use of a tape recorder as a therapeutic tool for auditory perception and discrimination, awareness of self and others, self-esteem
- use of nonmusic materials, such as flashcards, pictures, mirrors, puppets, hoops, scarves, balls, paper streamers, crayons, construction paper, and various kinds of costumes, for added sensory stimulation and comprehension
- use of manual signs for *start, stop, play*, and *wait*, with simultaneous singing/chanting or verbalization when possible (e.g., for impulse control, attending behavior, speech stimulation, fine motor skills)

The following sections deal with music therapy methodology: (a) categories of music, (b) modes of therapeutic music activity, and (c) therapeutic uses of the components of music.

METHODOLOGY

Categories of Music

The categories of music used in music therapy are:

- clinical music improvisation—instrumental and vocal (with or without text)
- composed music of all genres, idioms, styles, and origins—instrumental and vocal

- adaptation of composed music of all genres, idioms, styles, and origins—instrumental and vocal

Clinical Music Improvisation

Clinical music improvisation is the spontaneous, extemporaneous expression of music and its components, vocally and instrumentally, for therapeutic purposes. It is a uniquely potent path to the kind of musical rapport that promotes the client–therapist relationship and the client's sense of self. When used to reflect the here-and-now person or to engage a person or group in free as well as structured musical exchange and expression vocally, instrumentally, and bodily, this category of music is a highly individualized method of contact and communication. In reaching and acknowledging others on deep levels of inner experience and outer expression, it takes many musical forms. It is used to:

- establish contact with the individual and/or group
- establish a musical bond between the client and therapist
- bring about congruence and synchronicity with the person (feelings, moods, body movements, behavior)
- acknowledge the client by structuring and translating behavior into musical forms
- assist the client to gain inner control over behavior through musical guidance
- stimulate responses and aliveness
- encourage and stimulate communication, both musical and nonmusical
- reflect/match, support, or change/redirect behavior
- personalize and individualize client needs, problems, symptoms, interests, strengths, behaviors, and affective states

Clinical music improvisation requires that the therapist develop the ability and sensitivity to accept clients nonjudgmentally and to respond musically in empathic and intuitive ways to the person moment by moment. This necessitates that the therapist, while developing the client's awareness, is constantly honing his or her own acuity.

The use of clinical music improvisation requires the capacity to give musical form and expression in different musical styles, idioms, and modes instantaneously and to project musically, giving wide latitude and flexibility to the therapy process. The use of oneself creatively, as an instrument of musical expression and ideas, combines musicianship with knowledge and understanding of the characteristics of the client population. The style and musical idiom, the quality of melodic expression, the chordal structures and modes, and the kind of accompaniment used are chosen by the therapist extemporaneously in response to a person's condition at the moment. In using clinical music improvisation, the trained therapist must have available a wide variety of musical skills and knowledge.

Composed Music

In using composed music, the music therapist must be able to play and project the music without being dependent on the printed page. The music must be a natural expression of the therapist, not a performance. The significance of this distinction lies in the therapist's ability to project the power of music freely and fully to meet the client's needs and goals.

When selecting composed music—whatever the style, idiom, or ethnic origin—the music therapist asks questions such as: Is the music suitable for achieving specific predetermined objectives and goals? Is the music or song age appropriate? (A special concern is that the music not be childishly simplistic for adolescents and adults.) Is the melodic line of a song within a comfortable voice range (an octave or less)? Is the text/lyric of a song concrete and within the comprehension level of the person or group? Is the melody simple and uncomplicated rhythmically? Are the words repetitive and uncomplicated? Is the musical structure repetitive and uncomplicated? Does the music/song have appeal for the person or group? Is the music/song familiar to the person and accessible for the person's functioning level?

In building a repertoire, various criteria are used for selecting suitable music:

- *wide applicability:* can be used with a wide range of functioning levels and for a wide range of therapeutic music activities
- *specific applicability:* lends itself to working on (a) accomplishing specific objectives and goals; (b) problem areas (e.g., motor skills, communication skills, cognitive skills); (c) problematic behavior (e.g., lack of impulse control, stereotypes, self-abuse, perseveration); and (d) specific skills (e.g., directionality, laterality, basic locomotion, learning of body parts, numeration)
- *versatility:* lends itself to use with diverse kinds of situations and divergent groups
- *potential for improvisation:* lends itself to musical variations, to accompaniment changes, and to changes in dynamics, tempo, and mood
- *potential for adaptation and simplification:* lends itself to melodic, harmonic, and structural changes
- *content of text of song:* is concrete, deals with daily living, familiar ideas and objects, familiar people, or the immediate environment and can be used to reinforce other disciplines (e.g., special education, speech therapy)

- *form or structure of music:* has simple repetitive form such as verse–chorus song form or rondo form (vocal or instrumental)
- *quality of music:* conveys a particular spirit, mood, or feeling
- *dominance of a component:* either rhythm, melody, harmony, pitch, tempo, dynamics, timbre, or text of song
- *musical idiom:* folk,* popular, classical, ethnic, jazz, rock, or disco
- *familiarity:* a song that is known to or requested by the client or group

Adaptation of Music

Adaptation of music for clinical work puts similar demands on the therapist's competency and creativity and serves many of the same purposes as does clinical music improvisation. It requires musical skills, the capacity for spontaneous musical expression, knowledge of a wide range of music in all idioms and styles, and a high degree of selectivity. This means careful choice of musical material that lends itself to adaptational changes for meeting therapeutic needs and purposes, as well as the ability to exercise appropriate choices for the individual or situation. Retaining the original attributes of the music/song, the therapist may change the tempo and words or simplify rhythmic patterns, melodic lines, and structure. Musical phrases may be contracted or augmented; sections may be deleted; melodic phrases and words may be repeated or excerpted—all to adjust to the client or the flow of the therapy process.

Adaptation of music is based on a number of factors. When creating and designing therapeutic music activities, changes and adaptations in the music selected are in accordance with:

- functioning levels (e.g., simplification of music, words, form)
- functional needs (e.g., variations in quality of music for specific kinds of skills, voice ranges, physical conditions)
- individual emotional conditions and moods
- individual pace and rhythm of client
- individual and group interests and suggestions for activities
- actions initiated by the client
- specific therapeutic music activities planned, shaped, and molded by the therapist
- creative expression
- musical dramatizations

---

*Folk music of all origins has characteristics that make the music and songs particularly appropriate and suitable. These characteristics are repetitiveness of melody and words, familiarity of subject matter, and simplicity of melodic line and musical form. Their properties make them accessible to most people and create cultural or ethnic connections with a diversity of individuals and groups.

In exemplifying how material is adapted to suit the level of functioning, we see that the song, "I've Got Two" (Raposo & Moss, 1971; see Chapter 6), can be used in the following ways: (a) with severely and profoundly retarded clients, for awareness of body parts—hands, feet, arms, legs (the numbers are incidental); (b) with moderately retarded clients, for numeration and comprehension of number concepts in addition to body parts; and (c) with mildly retarded clients, for both comprehension of number concepts and learning the functions of body parts. The words would be adapted in ways such as:

I've got two hands, *one, two.*
I've got two hands, *one, two.*
I've got two hands,
One, two.

I've got two feet (legs, arms, eyes, ears, etc.) . . .

I've got one nose (mouth, neck, etc.) . . .

I've got five fingers on this hand . . .

I've got five fingers on this hand . . .

I've got two hands, one, two.
I've got two hands, one, two.
I've got two hands,
And what can I do with my hands?

I *clap* my hands, *clap, clap* . . .
(Continue to clap in rhythm of song)

Other parts of the body and their functions would be:

I've got two feet and I *walk* with my feet . . .

I've got two arms and I *push* with my arms . . .

I've got two eyes and I *see* with my eyes . . .

I've got two ears and I *hear* with my ears . . .

Visual aids (flash cards with numbers, pictures of body parts) and instruments can be used for "I see (instrument) with my eyes," and instruments can be played for "I hear (instrument) with my ears."

Adaptation (like improvisation) for the purpose of *matching* or *reflecting* a person's mood, pace, or dynamic level serves the needs of a client by bringing about congruence and synchronicity, whereas *unmatching* a person's condition by adapting (or improvising) music to express the opposite mood, pace, or dynamic level can also serve the person's needs in an empathic and clinically skilled way. For example, since rhythm is an energizing and integrating force, music that has a strong beat or rhythmic pattern would seem the obvious choice to arouse and raise the energy level of a hypoactive or withdrawn person. However, the therapist who is attuned to the person's needs and understands that responses to music are not only subjective but also unpredictable will not be caught up in a prejudgment of the effect the music will have. Matching or reflecting the person's low energy state might be energizing in that it acknowledges the person's affective state, whereas energetic music might at the moment be intolerable or felt to be a denial that could cause further withdrawal. Therefore, the therapist experiments with matching or unmatching to discover how best to meet the person's needs.

Modes of Therapeutic Music Activity

Three modes of therapeutic music activity used singly or in combination are:

1. singing/chanting
2. instrument playing
3. music-movement

Mind–body integration, which develops through sensory stimulation and leads to action, is basic to habilitation. On a continuum, intrinsic learning proceeds relative to a person's potential. The three modes of therapeutic music activity are direct paths to developing this mind–body awareness through experiential situations. Four or five domains of functioning may be worked on simultaneously through these three modes in order to expand the person holistically. For example, singing a song, playing an instrument, and music-movement may all deal with speech stimulation, coordination, impulse control, and auditory perception. One might think that combining the various modes would be complicated or confusing. On the contrary, it has been found that when singing and playing an instrument or singing and moving are simultaneous, one mode of activity reinforces and enhances another. When these modes are interwoven, the synergistic effect of the multisensory approach stimulates learning.

Therapeutic music activities designed in accordance with the developmental and social levels of functioning, as well as specific dysfunctions, involve the person as an active doer. Such activities are organic components of the multidimensional music therapy process. What makes it a therapeutic music activity (as distinguished from recreational) is the purpose for which it is designed by the therapist and its direct application for accomplishing long-term goals and short-term objectives. It is important to be mindful that music therapy as process is not merely a succession of therapeutic music activities, nor is the design of a therapeutic activity adhered to rigidly. A therapeutic music activity may be centered in any one of the modes of activity or in a combination of two or three of the modes. Furthermore, the treatment process may start out in one mode and evolve into any one or more of the other modes. The design may be open-ended or structured by the framework of a concrete theme or musical form or it may follow a preplanned pattern of movements such as an Orff-like sequence. The choice of music may be clinically improvised or composed music selected for its potential to serve many predetermined objectives and goals. On one hand, an activity, whether used in one session or many, may undergo changes in various ways (additions, deletions, and adjustments in the music) in relation to client responses and needs and the flow of the treatment process. On the other hand, an activity may be replicated exactly as originally designed if the therapeutic purpose is thereby served (e.g., exact repetition is a necessary and important law of learning that provides familiarity and security through recognition, recall, and retention).

Singing/Chanting

Developmentally, singing is the first form of spontaneous musical expression. In the normal course of maturation and development, the child "improvises" bits and pieces of songs, sings while playing. This natural experience is largely denied the mentally retarded child. As already mentioned, singing is rarely a spontaneous behavior for the mentally retarded person at any age.

Singing to, for, and with the client is a means of contact and communication that stimulates the awareness of self and others. To sing or hum a melody is to use the musical instrument that is an extension of the self—the human voice. The music therapist, knowledgeable about the influence of the melodic element of music, applies it skillfully for specific therapeutic purposes. For example, an agitated, hyperactive person, when encouraged to hum a melody, may create his or her own sense of calm through the vibratory effect of the music, as well as the emotional gratification it affords. Even on the most elementary level, singing and musical vocalizations mobilize energy and are a means of focus that create feelings of wholeness, for individuals and groups. When a person sings, he or she is the instrument of musical sound and, at the moment of producing it, becomes an integrated whole. And when people share the experience of singing together, the mutuality of their experience and the energy it generates integrate a group of separate individuals into a unified, cohesive whole. The benefits are individual and collective.

Singing all kinds of songs—whether folk, traditional, spirituals, rounds, rock, country, popular, or classical—serves many therapeutic purposes. Applied to everyday situations, holidays, transportation, animals, colors, numbers, the environment, and individual and group interests, songs can be:

- adapted musically and textually to persons of all levels of functioning
- a source of emotional security and stability
- a source of stimulation in all domains of functioning

- a pathway to verbal communication
- an aesthetic and liberating experience

An important aspect of treatment based in singing/chanting is the extensive opportunity it offers the therapist for shaping musical activities in various communicative and improvisational ways. Songs can be used in their entirety and in their structural parts—song phrases, song sentences, song sections (verses). Melodic rhythmic patterns can be extracted for chanting. The text and melody can be used to evoke feelings, moods, movement, dramatizations. Textual improvisation is used extensively in the strategies of Reflection, Identification, and Our Contact Song (see Chapter 4) by singing about what a person is doing and experiencing. The possibilities are as extensive as the therapist's inventiveness.

Speech stimulation is intrinsic to the use of song. A person may not understand the meaning of words that are sung, yet may experience them on some level of sensory or emotional awareness. Attempts to sing words and phrases that a person usually does not or cannot articulate are often successful. Once a flow of melodic line and rhythmic patterning occurs, producing preverbal sounds, isolated words, and groups of words that are received and acknowledged by another is an exhilarating and gratifying experience for the client and opens up a new dimension in communication. The musical characteristics of song—melodic line combined with words—directly influence a person's mode of expression and communication.

Furthermore, in stimulating communication through song by applying a particular technique, if an action—however outlandish—serves a therapeutic purpose, it is justified. For example, if a child with Down syndrome extends his or her oversized tongue and emits an "eee" sound, the therapist, by extending his or her tongue and singing in the same tonality, acknowledges the child and establishes trust—trust that is necessary to carry on the work. As this sound is matched tonally, it can be transformed into a first musical experience, a song.

Songs that have repetitive sections and words develop memory. Short-term memory, sometimes referred to as iconic memory, is considered the sensory representation of stimulus events (Detterman, 1974). The constant stimulation of recurring words and musical phrases thus enables the client to anticipate the repeated parts of the music motorically or cognitively or both. This is how Ronny, for example, entered the world of singing. It occurred through the repetition and slow, exaggerated enunciation of the word *home* at the end of the phrase, "Comin' for to carry me home" (lining-out singing) of the song, "Swing Low, Sweet Chariot" (Johnson, 1940). The therapist directed Ronny and the other members of the group to lift their arms as they sang the word *home*. After singing the word many times at many sessions, Ronny began to sing song phrases and gradually the entire song (on pitch).

Songs provide a base for a concrete understanding and interpretation of words. For example, the word *light* in the spiritual, "This Little Light of Mine" (Boxill, 1976, side 2, band 3), when considered as a part of the environment rather than in its original meaning of an inner light, can be an effective means for conveying the idea of what a light is and what it does, that is, it shines. Each time the word is sung, the client points to a light in the room, thus connecting the actual light with the word being sung. The act of lifting an arm toward the light that the client locates on the ceiling combines gross motor activity with singing the word, reinforcing the learning that is taking place. The ability to use words functionally emerged in this way for Jamie, who tests in the severe range of retardation. Jamie, who was able to articulate isolated words echolalically, had never before used speech with any sense of the meaning of his utterances. When he sang "light" and "shine" and was directed to point to the light, his face became animated and he showed signs of making an association between the words and the light that he pointed to when we sang together (using the lining-out singing technique):

> This little *light* of mine,
> I'm gonna let it *shine*.
> This little *light* of mine,
> I'm gonna let it *shine*.
> This little light of *mine*,
> I'm gonna let it *shine*.
> Let it *shine*,
> Let it *shine*,
> Let it *shine*.

With the next verse he stretched his arms rhythmically toward the light as the song led him around the room:

> All around the room,
> I'm gonna let it *shine* . . .
> (The same sequence of words as in the first verse was followed.)

The next verse heightened his awareness of the environment by leading him to various parts of the room as he waved his arms and sang:

> Everywhere I go,
> I'm gonna let it *shine* . . .
> (The same sequence of words as in the first verse was followed.)

Jamie began to transfer this experience by pointing to lights in other areas of the building. He would say "light," pointing to lights on the ceiling. As therapy progressed, many words were added that he assimilated and used functionally.

As noted previously, the range of the singing voice of the mentally retarded person is usually in the low register. The therapist, in order to be in synchrony with the client, must develop the ability to match the person's tones. This initial relatedness, made by means of reflecting/matching the person's voice vocally and tonally, establishes a bond—a "tuning-in" on a very basic organismic level. Once this connection is made, the tonal quality and range of the person's voice can improve through using the components of music that are "natural" expressions for change: melody, pitch, dynamics, and tempo.

Singing and making musical vocalizations, even on the most primitive level, serve to mobilize energy and are a means of focus that create feelings of wholeness, individually and as a group. Table 5–1 offers an example of a singing/chanting activity and a number of its therapeutic purposes.

Table 5–1 A Singing/Chanting Activity and Possible Therapeutic Purposes

Activity	Therapeutic Purposes
Therapist sings greeting song, "Hello, Everybody, Yes Indeed"*	Warm up for setting structure of session
Therapist sings greeting song to each client individually, shaking hands while singing	Awareness of self and self-identity
Clients look at each other or point to each other while song is sung for each individual	Awareness of others; peer interaction
Therapist encourages clients to sing their own names	Awareness of self; communication skills/speech
Therapist encourages client to sing names of others	Awareness of others; communication skills/speech; peer interaction
Clients clap hands to music	Involvement of entire group in active participation while singing about each client individually; gross motor skills
Therapist acknowledges each individual's pace, rhythm, and way of clapping	Self-direction; self-esteem
Therapist encourages others in group to clap the way the individual client is clapping (tempo, dynamic level, etc.)	Interrelatedness; imitative skills; gross motor skills

*For low-functioning multiply handicapped clients, the use of the same song to sing "goodbye" to everyone brings a satisfactory closure to sessions.

Instrument Playing

At all levels of awareness and functioning, instrument playing is an avenue for musical commitment that stimulates communication, cognitive development, and self-expression, both musically and nonmusically. The severely and profoundly retarded are able to use, in the main, rhythm/percussion instruments, although with the assistance of the therapist even the profoundly multiply handicapped person can be given the experience of strumming an Omnichord® (with the therapist pressing the chord buttons to provide musical structure). The person who functions in the mild and moderate ranges can use, in addition to rhythm/percussion instruments, instruments such as the Autoharp®, Casiotone®, Omnichord®, piano, and guitar with the support of the therapist, who seeks ways to make the client's playing of these instruments successful and musically expressive.

As a nonverbal means of communication, instruments, singly or in combination, can "speak" to each other with meanings of their own or with meanings conveyed by the person using them. Through instruments, high-functioning clients can engage in musical dialogues, conversations, arguments, and messages that have concrete meaning. At lower levels of the continuum, shaking tambourines together or at each other is a communication between two people that might never have been possible in any other form. At higher levels of the continuum, instrument playing offers opportunities for communication that can open up pathways to many forms of interaction, interrelatedness, and interpersonal skills. Playing rhythm instruments is particularly suitable for severely, profoundly, or multiply handicapped persons who, because they are restricted and often immobile, have very little opportunity to enjoy themselves. Instrument playing offers them participation in the external world through a form of expression that provides physical and emotional gratification. With musical support vocally and on the piano, guitar, or Autoharp®, the therapist creates sound stimuli that can motivate the person to grasp and shake a handbell or beat a drum or tap rhythm sticks or strum an Autoharp® with an adapted pick. For extremely handicapped people, playing instruments can be a source of joy and energy, something they do not experience often enough.

Overall, instrument playing provides a focus for energy and serves to:

- structure and give tangible form to musical behavior
- offer the opportunity to perform (make music) from simple manipulation to complex group instrument musical arrangements
- increase involvement and participation in musical activity
- stimulate and release emotions
- give an immediate sense of accomplishment and success

- increase individual and group relatedness to musical stimuli
- increase group cohesion and social skills
- increase attention span
- improve gross and fine motor coordination
- improve eye–hand and ear–hand coordination
- improve perceptual-motor skills
- improve auditory, visual, and tactile perception
- redirect inappropriate and maladaptive behavior
- offer an avenue for adaptive behavior

Instruments provide means of making music on many levels of relatedness, ranging from manipulation to produce simple sounds to using them expressively in simple to complex arrangements. The act of producing sound from an instrument is often an end in itself. Whether the instrument selected is a percussion, tonal/ melodic, or stringed instrument, each offers concrete, direct involvement in experiences requiring that energies be focused in the reality of the present. The person who beats a drum hears the sound and knows, on some level, that he or she did something to make it happen. This sensorimotor activity yields instantaneous kinesthetic and auditory feedback that activates awareness physically and emotionally. The immediacy of the results motivates further action. The reward is in the doing. Brought into play are psychomotor skills (voluntary action), kinesthetic experience (proprioception or deep muscle sense), coordination, and perceptual-motor skills.

Essential aspects of the therapeutic usefulness of instruments are that they can both influence affective states and serve as outlets for emotional expression. Another interesting aspect is that the production of different kinds of musical sounds emerges from the combination of physical and emotional expression. For example, when a person beats a drum with force in a rapid tempo, not only is there a heightening of energy, there is literally bodily motion activated by the emotions (as the word *emotion* signifies). Also, the potential for using an instrument to sublimate, express, or ventilate the gamut of feelings and emotions—sadness, joy, anger, apathy, anxiety, enthusiasm, frustration—lies to a degree in the nature of the instrument. Its range of sound, its timbre, its size, its shape, its method of sound production (strumming, striking, beating, fingering, blowing, shaking) determine in large measure how and why the instrument is selected. To illustrate, the therapist or client may select a drum to aid in the release of pent-up anger. If a drum is selected, the therapist must be on the alert for excessive beating that could escalate into an agitated, uncontrolled state and defeat the therapeutic purpose for which the instrument was selected. When this happens with any instrument, the client must be guided through the experience and have it brought to a satisfying closure.

If the use of an instrument is unrelated to the musical stimuli, the therapist works with the individual within the group on a one-to-one basis. In order to help the person acquire the ability to play an instrument in ways related to the musical stimuli, it is necessary to establish objectives that allow the client to attain that ability through a series of developmental steps. The therapist may use one instrument, such as a large timpani drum, for the entire group, with each person beating individually. Over a period of time, other instruments are added as the client becomes able to manipulate them in relation to the music. Eventually, a group of clients may develop the capacity to play instruments rhythmically and musically together.

The therapist chooses instruments for a variety of reasons: for working on specific objectives and goals; for working on specific developmental skills; for dealing with an immediate need of the client; for accommodating, ameliorating, or improving a particular physical condition; and, not least, for aesthetic and emotional gratification. Whenever possible or feasible, the therapist allows or encourages clients to make their own choices of preferred instruments, thus broadening their musical experience as well as fostering independent action.

In guiding the client's selection of an instrument, the therapist fosters the client's ability to make choices and be independent while acknowledging the person's interests. A person may select a particular instrument because of the comfort or satisfaction, physical and emotional, it provides. If the choice becomes perseverative, however, a change of instrument may counteract the autistic behavior pattern of the need for sameness.

Offering a variety of instruments that the person learns to manipulate and play appropriately broadens horizons musically as well as develops a healthy respect for the instruments themselves. As an intrinsic part of sessions, clients should be directed to handle instruments carefully and, when possible, select them as well as return them to their places. When this occurs, the instrument playing activity is organized; it has a beginning, a middle, and an end that clients learn to bring about in a self-regulating way.

For the multiply handicapped, clinically adapted instruments are not only recommended, they are necessary. As Clark and Chadwick point out (1980):

> Traditional instruments have long been included in music therapy, but for many clients their use has been frustrating or impossible. This experience, in turn, damages self-concept and hinders further efforts. For individuals with involuntary neurological impulses, missing limbs, and restricted motor abilities, adaptive equipment or assistance is necessary. (p. 7)

By adapting instruments and other equipment, the possibilities for instrumental activity are increased markedly and more independent participation is made possible.

To help clients with poor or no palmar prehension, mallets, shakers, bells, and oversized picks can be attached to the hand, arm, finger, wrist, leg, foot, or ankle with cloth or knitted bands with adjustable Velcro® fasteners. For those who have some degree of palmar prehension, mallets and instruments with narrow handles, such as maracas and rhythm sticks, can be built up by wrapping cotton batting or felt around the handles. All-purpose stands that have hooks and clamps for holding percussion instruments at various levels make it easier for clients in wheelchairs to reach these instruments. Additional aids are standing tone bars with a large striking surface and timpani drums that have drumheads 16 to 18 inches in diameter and adjustable legs for varying heights.

For clients who have the potential to grasp and hold, the therapist encourages the use of unadapted instruments, such as finger cymbals, jingle bell sprays, wrist bells, handbells, lightweight aluminum tambourines, resonator bells, rhythm sticks, and clappers. Because of their size and weight, these can be held more easily than other instruments, first with the assistance of the therapist and, as strength and skill improve, independently.

Table 5–2 provides an example of a group instrument activity and its possible therapeutic purposes.

Music-Movement

The concept of music-movement is more than movement to music. Music itself is time-ordered tonal sound moving in space. In translating sound into bodily movement and bodily movement into sound, the two modes of expression are inextricably interwoven. Music-movement encompasses rhythmic gross motor activity, basic locomotion, structured and free psychomotor movements, perceptual-motor activities, creative movement/dancing, social dancing, movement combined with rhythmic speech/singing/chanting, and movement combined with playing instruments. Such music activities proceed from simple to complex, depending on their therapeutic purposes and the levels of functioning and conditions of the clients—from the fully ambulatory to the wheelchair user, from the spontaneously independent to the completely dependent.

In persons who are developmentally disabled, motor/movement disabilities range over many gradations of gross motor, fine motor, and perceptual-motor deficits to a complete lack of ambulation. In the severely and profoundly retarded and multiply handicapped, the inability to stand, sit, hold the head erect, or move arms and legs with intention and in coordinated ways exists in varying degrees. Also, in varying degrees, there are sensorimotor deficits and imitative and voluntary movements have not been stimulated or developed because of retardation and/or psychosocial deprivation. These deficits, which seriously affect all domains of functioning and restrict the person's interaction with the environment, are dealt with directly through the sensorimotor stimulation of music-movement.

Table 5–2 A Group Instrument Activity and Possible Therapeutic
Purposes

Activity	*Therapeutic purposes*
Therapist selects specific instrument for each client or clients choose instruments preferred	Individual goals and objectives; self-direction; independence
Therapist leads clients in counting 1–2–3 on their fingers (verbalizing when possible); clients then use manual sign for *play*	Attending behavior; fine motor coordination; functional academics (ability to count); speech stimulation; group participation
Therapist plays steady beat of music on the piano, guitar, or Autoharp®	Auditory perception; cohesiveness of the group
Therapist continues steady beat, adjusting to predominant pace of the group	Perceptual-motor skills; relatedness to musical stimuli
Therapist provides musical support and structure using a specific song or clinical music improvisation (vocally and/or instrumentally) for the instrument playing	Integration, intrapersonally and interpersonally
Therapist improvises text of song or sings words to music identifying the instruments the clients are playing	Awareness and learning names of instruments
Therapist changes dynamics and tempo of music	Auditory perception; attending behavior; perceptual-motor skills; expressivity
Clients take turns playing the instruments alone, starting and stopping (use manual signs for *start, stop,* and *wait*)	Impulse control; self-esteem; creative expression
Clients carry on musical dialogues on the instruments	Intercommunication; expressivity
Clients play an entire composition with exact repetitions	Attention span; physical and emotional stability through structure and rhythmic flow of music
Clients play a musical arrangement as directed by the therapist	Participation as a team in music making

Child psychologists such as Piaget (1950) affirm that early sensorimotor experience is critical to the development of body awareness, self-awareness, and learning. Music educators such as Carl Orff (Orff & Keetman, 1956) emphasize sensorimotor development as being essential to readiness for cognitive tasks. The building of a healthy self-image and the potential for symbolic thought and oral language inhere in the assimilation of sensorimotor experiences. For the music therapist Gertrud Orff (1974), music and movement are an indivisible entity. Therefore, movement/motoric activity is basic to the Orff approach to music therapy with the handicapped person. "In our work, movement has various forms from mime and gesture . . . through locomotor movements . . . up to the composition of movement sequences" (p. 45). Experiencing music through body movement and body movement through music aids the promotion of attention, concentration, memory, perception of space and perception of the body, contact with others, social interaction, imagination, sensitivity, and creativity (Jaques-Dalcroze, 1976).

Increasingly, educators agree that movement and learning are inextricably connected. Movement educators such as Cratty (1964, 1969) tell us that by achieving competency in motor tasks a person's body-image and self-image improve and that improving physical skills in a concrete way may help increase the ability to function at higher cognitive levels. In recognizing that motivation and learning can be stimulated by pleasurable experiences derived from music, Cratty (1969) has investigated music therapy techniques and has applied them, using rhythmic sequences with music for adjustment of arousal level, improvement of attention, and for increasing the ability to sustain an activity—in general, improving the performing self through the use of music.

Montessori (1967) (whose first educational work was with retarded children at the Casa dei Bambini, which she founded in Rome in 1906) underscores the relation of movement to development: "When the child begins to move, his absorbent mind has already taken in the world. . . . It is through this experience of objects in his environment, in the guise of playing, that he does over again the impressions that he has already taken in" (p. 21).

When sensory mechanisms are not functioning adequately, a distorted body image results. Because body image is considered critical to the development of the total person, it is imperative to find methods to help people acquire a realistic body image. Much of the work with the developmentally disabled begins with stimulating awareness through the kinesthetic experience of the body and specifically developing awareness of body parts. For the person who does not initiate movement, or the person who is incapable of executing a psychomotor movement as basic as putting hands together in the act of clapping, or the person whose coordination is faulty, physically assisting the person to experience on a feeling or sensate level can lead to a knowledge of body parts and their functions.

The kinesthetic body has a mind of its own. In varying degrees, when stimulated, it knows what to do and how to do it without bringing the intellect into play. Since music stimulates the senses, the work involves making the body become an expressive instrument that remembers movements through deep muscle sense. In this process of receiving information through internal and external excitation of the senses, energy is generated, energy that needs direction and focus from moment to moment. The individual is encouraged and assisted in the treatment process to explore a full range of this kind of experiencing through music. Once the senses are awakened and stimulated, the person opens up to learning.

Awareness of body parts, which is basic to the development of body boundaries and body image, as well as awareness of the many ways the body can move, are best learned experientially. In the activity of rolling across the floor, the person begins to define such parts of the body as the chest, back, sides, shoulders, feet, hands, and head by experiencing them through kinesthetic and tactile receptors. Then comes experiencing how these parts move through space—walking forward, backward, sideways—and at different rates of speed, culminating in coordinated movements of higher levels of skill, such as hopping, jumping, galloping, skipping, and climbing, as control and awareness of the body increase.

Factors (adapted from Cratty, 1969) in the development of coordinated basic body movements, such as eye-hand, eye-ear, eye-foot, and ear-foot coordination, are:

- *Body image:* Body image is the total perception a person forms of his or her body, including its movement capabilities, shape, and size. It involves the relationship of the body to the surrounding space and awareness of direction.
- *Balance—static and dynamic (in space):* Balance involves the ability to maintain equilibrium relative to gravity and the kinesthetic awareness of body position. (Static balance is the ability to maintain postural adjustment while standing or kneeling. Dynamic balance is the ability to maintain equilibrium while engaging in various movements in space.)
- *Locomotion:* Locomotion is motor behavior that permits a person to move from one place to another and includes crawling, walking, running, skipping, etc.
- *Agility:* Agility is the ability to integrate body parts quickly and accurately.
- *Mobility/muscular flexibility:* Mobility/muscular flexibility is the ability to move a limb or limbs through a range of motion.
- *Strength:* Strength involves the ability to use muscle groups for gripping, moving, lifting, pushing, etc.
- *Laterality and directionality:* Laterality and directionality are the conscious awareness that one side of the body differs from the other, that one is called

left and the other *right*, and that people can move and locate themselves relative to these two sides.

We must guard against taking gross motor movements and basic locomotor skills for granted. A cursory glance at a group of mentally retarded people tells us otherwise as even those who appear well coordinated usually exhibit such dysfunctions as awkwardness of gait, excess motions, or rigidity of extremities.

The musical circle formation is especially effective for developing and enhancing basic movements through the rhythmic flow that can be transmitted from one person to another. Table 5–3 is an example of a music-movement activity using the circle formation and its possible therapeutic purposes.

Therapeutic Uses of the Components of Music

The components of music are rhythm, melody, harmony, pitch, tempo, dynamics, timbre, and, for the purpose of therapy, the text of song. The conscious, deliberate use of these components for therapeutic purposes is at once a simple yet exceedingly complex aspect of the use of our tool. Although no one component can be completely isolated (e.g., tempo and dynamics are intrinsic to any form of musical expression, and rhythm and tempo are inseparable in a melodic line), a specific component can be emphasized or made predominant in order to accomplish a particular objective. With its own unique attributes, properties, and qualities, each component can be used for the therapeutic purpose of reflecting and affecting emotional and/or physical states of an individual, as well as the prevailing mood of a group. In other words, playing music in a moderate tempo might reflect/match the behavior of an individual or group, whereas changing to a slow tempo might influence changes in behavior—musically and nonmusically. If the dynamics are changed, with the same tempo retained, responses may change. Then again, music—whether improvised or composed—may be used because it has a component that is inherently dominant. For example, the outstanding musical quality of the Brazilian folk song "Zinga Za" (Landeck, 1961) is its rhythm. The melody of the English folk song "Greensleeves" (Landeck, 1951) is its outstanding musical aspect. Obviously, there are no formulas. It can only be said that the more that music therapists understand, investigate, and learn about the nature of our tool, the more clinically skilled and creative they can become in using specific components for diverse therapeutic purposes and as agents of change.

The following discussion suggests ways that therapists can use each component based on its unique attributes and possible therapeutic effects. It is intended to stimulate further exploration of their use and influence on the individual or group. This area has not received the attention it warrants and is sometimes completely overlooked. The suggestions given are intended as catalysts for the therapists' own ideas and discoveries.

Table 5–3 A Music-Movement Activity and Possible Therapeutic
Purposes

Activity	*Therapeutic purposes*
Clients are directed to hold hands and, as circle is formed, therapist sings names of clients and what they are doing	Awareness of self; awareness of each other; group unity
Clients move around the room in various tempi as they act out the words of the song	Bodily expressivity; spatial balance; mobility and agility
Clients suggest actions and act out words of the song	Self-expression; comprehension
Clients are directed to choose partners and clap each other's hands; swing arms; raise arms up and down; stamp feet; turn around and face each other	Awareness of body parts; peer interaction
Clients reform circle and are directed by song to move to the right, left, forward (into the middle), backward to a full circle	Laterality and directionality
Clients move in space to various tempi and dynamic changes in music	Creativity; independent, self-initiated activity
After moving in space freely, clients come back to the circle and hold hands and the activity is brought to a close	Group cohesion; experience of structure engendered by structure of music

Note: The music selected should be a song with words designed to develop self-image and peer relatedness and should lend itself to acting out many different ways of moving (locomotor, creative and social dancing) in different tempi. Hoops, scarves, pictures, and other nonmusic materials can be used to facilitate imaginative movements, provide multisensory stimulation, and aid comprehension. Examples of music for this purpose appear in Chapters 6 and 7.

Uses of the components of music are illustrated and explored in the process-oriented descriptions of treatment contained in Chapter 6 and in the vignettes in other chapters.

Rhythm

The prime mover, the universal element that regulates and orders the macrocosm and the microcosm is rhythm. From the Greek *rhythmos,* meaning measured motion, it is a flow or movement characterized by a regularly recurring beat or accent that is interspersed with periods of relaxation. Rhythm may be broadly defined as everything pertaining to the duration (long-short) of musical sounds. It denotes the innumerable patterns formed, within the basic metric framework, by the various arrangements of smaller or larger note values.

Rhythm serves as energizer, unifier, stabilizer, and organizer of the individual and group. Because rhythm works on the organism on a primary level and is "absorbed" physically, its therapeutic use is basic to work with this client population. Auditory rhythmic cues can give immediate feedback that enables the person or group to adjust motor responses for maintaining perceptual-motor activity and coordinating gross and fine motor movements. Chanting and singing in rhythmic patterning of words stimulate verbalization and aid cognitive skills and learning in general. A strong rhythmic pulsation that is repeated over and over in the same tempo and on the same dynamic level can have a stabilizing effect both physically and emotionally.

To illustrate the latter, imagine that a group entering the music therapy room in a highly disorganized, agitated state is unable to settle down. Immediately, the therapist plays vigorously, repeating a rhythmic pattern in a visibly as well as auditorially spirited and exaggeratedly forceful manner, one that reflects the prevailing level of the group's energy. This is continued until the group is gradually brought into a state of equilibrium. In the process of gaining a sense of internal and external order, the group may then be directed to clap their hands to enable them to focus energy through active participation. This nonverbal communication through music, equally effective with verbal and nonverbal clients, is nonthreatening and has properties that can galvanize the group, whereas verbal commands in such situations may be threatening or ineffectual.

Melody

Melody is the horizontal arrangement of musical tones related to one another and to the whole in such a way as to express a coherent musical idea or entity. Such terms as *melodic line, theme,* and *tune* are interchangeable with *melody.* In song, the rising and falling of tones reflect the quality of the text, or the text may reflect the quality of the melodic line.

Melodic line and melodic rhythm patterns can set or reflect moods, feelings, and emotions. Because of the natural union of melody with speech, singing melodies and melodic phrases directly affects phonation, prosody, cadence, intonation, inflection, and the quality of voice. Also, the flow of a melody and changes in pitch often influence the flow of bodily movements and help a person move in a coordinated manner. This is a particularly important aspect of the use of melody with the spastic cerebral palsied person and numerous mentally retarded people whose bodies are tensely rigid and whose movements are uncoordinated.

Sandy is a case in point: In a constant state of extreme rigidity from head to toe, he would visibly release his tense stance in response to the melodious "Greensleeves" played with a lilting arpeggio bassline. As he began to move his head and arms to the music, he vocalized, at first in harshly emitted sounds quite unrelated to the melody. With many repetitions (in the same session as well as ongoing sessions), Sandy's vocalizations became more related to the quality and tonality of the melody. A relaxed smile, rarely seen on his face, gave evidence of the sense of well-being this experience gave him.

Harmony

Basic to much of Western music, harmony is the simultaneous sounding of related tones known as chords. This element provides texture to music through consonance and dissonance, through the relationship of one chord to another, through the relationship between the chords and the melody, and through the number of tones in the chord.

In exploring the impact of harmony, many different meanings and applications emerge. This component is used for a variety of musical textures and effects. Harmonic effects can so intensify singing and instrument playing as to make them highly pleasurable musical experiences, thus increasing expressivity and the motivation to learn.

Chordal progressions as accompaniments/basslines in the various modes— major, minor, pentatonic—and musical styles or idioms change the quality of the music and, consequently, the effect it might have on a person, emotionally and physically. An arpeggio bassline in a slow tempo may elicit motoric responses that are harmonious (coordinated), whereas a sharp, staccato chordal bassline could be overstimulating and cause a reaction such as stereotypic arm flapping or hyperventilation. The therapist must, therefore, be judicious in choices and alert to the effects a component is having.

In using chordal progressions independent of melody, we find as an illustration that chords in the pentatonic mode are particularly useful for supporting a client's random vocalizations or music making on a rhythm instrument. With the client playing selected resonator bells or bars on a metallophone (D♭ , E♭ , G♭ , A♭ , B♭), there cannot be any "wrong" notes. The therapist and client are in a completely harmonious blend of chordal tones that convey the therapist's acceptance of the client and ensure a successful musical experience for him or her.

Another use of harmony is for attention and arousal. If a person's attention has receded or there is a retreat into an autistic state, dissonant harmony—perhaps a sudden dissonant chord in contrast to consonant harmony being played—can bring the person into the vivid present.

Pitch

Pitch is the highness or lowness of sound. It is the property of sound, especially a musical tone, that is determined by the frequency of the sound waves producing it, that is, a definite number of vibrations per second.

Gross contrasts in pitch, from very high to very low and from very low to very high, are used to develop auditory discrimination, to capture attention (arousal), and, when appropriate, to work on directionality (up and down). In the latter instance, motoric activity stimulated by extremes in pitch would involve raising arms and body upward in response to high tones and bending to the floor in response to low tones. Even if the concept of high and low is not comprehended, the physiologic effect of high and low tones is experienced through psychomotor activity that increases auditory perception. (The therapist may wish to raise arms and body up when singing high notes or playing the high register on the keyboard, and lower arms and body when singing low notes or playing in the low register, to reinforce upness and downness.)

Pitch is used therapeutically to improve speech. This is an especially important area of treatment for mentally retarded, cerebral palsied, and autistic clients who are verbal or capable of using isolated words. Very often the quality of the voice may be nasal or harsh, or the voice may be a monotone, lacking intonation, inflection, and cadence (prosody). One way of working on these conditions is through changes in pitch, beginning by intoning intervals of ascending and descending thirds and fifths on words of two or more syllables (such as *hello, goodbye,* or the person's name). The rising and falling pitch of melodic lines, discussed in the section on melody, is an expansion of the therapeutic use of pitch that furthers the development of a pleasing quality of voice and fluidity of speech.

Tempo

Tempo is the rate of speed of music. Gradations in tempo may range from *prestissimo* (as fast as possible) to *adagio* (very slow). Each person has an inner tempo. The therapist observes and becomes attuned to the person's pace upon their initial meeting. At times the inner tempo is immediately obvious, particularly if the person is at one extreme of the spectrum or the other, that is, hypoactive or hyperactive. In working either to increase a person's energy level or decrease it (because both extremes interfere with functioning and development), the therapist uses tempo as one means of bringing about change in the form of eventual relatedness between the musical stimuli and the person's output of energy. Once a quickening of pace is experienced, the hypoactive person may be motivated and activated into self-initiated behavior. Conversely, once a slowing down is experienced, the hyperactive person may be able to mobilize and control energy that has been randomly diffused.

In using tempo for auditory perception and perceptual-motor activity, gross contrasts from very slow to very fast are used at first. Gradually there may be progress to more subtle changes, particularly with moderately and high-functioning persons. One example of this is the dramatization of a train activity in which the text of song indicates the tempo of the music, starting in the station slowly and getting faster (*accelerando*), then slower and slower (*ritardando*) until the train stops. Another example is speech articulation, the pace of which is exaggeratedly slow and, over a period of sessions, is speeded up to stimulate a more natural flow. Also, for developing mobility and agility, tempo can be stepped up relative to the person's condition and changes in capabilities. This flexibility in the use of tempo is possible only by using live music.

Dynamics

Dynamics denote the degree of variation and contrast in volume—loudness or softness and the many gradations between the extremes of *fortissimo* (very loud) and *pianissimo* (very soft). Changes in dynamic levels (volume) have psychologic and physiologic effects on a person's ability to perceive auditorially, perform perceptual-motor tasks that require sound discrimination, and tolerate loud sounds, as well as on emotional states and moods. As with gross changes in tempo, gross changes in dynamics from very loud to very soft and from very soft to very loud are among the first steps in laying the foundation for awakening awareness through auditory perception. In dealing with the multiple handicaps of this population, the therapist must understand that certain conditions require special attention. For example, the visually impaired or blind person or the autistic child (who is sometimes characterized as having "psychic blindness") may recoil from loud musical stimuli because of aural superacuity or sensitivity. Then, again, the therapist, knowing that a whisper often gains more attention than a strident tone of voice, will sing a song very softly to increase attending behavior.

Much of what is indicated in the use of tempo applies to the uses of dynamics, especially with regard to influences on motoric responses, the quality of voice (intonation, inflection, prosody), and affective responses, states, and adjustments. A gradual increase in volume (*crescendo*) may be used for arousal or raising the receptivity to sound and the spoken word. The increase and decrease (*decrescendo*) of volume used alternately are musical devices designed to expand and heighten awareness through changes in sound levels.

Timbre

Timbre, or tone color, is defined as that characteristic quality of sound that distinguishes one musical instrument, including the human voice, from another. It is basic to the sentient and vibratory experience of both the producer of sound and the one in whom it resonates. Timbre has direct application in developing auditory perception and auditory discrimination. Being able to distinguish between two simple rhythm instruments such as a bell and a drum is a beginning step in awakening awareness of the environment. Recognition and identification of rhythm and other musical instruments (by naming them, pointing to them, looking at them, matching them with a flash card picture) is designed to develop higher and higher levels of auditory perception. These levels can transfer to the ability to distinguish between and recognize environmental sounds (such as a telephone bell, automobile horn, etc.) and the voices of various people—to become more sensitive and responsive to the human and nonhuman environment.

Physiological and psychological effects of the timbre of instruments need exploration. Of great importance to the therapist is the discovery that a specific kind of instrument—stringed, percussion, wind—has appeal for a person and, as a consequence, can be the means of arousing attention. The experience with Carlo is particularly illustrative of this: Working on the goal of developing eye contact with him, the therapist explored various ways to establish this contact. The timbre of a flute was the first musical sound to which he responded. Until he was exposed to the penetrating vibratory sounds of that instrument, he had remained oblivious (observably) to his surroundings and the people in the immediate environment. When the therapist bent toward him and looked directly at him while playing, he looked up and focused his eyes, first on the source of sound, then on the therapist's face, and then directly into the therapist's eyes. This eye contact signaled the first overt contact between client and therapist.

The Text of Song

The text of song is included as a component of music because it is an inextricable and integral part of therapy that is strongly song oriented. As a referent, words of song are a potent catalyst for the release of emotions, the recall of experiences and feelings, and a means of stimulating comprehension, speech, and imagination. Words may be used as written in a given song or chant, or they may be improvised by the therapist for specific therapeutic purposes in response to the momentary needs of the client. Words may also be spontaneously offered by the client or encouraged by the therapist.

Words of song—whether used as written, adapted, or improvised—are indispensable to the three main strategies of music therapy based in the context of *a continuum of awareness,* namely, Reflection, Identification, and Our Contact Song. When combined with tonal sound, words can be a direct path to awareness, whether they are comprehended cognitively or experienced on a purely sensory level. The way the therapist projects words musically is a key to the effect they have on the lowest- to the highest-functioning client. The varied usages of text of song have special significance, application, and efficacy for this client population.

CONCLUSION

It is not enough to know *about* music, to know *about* its power. We must be able to project and communicate this power in the service of therapeutic purposes. Whatever the musical idiom or style—classical, folk, ethnic, pop, jazz, rock—the music therapy session must be rich with structured musical sound. We must be able to use our therapeutic tool and ourselves with musical sensitivity, sensibility, and expressivity that meet and reflect the needs of the person in treatment. This means that the therapist projects musically not only through vocal and instrumental modes of expression but also through bodily movement. The therapist who is fully involved must necessarily move freely with and among the clients, actively engaged in the coexperience.

Going a step further, it is not enough to know that we must be able to project and communicate the power of music. We must be able to improvise music for clinical purposes and acquire a large repertoire of carefully selected music materials. Composed as well as clinically improvised music can be used spontaneously, or it can be used as the basis of a therapeutic music activity that may be repeated many times over with or without changes and adjustments. Whatever the category of music and whatever the musical instrument, therapists must be able to express themselves with freedom and assurance. The printed page and the musical instrument must never be barriers between therapist and client.

Ultimately, it is not enough to say that treatment through music therapy differs in a basic way from other therapies. What is essential to convey is the deep-rooted reason for this difference. The health-giving nature of the modality itself gives overall direction to treatment. This direction, as leading music therapists affirm, is wellness—an optimal state of wholeness of the physical, emotional, and mental self.* In a word, music therapy concentrates on the wellness, not the illness, of a person. It is the healthy parts of us that constantly stretch up and push forth, seeking expression. Whether aware of it or not, people at all levels strive to feel better, to know, to learn, to experience a sense of satisfaction, to be in harmony and accord within themselves and with others. Just as we nourish the seedling that has its full potential imbedded in it, so, too, must we nurture whatever is "growable" in us.

REFERENCES

Ashton-Warner, S. *Teacher*. New York: Bantam Books, 1964.

Boxill, E.H. "The people in the room today." *Music adapted, composed, and improvised for music therapy with the developmentally handicapped* (side 1, band 1). New York: Folkways Records, 1976. (Record, FX 6180, booklet included)

Boxill, E.H. "This little light of mine." *Music adapted, composed, and improvised for music therapy with the developmentally handicapped* (side 2, band 3). New York: Folkways Records, 1976. (Record, FX 6180, booklet included)

Bugental, J.F.T. *Psychotherapy and process: The fundamentals of an existential-humanistic approach*. Reading, Mass.: Addison-Wesley Publishing Company, 1978.

---

*As delineated at the International Symposium on Music Therapy at New York University, New York City, June 1982.

Clark, C., & Chadwick, D. *Clinically adapted instruments for the multiply handicapped: A source-book*. St. Louis: Magnamusic-Baton, 1980.

Cratty, B.J. *Movement behavior and motor learning*. Philadelphia: Lea & Febiger, 1964.

Cratty, B.J. *Motor activity and the education of retardates*. Philadelphia: Lea & Febiger, 1969.

Detterman, D.K. Memory in the mentally retarded. In R. Ellis (Ed.), *Handbook of mental deficiency: Psychological theory and research* (2nd ed.). Hillsdale, N.J.: Lawrence Erlbaum Associates, 1974.

Dubos, R. *Man adapting*. New Haven: Yale University Press, 1980.

Erikson, E.H. *Childhood and society* (2nd ed.). New York: Norton, 1963.

Jaques-Dalcroze, É. [*Rhythm, music, and education.*] (H.F. Rubenstein, trans.). New York: Arno Press, 1976.

Johnson, J.W. (Ed.). *The book of American Negro spirituals*. New York: Viking, 1940.

Landeck, B. (Compiler). *More songs to grow on*. New York: Edward B. Marke Music Corporation, 1954.

Landeck, B. (Compiler). *Echoes of Africa in folk songs of the Americas*. New York: David McKay Company, 1961.

Madsen, C., Madsen, C., & Cotter, V. A behavioral approach to music therapy. *Journal of Music Therapy*, 1968, *5*(3), 69–72.

Maslow, A.H. *The farther reaches of human nature*. New York: Penguin Books, 1976.

Menuhin, Y. *Theme and variations*. New York: Stein and Day, 1972.

Montessori, M. *The absorbent mind* (3rd ed.). New York: Dell, 1967.

Moss, J. "The people in your neighborhood." In J. Raposo & J. Moss, *The sesame street song book*. New York: Simon & Schuster, 1971.

Orff, C., & Keetman, G. *Music for children: Orff-Schulwerk* (Eng. adaptation by D. Hall & A. Walker). New York: Schott Music Corp., 1956.

Orff, G. *The Orff music therapy: Active furthering of the development of the child* (M. Murray, trans.). London: Schott & Co. Ltd., 1974.

Pearce, J.C. *The crack in the cosmic egg*. New York: Pocket Books, 1971.

Piaget, J. *The psychology of intelligence*. New York: Harcourt Brace, 1950.

Raposo, J., & Moss, J. "I've got two." In J. Raposo & J. Moss, *The sesame street song book*. New York: Simon & Schuster, 1971.

Rogers, C.R. *On becoming a person*. Boston: Houghton Mifflin, 1961.

Rogers, C.R. Characteristics of a helping relationship. *Canada's Mental Health*, 1962, *27*, 1–18.

Yalom, I.D. *The theory and practice of group psychotherapy*. New York: Basic Books, 1970.

Zinker, J. *Creative process in gestalt therapy*. New York: Vintage Books, 1978.

Chapter 6

Clinical Practice: Process-Oriented Descriptions of Treatment

Special person, sing with me,
Special person, sing with me,
Sing with a sound that is clear and bright,
Sing with me . . .

Special person, beat your drum,
Special person, beat your drum,
Beat a rhythm that for you is right,
Beat your drum . . .

Special person, move with me,
Special person, move with me,
Move to the music with joy and light,
Move with me . . .

INTRODUCTION

Divergent problems, behavioral disorders, and conditions commonly presented by developmentally disabled persons are illustrated in the process-oriented descriptions of treatment comprising this chapter. The client conditions dealt with are primarily subcategories of mental retardation of various etiologies. These accounts demonstrate the positive changes that occur in functioning and behavior through the development of awareness of self, others, and the environment. Some accounts concentrate on the process during one session; others cover a span of time. They are divided into three categories: (a) individuals within the group setting; (b) group therapy; and (c) one-to-one therapy. Each description is designed to provide different aspects and dimensions of the music therapy process as well as varied applications of music therapy strategies and techniques. The

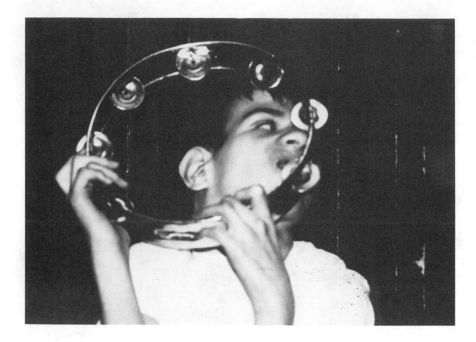

accounts demonstrate (a) evolvement of therapeutic music activities—at times from a preplanned idea or a specific design, at others from here-and-now situations; (b) reasons for the selection of music and uses of the components to attain long-term goals and short-term objectives; and (c) stages of therapy involved in establishing and maintaining a therapeutic relationship. As the process deepens and as clients gain control over their behaviors and their immediate environment, their sense of self is strengthened and their sense of living expanded.

Occasional verbatim excerpts from tape recordings of sessions, which accentuate the impact of the treatment on the client and give the flavor of the experience, are included in these accounts. Each description is preceded by a guide to the salient features of treatment:

- long-term goals
- modes of therapeutic music activity used
- components of music used
- rhythm and musical instruments used
- music materials used
- nonmusic materials used
- some strategies and techniques used

DESCRIPTIONS OF THERAPY

Individuals within the Group Setting

Emanuel D.: *18½ years; severe to profound range of mental retardation; etiologic factor: microcephaly (chronic nonprogressive encephalopathy of unknown etiology).*

Long-Term Goals: to awaken awareness of self, to develop attending behavior, to reduce self-abusive and abusive behavior, and to develop communication skills.
Modes of Therapeutic Music Activity Used: singing and instrument playing.
Components of Music Used: rhythm, tempo, melody, pitch, and timbre.
Rhythm and Musical Instruments Used: conga drum, maracas, temple blocks, clavés, and piano (therapist and client).
Music Materials Used: clinical music improvisation, "Emanuel" (Our Contact Song), and "The Merry Old Land of Oz."
Nonmusic Materials Used: hoop and mirror.
Some Strategies and Techniques Used: Reflection, Identification, Our Contact Song, physical and gestural prompts, pacing and tempo adjustments of activities and musical stimuli, exaggerated articulation of words of song, modeling of body movements, call-and-response singing, sequential movements with syllables/words, and action words with appropriate movements.

Emanuel is the youngest of six children. His birth weight was seven pounds, five ounces, and he was assumed to be normal at birth. Developmental milestones were delayed, however. He rolled over at 9 months, held his head erect at 1 year, sat unsupported at 2½ years. At 4½ years he began to walk with a loose, awkward gait. His hearing was reported within normal limits, and speech apparatus was intact, yet no speech developed. The Vineland Social Maturity Scale administered at the age of 5 yielded an MA of 18 months. According to a neurological evaluation, severe to profound psychomotor retardation resulted in failure to thrive.

Persons who are mentally retarded have, on the whole, little control over their lives and environment. Having a say in their lives is a deep-seated need that exists in all human beings. If they have not had opportunities to express their needs in positive ways, their behaviors will become destructive to themselves and others.

At the time treatment began, Emanuel exhibited abusive behavior that took the form of scratching others and self-abusive behavior in the form of trichotillomania (pulling out hair). Aggressive and assaultive behaviors occurred when there was such a buildup of frustration from not being able to communicate fully that he exploded. Assaultive behaviors were directed at adults whom he would punch. On occasion, he threw chairs and, in the music therapy room, knocked over his favorite conga drum. Clearly, his greatest need was to have all possible lines of communication and expression open to him. The interdisciplinary treatment team agreed upon a long-term goal of developing gestural and preverbal communicative skills. He was to be in a group of five clients from his regular classroom for two half-hour sessions a week.

The first contact with Emanuel was through an improvised song, "Emanuel" (see Figure 6–1):

> Emanuel, Emanuel, I'm here with you,
> Emanuel, Emanuel, I'm here with you.
>
> Emanuel, Emanuel, do you see me?
> Emanuel, Emanuel, I'm looking at you.
>
> Emanuel, Emanuel, do you hear me?
> Emanuel, Emanuel, I'm singing to you.

The therapist explored ways to awaken his awareness and develop attending behavior. Hoops and a mirror were offered to no avail. *Seemingly* unaware of his environment, he would nevertheless extend his arm toward these objects, fending them off brusquely.

It was in the third month of sessions, while playing and singing "Emanuel," Our Contact Song, that the large blue conga drum caught his attention (the therapist had placed it near his chair and had used it to accent the rhythmic pulse of the song). Emanuel reached over and slapped the drum with his right hand. The therapist reflected this as she continued to sing and play a chordal accompaniment with her left hand. He swayed back and forth, his face lighting up with a spark of awareness. His chest expanded in what seemed an expression of satisfaction in his newfound accomplishment. The therapist identified what Emanuel had done, pointing out to the group that Emanuel had beat the drum. A rhythm instrument activity was built around the song that had been the catalyst for Emanuel's first self-initiated participation.

At the following sessions, when Emanuel entered the music therapy room, he claimed ownership of the large blue conga drum. Silently he would place himself on a chair next to the piano, the conga drum safely between his legs. Then he would wait.

Participation in group rhythm instrument playing began to have a special appeal for him. He began to relate to vigorous rhythmic music, perceiving the pulse of the music by beating the conga drum with alternating hands in a steady, firm beat. Using these movements as a path to vocal and gestural expression, work began on stimulating conscious vocal expression through bodily movement with the playing of *his* blue conga drum.

The therapist searched for music materials that would meet his needs as well as the group's. She observed that as she sang "The Merry Old Land of Oz," (Harburg & Arlen, 1966) Emanuel would look directly at her lips, moving his lips

Figure 6–1 Emanuel

Note: Improvise words, adjusting rhythmic patterns to here-and-now person, situations, and therapeutic purposes. For example:

Emanuel, Emanuel, do you see me?
Emanuel, Emanuel, I'm looking at you.

Emanuel, Emanuel, do you hear me?
Emanuel, Emanuel, I'm singing to you.

Emanuel, Emanuel, we're here together,
Emanuel, Emanuel, Emanuel and Edi.

Source: © Adapted from a clinical improvisation by Michael Stocker (music therapy intern, 1980).

in what seemed to be an attempt to imitate the therapist as she enunciated the words and sang in an exaggerated manner. He lifted his arms and, catching the rhythmic pattern of the words ''Ha-ha-haaaa, ho-ho-hoooo,'' his hands came down on the drumhead. At the same time he moved his lips. There was no sound from his throat. He was silent except for the beating of the drum.

Three sessions later, Emanuel settled in with his drum. This time, however, when he heard the now familiar song, he watched the therapist's lips intently, stretched his neck upward, and with an all-out effort, emitted an unmistakable "haaaa." He appeared triumphant. This was Emanuel's first intelligible consciously produced sound.

As he repeated the syllable and then followed it with an imitation of the therapist's "hoooo," he broke into a laugh and moved his body excitedly with pleasure. It seemed that he was making a connection between these sounds ("ha" and "ho") and the sounds of laughter. The emotional gratification from the intentional production of sounds had a strong impact on him. In the first sessions he had responded to musical stimuli in a robotlike, stereotypic fashion, for the most part beating the drum in the same tempo and dynamic level, but now he began to be more aware of changes and variations as his ability to be more spontaneous emerged.

In the months that followed, using the song "The Merry Old Land of Oz" to build upon, further communication skills were explored through an adaptation of Orff-Schulwerk (a method of experiencing music by incorporating movement with vocalizations or speech). Sequential movements were used to expand his repertoire of movements and to help release him from an autisticlike need for sameness. (Perseverative behavior took such forms as insisting on sitting in the same seat, playing the same instrument, and wearing the same kind of T-shirt.)

The other members of the group varied in speech and verbalization skills. Some sang isolated words of songs, others were able to sing word phrases. All participated in varying degrees of motoric skill in the sequence of movements that was designed to interweave motoric with vocal expression. The therapist demonstrated the following sequence of movements while singing:

Ha-ha-haaa (clapping hands to the left),
Ho-ho-hooo (clapping hands to the right),
And a couple of tra-la-laaaas (slapping knees with alternate hands),
That's how we laugh the day a-waaaay (stamping alternate feet),
In the merry old land of Ozzzz (rolling arms in front of chest).

Gradually, Emanuel was able to imitate all the movements while emitting the syllables *ha, ho,* and *la* as they were sung by the therapist. He would sustain the activity for the duration of the song, repeating the syllables with enthusiasm and an increasing willingness to enter into the group process.

The therapist offered him a variety of rhythm instruments—clavés, temple blocks, maracas—which he accepted, sometimes hesitantly, sometimes grudgingly. It was obvious that he still preferred the conga drum. Gradually, the therapist asked him to indicate, by pointing, his choice of one of two instruments offered.

In action songs in which the therapist played extremes of high and low tones on the keyboard, he approximated the sound of the word *up* while lifting his arms in the air and the sound of the word *down* while bending down to the floor. Moving in space, he had sensory experiences of a combined kinesthetic and vocal nature that facilitated word retrieval (e.g., retrieval of the words *walk, run, jump*).

Constant acknowledgment of his efforts, time to assimilate, and repetition were essential in the ongoing process of encouraging and nurturing his ability and motivation to use sounds and gestures. As more and more functional words were worked on, Emanuel began to use sounds and gestures to make his needs and wants known. Although Emanuel will not develop speech for communicative purposes, the emotional release that came from this means of gestural and vocal communication had a positive effect on his behavior. Finding that his needs and wants were understood by others, he was less subject to extreme frustration. Accepting a variety of rhythm instruments and participating increasingly in group music-movement activities produced a reduction in stereotypic and assaultive behaviors.

Reports from his teacher and the supervisor of his living quarters were very encouraging. His attempts to make himself understood through gestures, at times accompanied by vocalizations and functional words, were becoming more frequent and more successful.

Irma N.: *20 years; severe mental retardation; etiologic factor: tuberous sclerosis (face and trunk).*

Long-Term Goals: to increase attending behavior and to reduce resistive/ oppositional behavior.

Modes of Therapeutic Music Activity Used: singing/chanting, instrument playing, and music-movement.

Components of Music Used: melody, harmony, tempo, dynamics, pitch, and text of song.

Rhythm and Musical Instruments Used: tambourine, handbell, and hand cymbals.

Music Materials Used: clinical music improvisation and "Go to Sleep, My Dear."

Nonmusic Materials Used: puppets and scarves.

Some Strategies and Techniques Used: Reflection, Identification, hand-overhand assistance, and pacing and tempo adjustments.

At the onset of therapy, Irma's behavior was described as hostile and frequently unmanageable. She tore off her clothes in bursts of agitation, lying on the floor flailing her arms and legs uncontrollably and banging her head against the wall.

During the assessment process, Irma revealed extreme swings of mood for no observable reason. She changed from having a flat, blunted facial expression to marked arousal. During this time she would hyperventilate.

In understanding the impact of music, the therapist must be aware that music can arouse negative as well as positive feelings. Some reasons for this are:

- Music or words of a song may be associated with an unpleasant or painful experience.
- The quality of the music may be momentarily unsuitable.
- The person may become overstimulated, unable to tolerate good as well as unpleasant feelings generated by the music.
- The person may be negativistic generally or because of a temporary mood.
- There may be an inability to tolerate sound above a certain pitch or volume.
- The person may not be able to accept music that is unfamiliar.
- There may be rejection of certain idioms or styles of music.

In the case of Irma, her pattern of hostile behavior had become so ingrained that she seemed overwhelmed by feelings that welled up in her when affected by music. However, negativistic behaviors, which had been habitual, lost their strength when she was eventually able to respond with "good" feelings to music that appealed to her.

For the first month of therapy, Irma was seen individually for one-half hour a week and in groups with her class for one-half hour a week. At her first individual session, she rejected any contact with the therapist, lashing out, scratching, and kicking vehemently. At moments, aware of the music the therapist played and sang, she would slump down in her chair, cover her ears with both hands, and close her eyes. At each successive session, though withdrawn or openly resistive, she directed occasional surreptitious glances toward the therapist. At those moments, she would begin to hyperventilate, turn her back to the therapist, and start to tear off her clothes. She would calm down as the therapist chanted words such as:

> Irma doesn't want to sing or play,
> And that's okay.
> Irma doesn't want to sing or play,
> Maybe she will on another day,
> On another day.
> Not today, not today.

Irma understood this acceptance on some level, either from the tone of voice or manner of the therapist, or the repetitious rhythmic chant that was designed to have a stabilizing effect, or perhaps all of them combined. She would begin to sway back and forth in time to the chant. Cautiously, the therapist would approach her, touch her hands, hold them ever so gently, and sway back and forth, from side to side with her. In a very subtle upward movement they would stand, swinging arms, swaying back and forth, as the therapist identified what Irma was doing, singing words such as:

> Irma is swinging her arms,
> Back and forth, back and forth,
> Irma is swinging her arms,
> Back and forth.
> We are swinging our arms,
> Back and forth together,
> We are swinging our arms,
> Back and forth together.

She would passively *allow* this to happen, yet this was an advance from the resistive behavior she originally exhibited.

It was not until many sessions later that she became actively involved. At a group session, her agitated behavior began to escalate into a full-blown tantrum. While a therapy aide sat with her, the therapist played a lullaby with a flowing melody line and a hypnotic rhythmic pattern in an attempt to relax her. The therapy aide was instructed to take Irma's hands (gently) and sway back and forth with her, humming the song along with the therapist. The song (originally an improvisation) was "Go to Sleep, My Dear" (Boxill, 1976, side 2, band 1). (See Figure 6–2.) As the therapist watched attentively, playing flowing arpeggios in a steady, slow, and hypnotic accompaniment to the melody, she became aware of a sound emanating from Irma—a throaty dronelike hum. *This was Irma's very first sound in response to music.* Immediately, the therapist reflected the throaty hum in the same register. From a fixed averted stare, Irma looked toward the therapist; her bodily movements eased up perceptibly. A "chord" had been struck in her. The words "go to sleep, my dear" were changed to:

> Irma, Irma,
> Sing with me, my dear,
> Sing with me, Irma,
> Sing with me, my dear.
> Mmmmmmm, mmmmmmmm,
> Mmmmmmmm, mmmmmmmm,
> Mmmmmmmm, mmmmmmmm,
> Sing with me, my dear.

The group was brought into the music-movement activity with the therapist and assistants (a music therapy intern and a therapy aide) engaging the members in a humming and swaying activity. The entire room took on a peaceful atmosphere.

Two months later, Irma entered the group for two sessions a week (individual sessions were suspended).

At a case conference the therapist reported that Irma had become much less resistive, allowing the therapist to use hand-over-hand assistance. She had begun to accept and appropriately manipulate rhythm instruments such as handbells, a tambourine, and hand cymbals and sustained attention for longer periods of time.

Figure 6–2 Go to Sleep, My Dear

Words and Music by
EDITH HILLMAN BOXILL

*If sung for a group, substitute word "everyone."

Source: © Edith Hillman Boxill, 1975.

She increased her eye contact, hummed to music, and occasionally sang isolated words, particularly to a favorite song such as "Day by Day" (Boxill, 1976, side 1, band 2). She still refused to leave her chair when the group engaged in a circle song game. However, she would participate at times when a circle was formed around her. Scratching had diminished, as had her tantrums. Hyperventilation occurred less frequently and with less intensity. She now showed evidence of being able to tolerate pleasurable feelings in response to music. As she became more aware of herself and others, her motivation to participate spontaneously became evident.

Other members of the interdisciplinary treatment team concurred that Irma was attending on a more sustained basis. As a consequence, she was making considerable strides in the area of prevocational tasks, such as matching colors and shapes and identifying objects in the immediate environment, and was performing fine motor tasks such as stuffing envelopes.

The next stage in the music therapy process was to increase her ability to participate in music-movement to reduce further her resistive behavior. Another goal was added to her treatment plan—namely, to increase motoric skills and ability.

Perry G.: *29 years; moderate mental retardation; etiologic factor: gross postnatal brain disease.*

Long-Term Goals: to improve coordination and articulation.

Modes of Therapeutic Music Activity Used: singing/chanting and instrument playing.

Components of Music Used: rhythm, melody, tempo, dynamics, pitch, and text of song.

Rhythm and Musical Instruments Used: timpani drum (with adapted mallet).

Music Materials Used: clinical music improvisation, "Guantanamera," and "Kum Ba Ya."

Nonmusic Materials Used: plastic hoop.

Some Strategies and Techniques Used: Reflection, Our Contact Song; lining-out singing; call-and-response singing; pacing and tempo adjustments; and exaggerated articulation of words of song.

Perry, a wheelchair user, is hemiplegic, with limited use of his left arm and hand. His speech is dysarthric. Very much aware of his physical condition, Perry's lack of coordination caused him anguish and made him hold back. He had been unsuccessful in so many areas of functioning that he had retreated into a protective shell of nonactivity. The music therapy assessment process, which Perry reluctantly assented to, revealed the discrepancy between his auditory perception and his ability to execute physical responses. It was evident that if he gave himself the chance he could benefit from a music therapy experience. The therapist could provide the opportunity; he would have to "prove" it to himself.

In reflecting and matching a client's sounds and movements, the therapist brings about synchrony between two people. To borrow an acoustical term, it might be said that "sympathetic resonance" is the phenomenon that takes place. Just as one violin whose strings are in tune with those of another violin will vibrate sympathetically, so the therapist who is in tune with a client could be considered an analog for this musical phenomenon. What happened with Perry bears this out.

At the start of his therapy sessions, he resisted participation, negatively shaking his head when he was approached. A throaty "noooo" and a wave of his left hand accompanied the shake of his head. His eyes closed, punctuating his removal. Though individual sessions were recommended, he refused to be brought to the music therapy room. Group sessions were then attempted to enable Perry to be more comfortable participating and interacting with peers from the residential section of the facility. This proved to be a wise move. At least he was willing to attend the sessions.

At the first and second sessions he sat and observed. The therapist, accepting his resistance, was pleased to have him there. No overtures were made to engage him in the group activity. A timpani drum with a mallet lying on the drumhead was placed in front of him, giving him the choice to play it or not.

At the third session he was drawn into the group's music making by the nonthreatening energy that was generated. Subtly directing attention to him through words of songs and nonverbal communications, the therapist observed a melting of his resistant behavior. His body began to relax, his face took on a pleasant expression, his eyes dropped their glare.

It took two more sessions before Perry reached over, managed to grasp the mallet, and began to beat the drum. With deep concentration, holding the mallet awkwardly at a peculiar angle, he made a supreme effort to relate his drumming to the music. Though it was uncontrolled, arrhythmic, and spasmodic, he became utterly absorbed in what he was doing. Immediately, the therapist informed the group that it was Perry's turn and quickly matched his drumming in an improvisation on the piano.

Within the group setting, it was possible to give Perry individualized attention, dovetailing his needs and goals with those of other members of the group. In reflecting his erratic timing and bursts of intensity, the therapist picked up the signals Perry was sending out. He was aware that something new was happening. His face was taking on a more alert expression. He was drumming with more interest and involvement. He was gaining some control over his environment. The therapist took great pleasure in what was evolving, giving him goodly amounts of acknowledgment that made him puff up with pride.

During the next six sessions, with rhythmic music as a catalyst, the therapist would adjust to his drumbeating and, as he gained more control, would "stretch" him by bringing the music closer and closer to a steady rhythmic flow. The song that was the underpinning of this process was ''Guantanamera'' (Boxill, 1976, side 1, band 6.), selected for its highly rhythmic quality and its familiarity (to the entire group). The process took the following form:

- The therapist played the song in its original form.
- The therapist matched/reflected his drumbeating.
- The therapist, by these means, created successful experiences for him.
- Perry and the therapist were then in synchrony and communication.
- Through feelings of trust and pleasure generated by being accepted and acknowledged, Perry gradually was able to beat the drum in a more coordinated, controlled manner.
- With continued encouragement and acknowledgment through the use of Reflection and Identification, he gained a heightened sense of what he was doing.
- Kinesthetic learning was taking place as his drumming became more related to the musical stimuli.

Perry's therapy sessions continued for a year. Activities with nonmusic materials, such as swinging a hoop held by the therapist or other clients, were introduced to increase mobility in his arm movements. Improvement in his coordination and motoric control had direct transfer to his work in a sheltered workshop, where his task was to put foam rubber discs into plastic bags.

Although ''Guantanamera'' became Our Contact Song, it was ''Kum Ba Ya'' (1971) that was used to work on articulation. The syllables had a special appeal for him. When this song was introduced by the therapist, who used the lining-out singing technique, Perry would sing ''Kum ba ya'' at the end of each phrase, at first inaudibly and laboriously but in a highly motivated, determined way. He *wanted* to sing the words as clearly as possible. The pace was adjusted to his ability at first and then gradually the rhythmic pattern of the words was brought closer and closer to their natural rhythm. In the last sessions, he was singing *all the words*. His articulation had become clearer as he sang with his head thrown back in an expansive gesture of exhilaration and liberation:

> Perry is beating the drum,
> Kuuuum-baaaa-yaaaa!
> Perry is beating the drum,
> Kuuuum-baaaa-yaaaa!
> Perry is beating the drum,
> Kuuuum-baaaa-yaaaa!
> O Lord, Kuuuuuum-baaaaaa-yaaaaaa!

Victor T.: *18 years; profound mental retardation; etiologic factor: microcephaly.*

Long-Term Goals: to improve attending behavior and the ability to mobilize and focus energy purposefully.

Modes of Therapeutic Music Activity Used: singing/chanting and instrument playing.

Components of Music Used: rhythms, tempos, dynamics, text of song, and pitch.

Rhythm and Musical Instruments Used: xylophones, timpani drums, rhythm sticks, hand cymbals, and piano (by therapist).

Music Materials Used: clinical music improvisation, "The Xylophone Song," and "He's Got the Whole World in His Hands."

Nonmusic Materials Used: puppets.

Some Strategies and Techniques Used: Identification, Reflection, Our Contact Song, lining-out singing, hand-over-hand assistance, use of specific rhythm instrument for specific therapeutic purpose, and modeling of rhythm instrument playing.

Victor is a study in contrasts. He is heavily built, with small, delicate, thin-fingered hands that hang flaccidly by his sides. His gait is slow and shuffling and his bodily movements tenuous. When agitated, he becomes assaultive. Otherwise, his energy level is phlegmatic. He has a history of grand mal seizures (now controlled by anticonvulsant medication).

During the music therapy assessment process, Victor exhibited self-stimulatory and autisticlike behaviors. For the most part he appeared oblivious of the therapist and his surroundings and unaware of rhythm instruments offered to him and attempts by the therapist to sit near him. His only response to musical stimuli (therapist's improvisation at the piano) was a high-pitched vocalization on the notes C and E which he emitted as he rocked back and forth. When the therapist reflected his sound, she observed a flicker of a glance in her direction.

Victor was scheduled for two half-hour group sessions a week. In the initial sessions his autistic behavior made contact with him a remote possibility. He avoided all eye contact and seemed impervious to the musical stimuli. However, once he became comfortable and secure in the group, he gave evidence of the positive effect that music had on him. In imitation of the therapist's modeling of clapping, he attempted to clap his hands, managing to bring his fingertips together in a fluttering, soundless motion that simulated clapping. The therapist still could not use hand-over-hand assistance. Victor was not ready for direct physical contact.

Often, during the following sessions, he would laugh gleefully as his hand clapping became more defined, although it produced no perceptible sound. However, when offered a drum, hand cymbals, or rhythm sticks, he shook his head and pushed them away. When rubber puppets in the form of human figures were used with the song, "He's Got the Whole World in His Hands" (Ginglend & Stiles, 1965), Victor became interested in the group's activity. He not only accepted the puppets on his hands, he focused his eyes on them and vocalized in high-pitched tones. Each time the word *hands* was sung, the group was directed to hold up their hands (with or without puppets) and wave them in the air. This Victor also did, initially with physical prompts and, after many repetitions, on his own initiative. He began to focus his eyes more and more as his head turned directly toward the puppets on his hands.

Attentional problems that stem from mental retardation caused by organic deficits, and are compounded by environmental and sensory deprivation, often seem an unsurmountable challenge. For Victor, the puppets proved to be an added sensory and concrete stimulus that served two distinct purposes: (a) they helped gradually increase his ability to focus his eyes to make direct eye contact with the therapist, and (b) they diminished his tactile defensiveness, resulting in gradual acceptance of hand-over-hand assistance.

Before the start of a session in the fourth month of therapy, his classroom teacher informed the therapist that Victor had been acting out. He had assaulted another client and had knocked over several chairs. Though he had swung back to his phlegmatic behavior before coming to music therapy, his emotional state was still far from stabilized. As the group settled in the semicircle of chairs near the piano, the therapist made a quick decision to provide a new focus for Victor's attention. By placing a table with a xylophone in front of him, an environment was created that might have a stabilizing effect. When the therapist offered him two mallets, he eyed them with his characteristic sideways glance, his head tipped upward. The therapist stood with arms outstretched toward him. Everyone in the room waited silently, raptly intent on seeing what Victor would do. The therapist ran the mallets over the xylophone bars and then held them toward Victor. She repeated this glissando movement several times in quick succession. Then, without seeming to look toward her, he reached out with both arms and slowly drew the mallets from her hands. He moved the mallets toward the xylophone, tapping them tenuously; suddenly, a tinkling sound floated through the air. Victor became utterly absorbed in what he was doing. Now at the piano, the therapist reflected the delicate musical sounds that Victor was making. She improvised a song that matched the carousellike sounds and, as a carousel goes round and round, so the therapist played. Without interrupting the flow of the music, she instructed an assistant to distribute handbells, a tambourine, a triangle, and resonator bells to the other members of the group.

Victor had inspired Our Contact Song, "The Xylophone Song" (see Figure 6–3). It became a song the entire group sang, played, and moved to in many later sessions.

The therapist, by transforming Victor's tenuous tapping on the xylophone into a structured musical experience, made it a successful experience for him, stirring a sense of life and well-being in him. The musical contact between them became the source of emotional contact. Once this was established, Victor began to have a focus and positive purpose for his actions. His participation in the group was on a more consistent basis and his attention lasted as long as the music did when he was playing the xylophone. At other times his attention was sporadic and he needed to be reminded constantly to participate.

"The Xylophone Song" served as a building block on which to increase his ability to attend to a task. As he played the song over and over, he became more adventuresome. He tried running the mallets up and down, imitating the glissandos the therapist demonstrated. His auditory perception improved (demonstrated by his ability to follow changes in dynamics from very soft to very loud) and his receptivity to movement activities grew as did his willingness to use different instruments.

When Victor began to mouth and produce words of songs audibly, it was a signal that he was getting ready for another step up the developmental ladder. It was decided that the music therapist, speech therapist, and teacher would work on a transdisciplinary basis with Victor to develop the use of words.

Figure 6–3 The Xylophone Song

Source: © Edith Hillman Boxill, 1981.

Lenny C.: *12 years; profound mental retardation; etiologic factor: Down syndrome.*

Long-Term Goals: to awaken awareness and to develop body awareness/body image and motoric skills.

Modes of Therapeutic Music Activity Used: instrument playing and music-movement.

Components of Music Used: rhythm, tempo, and dynamics.

Rhythm and Musical Instruments Used: timpani drum and sleighbells.

Music Materials Used: clinical music improvisation and "Drum Song."

Nonmusic Materials Used: puppets, stuffed animals, plastic hoop, scarves, and mirror.

Some Strategies and Techniques Used: Reflection, Identification, hand-over-hand assistance, gestural prompts, onomatopoeic words, action words, modeling of body movements, and exaggerated articulation of singing/chanting.

Whereas many Down syndrome children's bodies are flexible (sometimes to an extreme), others such as Lenny's are rigidly immobile. Institutionalized since birth, he was underweight and undersized and moved (with assistance) very slowly and awkwardly with a slew-toed (feet turned outward), wide-based gait. His affect was flat (his face fixed and expressionless) and he made no eye contact.

As is true of Lenny, when sensory mechanisms are not functioning adequately, a distorted body image results and there may be little or no purposeful body movements in response to sensory stimuli. For the person with extreme deficits in sensorimotor development, intensive work to awaken and activate the person's kinesthetic body is primary. Because each individual's rhythm and pace are different, clinical skills that aim to stimulate bodily sensations and activate bodily movement are applied on a highly individual basis by taking even the slightest cues from the person as a starting point. As kinesthetic learning takes place, self-initiated expression and conscious experiencing can develop.

During music therapy assessment, the only observable responses to musical stimuli were a slight upturn of his lips and a reflexive flicker of his eyelids. There was resistance to physical prompts (his body became completely rigid when approached). He tracked a bell horizontally and vertically but did not reach out for it. Otherwise, he remained passive. When a mirror was held in front of him, he showed no sign of recognition. There was no imitation of gross motor movements.

Shortly before the start of music therapy, Lenny had been placed in a sensory stimulation group for low-functioning clients. The interdisciplinary team recommended that Lenny be scheduled for music therapy sessions with two other clients. Inasmuch as the music therapist had the assistance of a music therapy intern and a therapy aide, it was possible to have this "group" take the form of three simultaneous individual sessions. In essence, Lenny was to receive one-to-one attention.

In the initial sessions, exposed to highly rhythmic music played on the piano, Lenny's body remained immobile except for his hands, which moved perseveratively close to the left side of his tilted head in a continuous slow, sinewy motion. This mannerism had not manifested itself during the assessment process. Was it his first overt response to music?

Taking this cue, the therapist sat opposite Lenny, singing directly to him, alternating between improvising melodies that matched his hand movements and playing vigorous rhythmic musical sounds on the Autoharp®. Gradually, as Lenny showed signs of arousal, the therapist would take Lenny's hands and gently rub them in time to the music. As he accepted her touch, she worked toward releasing bodily tension by swinging his arms to "swinging" music, lifting his feet up and down to marching music, and moving his torso back and forth to "swaying" music. With this close physical contact and careful handling, Lenny's body began to loosen up and his hand mannerism became less "necessary." He made attempts to grasp brightly colored crepe paper streamers and scarves that were waved before his eyes. He began to reach for sleighbells that were shaken vigorously while being offered to him. His eyes began to lose their listlessness as he followed the therapist's movements, which were supported by vocal and instrumental improvisations. Other nonmusic materials, such as stuffed animals, puppets, a mirror, and a red plastic hoop, were used to stimulate him visually and tactilely.

As Lenny became more trusting and aware of the therapist, a new element was introduced—a timpani drum. This drum was selected because of the quality of its sound and its potential to arouse Lenny's attention. For many sessions the drum was placed in front of him. When the drum mallet was offered to him, he extended his left hand toward it but made no move to grasp it. The next time it was offered, the therapist held it close, touched his hand with it, slipped it into his hand, and held her hand over his. He grasped it and then dropped it. When it was offered to him again, he reached for it with his right hand, grasped it, held it for one second, and then dropped it.

With hand-over-hand assistance and many weeks of repetition of the preceding process, Lenny began to manifest the effects of the kinesthetic experience of holding onto the drum mallet. Each time he held it, the therapist directed his hand to the drumhead, lifted his hand, and let it fall. There would be a very slight thud. It was not until the ninth session that he grasped and held the mallet with his right hand, then transferred it to his left. (He showed no hand preference when the mallet was offered to him in the initial sessions.) This became his pattern for a time. Then he reached for it, grasped it, and held it with his left hand quite consistently.

The therapist demonstrated beating the drum, but Lenny was not ready to imitate the complicated process of lifting his arm up and bringing it down with the intention of making a sound. He did begin to pick up the mallet (now placed on the drumhead), however, and direct it toward the drum, moving it in a soundless, circular motion that was singularly like his sinewy hand mannerism. The movement had the same slow, undulating quality. The therapist reflected this at the piano, playing softly in the same undulating manner. This was to be the way Lenny *played* the drum, until he was ready to take the next step. The significance, however, of what he was doing was that it was his *first self-initiated* movement in relation to an external object—*his first sign of awareness of his immediate environment*. He seemed to be making a connection between the drum and what he could do *to* it. His movements were becoming more purposeful with each repetition of the experience.

Lenny's way of entering the room began to change. His gait had been sluggish and awkward, but now it began to take on a little bounce. His body began to come alive. He no longer sat inertly when the drum and mallet were placed in front of him. In each succeeding session, he would pick up the mallet spontaneously and move it on the drumhead, covering more and more of its surface. As the therapist matched his movements, she would sing, "Lenny, that's very good. Lenny's that's *very* good." The tone of her voice conveyed how pleased she was, and Lenny began to look up at her with some traces of animation flickering on his face.

The next step was to develop the kinesthetic experience of lifting his arm up and bringing it down with enough energy to produce a drum sound. An aide (who had been instructed in using hand-over-hand assistance) sat beside Lenny, lifted his arm up and let it fall, over and over. As Lenny began to feel the sensation of lifting his arm and as he heard the sound of the drum as the mallet hit the drumhead, he became aroused—his body assuming a purposeful posture, his eyes brightening, his face losing its pallor. The therapist would improvise a chant in a steady rhythmic pulse with strong accentuation:

> Lenny is beating the DRUM!
> Lenny is beating the DRUM!
> BOOM! BOOM! BOOM! BOOM!
> BOOM! BOOM! BOOM! BOOOOOOM!

Over the months that followed, Lenny showed more initiative. One day, he lifted his arm up himself and brought it down with a lusty "Boom!" He was so pleased with his accomplishment that he lifted his arm up again. This time as he came down with a good strong beat, the therapist sang out in strong tones, "Lenny is beating the drum! Lenny is beating the drum!" Suddenly, his entire body came alive, his eyes focusing directly on the therapist. As the therapist improvised a "Drum Song," singing and playing it with vigor, Lenny beat with increasing vigor on the drum. This was the moment of a shift in awareness that opened up Lenny's ability to imitate and eventually execute gross motor movements spontaneously.

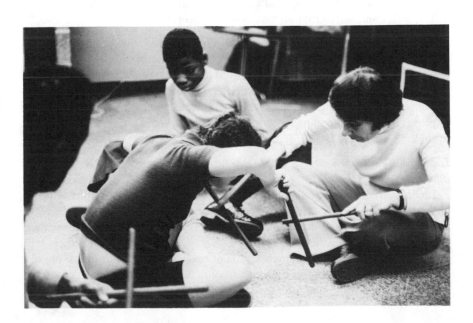

In addition to beating the drum with increasing relatedness to musical stimuli, he became aware of what he could do with his hands, his feet, his entire body. He learned to clap his hands, stamp his feet, bend his knees, turn around, and walk in a circle. He even started to attempt to run. Onomatopoeic words such as *boom* and actions words such as *walk* and *bend,* chanted and modeled by the therapist, were used as he began to move into space. Though he continued to need physical assistance and prompts, his movements became more spontaneous and, with increasing frequency, self-initiated.

In his classroom, Lenny's perceptual-motor skills were noticeably improved, beginning with an increased ability to place puzzle parts in their proper niches. His progress in general functioning and awareness was noted by the treatment team as being beyond previous "expectations."

Group Therapy

Group 1

Gio L.: *6½ years; moderate mental retardation; etiologic factor: Down syndrome.*

Gio has a systolic heart murmur, divergent strabismus, and a slight hearing loss in both ears. He speaks in two-word sentences, has good receptive language, and relates to peers, especially in structured classroom situations and organized group activities. During music therapy assessment he responded well to musical stimuli: he beat the drum with a steady pulse, intoned isolated words of songs (monotonally), and manipulated rhythm instruments appropriately.

Rodney A: *8 years; severe mental retardation; etiologic factor: phenylketonuria.*

Rodney has a history of convulsive disorder. At 6 months of age developmental delays were evident. He speaks in two-word sentences, omitting the final sounds of words. Hyperactivity and aggressive behaviors affect his ability to attend. His responses during music therapy assessment clearly indicated a potential for improvement of his attending behavior and eye–hand coordination through the use of rhythm instruments.

Linda W.: *8 years; severe mental retardation; etiologic factor: organic brain damage due to meningitis.*

Linda's behaviors, including her manner of speech and bodily movements, are characterized by bodily tension (hand wringing, teeth gnashing, stiffening of entire body) and hyperkinesis (involuntary movements). Her speech is dysphonic (characterized by misarticulation of words), yet intelligible. She interacts with peers and adults. Music therapy assessment revealed that her drumbeating was compulsive and unrelated to musical stimuli. Gross motor movements were spasmodic and unsustained. She sang on pitch and comprehended texts of songs.

Ramos N.: *7½ years; moderate mental retardation; etiologic factor: prematurity.*

Ramos was born at 28 weeks of gestation weighing 2 pounds, 1 ounce, and was in an isolette for 2 months. All developmental milestones were slightly delayed. He has cataracts in both eyes and a history of petit mal seizures. A neurological test at the age of 4 years disclosed a bilateral cerebral disorder secondary to prematurity. His speech is intelligible with some omissions and substitutions, his receptive language good. In the music therapy assessment sessions, his musical behavior was erratic and fragmentary. He rejected the drum, strummed the Omnichord® fleetingly, and performed perceptual-motor tasks with difficulty.

Carol R.: *8 years; severe mental retardation; etiologic factor: Down syndrome.*

Carol walked at 2 years and began to talk at 3½ years. All developmental milestones were delayed. Her articulation is poor, yet she is able to use words for communicative purposes, and her receptive language is good. Inappropriate laughing interferes with her ability to attend. Music therapy assessment revealed that, although the quality of her voice is raspy and muffled, she is able to sing syllables and words of songs on pitch.

Long-Term Goals: To increase body awareness/body image and to learn number concepts.

Modes of Therapeutic Music Activity Used: singing, instrument playing, and music-movement.

Components of Music Used: rhythm, melody, text of song, and pitch.

Rhythm and Musical Instruments Used: timpani drum, temple blocks, resonator bells, metallophone, cymbals, and Omnichord®.

Music Materials Used: "I've Got Two" (adaptation).

Nonmusic Materials Used: flash cards with numbers and pictures of body parts.

Some Strategies and Techniques Used: exaggerated articulation of words of song, lining-out singing, melodic intonation, modeling of body movements, use of music that is familiar, exact repetitions of rhythmic patterns, use of specific rhythm instruments for specific therapeutic purposes, and use of flash cards.

This group of children met for two half-hour sessions a week. The group was somewhat homogeneous: they were close in chronological age and functioning levels, and all had some degree of communicative speech. In their classroom they were learning body parts and numeration. Treatment plans were formulated to reinforce this classroom work.

Since these children watch the television program "Sesame Street" on Saturday mornings (they lived in the same apartment in the residential facility), the catchy tune "I've Got Two" (Raposo & Moss, 1971; see Figure 6–4) was selected not only for its suitability but also its familiarity. When the therapist played and sang it, there was an unmistakable spark of recognition on their faces. The song captured their attention immediately.

Figure 6–4 I've Got Two

Words by **JEFFREY MOSS**
Music by **JOE RAPOSO**

Source: I've Got Two, words by Jeffrey Moss, music by Joe Raposo, © 1970 Festival Attractions, Inc. ASCAP. © 1973 Jonico Music ASCAP. Used with permission.

The design of the therapeutic music activities, which were aimed at stimulating cognition through motoric action, was based on the rhythm pattern of two beats (1-2, 1-2, etc.), which is natural to our inner body rhythm and the symmetry of our body. Our breathing, our heartbeat, our walking are in duple (two-beat) rhythm. We have two hands, two feet, two arms, two legs, two eyes, two ears. Starting from this resource—their own bodies—working on learning body parts and their functions was done by adapting the words of the song, with fine and gross motor movements an integral component of the combined singing and music-movement activities:

I've got two *hands* (holding up both hands),
One, two (moving alternate hands rhythmically to the count of 1-2),
I've got two *hands* (same as line 1),
One, two (same as line 2).
I've got two *hands* (same as line 1),
And I clap with my hands.

Clap, clap, clap, clap,
Clap your *hands* (holding hands up in the air on word *hands*),
Clap, clap, clap, clap,
Clap your *hands* (holding hands up in the air on word *hands*),
Clap, clap, clap, clap,
Clap your *hands* (holding hands up in the air on word *hands*).

Various other movements ("Shake your hands," "Pull your hands," "Wiggle the fingers of your hands") were suggested nonverbally or verbally by the children or were directed by the therapist gesturally and vocally. Lining-out singing was used to encourage the singing of the body parts. (This activity can cover the entire body—from simple to complex body parts, i.e., hands, arms, legs to wrists, elbows, ankles, knees. The song can also be adapted rhythmically and textually to parts of the body, e.g., "We have one head" (mouth, nose, neck, stomach, and back) as well as to the more complex cognitive task of counting fingers and toes.)

Over months of sessions, the song was repeated with many changes in words and actions to reinforce the learning of body parts, on which the classroom teacher was also working. As a result, these children gained an awareness not only of body image and the functions of body parts but also increased their ability to count. A variety of rhythm instruments—timpani drum, temple blocks, resonator bells, metallophone, cymbals—were used to stimulate these activities as well as auditory perception and discrimination. When singing about their ears, the therapist would beat a timpani drum or shake a bell and sing, "What do we hear with our *ears*?" Either the children or the therapist or both would sing back, "We hear the drum (bells, cymbals, etc.) with our *ears*." Rhythm instrument playing also stimulated awareness of the use of body parts: "We play resonator bells with our *hands*," "We beat the drum with our *hands*." Motoric and locomotor actions were identified through singing and chanting rhythmic patterns within the framework of the song, "We walk/run/march with our *feet*," "We push with our *arms*," "We swing our *arms*."

Flash cards of body parts and numbers were used as visual aids. The concept of the numbers 1 (one nose, one mouth, one head, etc.), 2 (two hands, two feet, two eyes, etc.), 3 (three fingers, three objects such as resonator bells, etc.), 4 (four fingers, four drumbeats, etc.), and 5 (five fingers, five temple blocks, etc.) was woven into the process.

Through this multidimensional approach of combining motoric, sensoric, and cognitive learning, these children became highly motivated to learn names and functions of body parts and, at the same time, numeration.

Group 2

Lucy L.: *30 years; severe mental retardation; etiologic factor: hydrocephaly.*

Lucy is a spastic paraplegic with deformed feet. Though usually confined to a wheelchair, she is able to pull herself to the floor and crawl. She has a history of petit mal seizures and is subject to wide mood swings. Occasionally she utters words echolalically.

Danny D.: *24 years; profound mental retardation; etiologic factor: encephalopathy associated with maternal toxemia of pregnancy.*

Danny is blind from retrolental fibroplasia. He is nonambulatory, and all extremities are hypotonic. He has respiratory difficulty and a history of petit mal seizures; he has no speech.

Nick T.: *20 years; profound mental retardation; etiologic factor: multiple congenital anomalies of the brain.*

Nick is a spastic quadriplegic with more involvement of the lower extremities than the upper. Though his arms are severely contracted at the elbows, he reaches for objects, particularly with his left arm, which has more mobility than the right. Audiological testing revealed a hearing loss in both ears. He has a history of grand mal seizures and is nonverbal.

Carolyn S.: *31 years; profound mental retardation; etiologic factor: perinatal mechanical injury.*

Carolyn's behavior is characterized by impulsivity and distractibility. Though there is spasticity of her legs, she is ambulatory, capable of a wide-based, waddling gait (with assistance). She has a history of petit mal seizures and is nonverbal.

Long-Term Goals: to awaken and expand awareness of themselves and others and to improve motoric skills.

Modes of Therapeutic Music Activity Used: singing, rhythm instrument playing, and music-movement.

Components of Music Used: rhythm, melody, text of song, and pitch.

Rhythm and Musical Instruments Used: barrel drum, resonator bells, wristbells, rhythm sticks, flutophone, Autoharp®, guitar, and piano (by therapist).

Music Materials Used: "Hello Song," "The People in Your Neighborhood" (adaptation), "Rookoobay," and "Goodbye Song."

Nonmusic Materials Used: none.

Some Strategies and Techniques Used: Identification, manual signing for *start, wait, play, more,* hand-over-hand assistance, modeling of manipulating rhythm instruments, modeling of body movements, onomatopoeic words, matching the here-and-now person through vocalizations, physical and gestural prompts, and pacing and tempo adjustments.

For a group of individuals whose lives are isolated and fragmented and whose energies are not self-directed, the music therapy process provides a structured environment. It brings them together. These separate individuals can become a *group* on increasing levels of cohesion and integration when the energy generated by the music, as it is projected and used by the therapist, serves to bind them together.

No matter how simple the melodic line or harmonic structure may be, the therapist's ability to stimulate activity by projecting vocally and instrumentally is essential. As previously stated, whether the piano, guitar, Autoharp®, or some other instrument is used, it must *never* be a barrier between the therapist and the clients. The therapist must be ready to move freely among the clients, constantly alert to and meeting their needs, constantly working with them to accomplish individual short-term objectives.

Sessions opened with the group sitting (three in wheelchairs) in a circle as the therapist played an Autoharp® or guitar while singing a "Hello Song." Because the group needed individual assistance, a music therapy intern and therapy aides were trained to assist on a one-to-one basis.

It was several months before Danny would accept any physical contact. When approached, he screamed and flailed his arms in the air.

Carolyn, on the other hand, craved physical contact. When the therapist approached her, she reached out for the therapist to take her hands. With help, she could maintain balance statically and spatially. Often, after the therapist walked slowly and rhythmically with her, at the same time swinging her arms to music, she became more coordinated and peaceful, her random movements changing to focused and purposeful ones. She was then able to sit in one place long enough to have the therapist or assistant work on the short-term objective of having her clap her hands together in response to the music. First the therapist would clap hands toward her, then use hand-over-hand assistance, clapping her hands together to the rhythm of a chant, "Carolyn claps hands—clap, clap, clap."

Nick, who functioned at a mental age of five months, attempted to reach out for the rhythm sticks that were offered to him. Contrary to the report that he had a severe loss of hearing, Nick's auditory perception went beyond the level of tracking sound. He would sway back and forth rhythmically to the music. At a session one month after therapy began, as he moved his head back and forth in response to the song the therapist was singing, his face took on a "soulful" expression and he began to vocalize "aaah-aaah-aaah" *in the tonality of the music*. The therapist sang back "aaah-aaah-aaah" in acknowledgment. His eyes focused on her face for the first time. This was a moment of significant contact— musical contact that opened the door to developmental growth. It then became possible to work with him on grasping the rhythm sticks and subsequently on holding them. These short-term objectives were steps toward a long-term goal, namely, transferring this skill to holding a spoon, perhaps eventually to feeding himself.

Until it was found that Lucy preferred the barrel drum, she had maintained an isolation that was expressed bodily. She would fold her arms tightly, resisting all contact. However, she moved her head from side to side rhythmically to the music.

Carolyn, seated in front of a table, needed to be engaged in a concrete activity to reduce her hyperactivity. Resonator bells were selected to help her focus her energy. The immediate feedback of pleasant musical sounds that came when she struck the bells with mallets in both hands caught and held her attention. She needed guidance and hand-over-hand assistance in the beginning. Gradually, she would pick up the mallets placed on the table and strike the bells independently. This activity was the first that Carolyn initiated. The bells had a stabilizing effect.

The session described here took place seven months after therapy began. Following the "Hello Song," the therapist sang "The People in the Room Today" (Boxill, 1976, side 1, band 1), an adaptation of "The People in Your Neighborhood" (Raposo & Moss, 1971; see Figure 6–5), using each person's name as follows:

> (*Client's name*) is a person in this room today,
> In this room today, in this room today,
> (*Client's name*) is a person in this room today,
> A person in this room today.

As the therapist sang Danny's name, the intern moved his wheelchair back and forth to the rhythm of the music. He responded by moving his head and waving his arms in the air. His arm waving had become quite related to the flow of the music, and he was now able to tolerate having wristbells placed on both wrists. He, too, began to "make" music.

Though there was much starting, stopping, and waiting, the feeling of making music together was beginning to emerge. There was no overt interaction, yet a sense of energy was being transmitted, one to the other—an awakening of awareness as the bells, drum, and rhythm sticks blended with the Autoharp® played by the therapist.

As the therapist sang "Lucy is a person in this room todaaay," a lovely full-toned "tooo-daaay" rang through the room. Previously, Lucy occasionally said a word or two echolalically. However, until this moment she had not revealed that she possessed a beautiful rich singing voice. *No one had ever heard it before!* Once discovered, Lucy's singing was not only the pathway to her individual growth but also became a focal point of the group's musical experience.

When Carolyn's name was sung, her eyes sparkled and she began to move her hands in what looked like an attempt to clap them together. With assistance, her movements were organized into steady clapping. This had a visibly relaxing effect upon her—she liked the steady "clap, clap, clap, clap" to the pulse of the music.

Nick responded to the singing of his name by swaying back and forth in a movement that related closely to the tempo and pulse of the music. As his name was repeated, the therapist stood directly in front of him, putting her hands on his

Figure 6–5 The People in Your Neighborhood

Words and Music by
JEFFREY MOSS

Source: The People in Your Neighborhood, words and music by Jeffrey Moss © 1970 Festival Attractions, Inc. ASCAP. Used with permission.

shoulders and swaying with him. The vocalizations, which were becoming more frequent, came out in full force. The therapist, acknowledging these vocalizations, sang to the same tune:

Nick is singing a song today,
A song today, a song today,
Nick is singing a song today,
Singing a song today.

Nick smiled. He was receiving this acceptance.

Then rhythm instruments were distributed. Lucy happily sang as she beat the barrel drum; Nick was assisted in tapping the bright red rhythm sticks; Danny blew into a flutophone that an aide held to his lips, and the wristbells were tinkling as he waved his arms; and Carolyn was striking the resonator bells (independently but with close supervision to avert her tendency to strike her nearest neighbor). At the piano, the therapist played and sang a strongly rhythmic Trinidadian song, "Rookoobay" (see Chapter 7), inserting the names of each one in the group and identifying the instrument that each was using. A feeling of actively sharing and relating to the music together was generated:

> Lucy, Lucy is beating the drum,
> Carolyn is playing the resonator bells,
> Danny, Danny is blowing on the flutophone,
> Nick is tapping the sticks.
> We're playing together,
> We're playing together,
> We're playing together.

Though the actual words may not have been comprehended, the combined action and musical sounds created a sense of unity and purposeful activity.

The session was brought to a close with a "Goodbye Song." Saying goodbye in a familiar way (each session was brought to a close with this song) seemed to be understood to some degree by Danny and Nick as they were wheeled out of the room, and to a greater degree by Carolyn and Lucy, who waved their hands in imitation of the therapist's goodbye wave.

Group 3

Diane E.: *43 years; moderate mental retardation; etiologic factor: cultural-familial retardation.*

Sonia K.: *38 years; moderate mental retardation; etiologic factor: Down's syndrome.*

Robert G.: *32 years; severe mental retardation; etiologic factor: Klinefelter's syndrome (sex chromosome anomaly).*

Jan T.: *41 years; moderate mental retardation; etiologic factor: psychosocial deprivation.*

Harry M.: *39 years; moderate mental retardation; etiologic factor: disease due to unknown prenatal influences.*

Celia G.: *25 years; severe mental retardation; etiologic factor: Down's syndrome.*

Long-Term Goals: to improve cognitive skills (memory/recall/retention), to increase communication skills, and to increase socialization.

Modes of Therapeutic Music Activity Used: singing, rhythm instrument playing, and music-movement.

Components of Music Used: rhythm, tempo, dynamics, and text of song.

Rhythm and Musical Instruments Used: resonator bells, xylophone, cowbell, tone block, barrel drum, and Autoharp® (by therapist).

Music Materials Used: "The People in Your Neighborhood" (adaptation), "Ev'rybody" (adaptation), "When the Saints Go Marching In" (1962) (adaptation), "Turkey in the Straw."

Nonmusic Materials Used: pictures pertaining to Thanksgiving holiday, costumes.

Some Strategies and Techniques Used: Identification, call-and-response singing, lining-out singing, pacing and tempo adjustments, and dramatization.

This group of six clients met two afternoons a week for half-hour sessions after returning from a sheltered workshop. Their conditions and problems, though varied, had some commonalities: all had speech with diverse problems in articulation, phonation, inflection, and quality of tone. All were fairly well coordinated, with individual pace and rhythm that varied considerably. All had good perceptual-motor skills. They particularly enjoyed singing songs that applied directly to their daily lives and interests.

Sessions began as the clients entered the music therapy room to the therapist's singing of "When the Group Comes Marching In," to the tune of "When the Saints Go Marching In" (1962). The sessions ended with the same song to the words "When the Group Goes Marching Out," giving structure—an opening and closing—to the sessions.

After the group was seated in a semicircle around the piano, there was a warmup song in which everyone in the room, including therapy aides, interns, and the therapist, were sung about and greeted. One such song that stimulated awareness of others and encouraged interaction was "The People in the Room Today" (Boxill, 1976, side 1, band 1), an adaptation of "The People in Your Neighborhood" (Raposo & Moss, 1971). Each person had a turn to sing his or her name while initiating a movement that the rest of the group joined. They were encouraged to sing each others' names, look at or point to the person being sung about, walk up to the person and touch or shake hands, in some way to show awareness of each other. The therapist adapted the music and words of the song to the movements initiated by the client, changing tempo and dynamics to reflect the pace and quality of the individual movements:

> Let's clap our hands the way (client) does:
> High above our heads,
> And now down to the floor,
> Fast, fast, fast, FAST,
> S L O W L Y , S L O W L Y .

The therapist encouraged each member of the group to initiate a body movement. Some were eager to do so, others needed assistance and suggestions. Individual goals were interwoven into the process of working on socialization. Often, music-movement activities grew organically out of the kind of movement initiated. The group moved about the room, at times performing vigorous movements such as stamping or jumping or dancing to the music. Then a return to the seats was incorporated so that the flow of the session would not be interrupted.

The group engaged in verbal expression that emanated spontaneously from song material or was elicited by the therapist. In a session that was centered around the upcoming Thanksgiving holiday, the therapist asked, "What holiday is on Thursday?" Immediately, Harry and Jan called out, with a sense of pride, "Thanksgiving."

To the tune of "Ev'rybody" (Boxill, 1976, side 2, band 5), the therapist sang:

> Ev'rybody loves Thanksgiving Day,
> Ev'rybody loves Thanksgiving Day,
> Ev'rybody, ev'rybody, ev'rybody, ev'rybody,
> Ev'rybody loves Thanksgiving Day.

The first time, the song was sung in a spirited tempo to stimulate clapping and to project the joyous quality of the holiday. Then the tempo was slowed down in order to encourage and allow the group to sing key words. Lining-out singing of the words *Thanksgiving Day* was used, giving each a turn to sing at his or her own pace and capability. After several repetitions, the clapping and singing gained momentum. Then, using call-and-response singing, the song grew. The therapist called out, "What do we eat on Thanksgiving Day?" Each time a client called out the name of a food, a verse was sung. The process went like this:

> Call: What do we eat on Thanksgiving Day?
> Response: Turkey.
> Verse: We all eat TURKEY on Thanksgiving Day,
>   We all eat TURKEY on Thanksgiving Day,
>   We all eat TURKEY, we all eat TURKEY,
>   We all eat T U R K E Y on Thanksgiving Day.
> Call: What else do we eat on Thanksgiving Day?
> Response: Sweet potatoes.
> Verse: We all eat SWEET POTATOES on Thanksgiving Day
>   (repeat as in above verse).

Call: What else do we eat on Thanksgiving Day?
Response: Pumpkin pie.
Verse: We all eat PUMPKIN PIE on Thanksgiving Day
           (repeat as in above verse).

And on and on until many more foods, including hamburgers, were sung about. Work on social, cognitive (especially those that stimulate memory), and speech skills was interwoven into this process. Rhythm instruments—resonator bells, xylophone, cowbell, tone block, barrel drum—were used to emphasize the words *Thanksgiving Day* and the names of foods. Individual speech problems were being dealt with and musical interactions created through the singing and instrument playing. What emerged was a dramatization of a Thanksgiving Day dinner. With visual aids (pictures relating to Thanksgiving that were displayed during the singing) as scenery, the group enacted in pantomime the preparation of the foods to be eaten, the serving of food, and a square dance to "Turkey in the Straw," which ended the festivities.

As a result of these sessions, the entire group was inspired to plan to make decorations for the actual Thanksgiving Day dinner. They performed their playlet at the dinner and also at the "Home Talent Nite" on the Friday evening after Thanksgiving. Costumes simulating the Pilgrims' clothing added to the spirit of the performance. Other residents as well as staff members joined in the singing and square dancing.

"Ev'rybody" was used for different holidays: Halloween, Valentine's Day, Christmas, Easter. It became familiar throughout the center. Therapy sessions were the catalyst and "rehearsal" time for many events and performances by the clients.

One-to-One Therapy

Gregory R.: *10½ years; severe mental retardation; etiologic factor: brain damage due to perinatal asphyxia.*

Long-Term Goals: to reduce assaultive and compulsive behavior and to increase communicative speech.

Modes of Therapeutic Music Activity Used: singing/chanting, and music-movement.

Components of Music Used: rhythm, tempo, dynamics, and text of song.

Rhythm and Musical Instruments Used: conga drum.

Music Materials Used: "Pick a Bale of Cotton."

Nonmusic Materials Used: pieces of paper, and wastepaper basket.

Some Strategies and Techniques Used: Reflection; lining-out singing; manual signing for *start, stop, wait,* onomatopoeic and action words, call-and-response singing/chanting.

Gregory has a history of child abuse. He displays self-abusive, assaultive, and compulsive behaviors such as picking up specks of dust or scraps of paper from the floor. His speech is echolalic with some dysphonic anomalies (misarticulation). Compulsive giggling intrudes upon his activity and constantly short-circuits his energy. His forehead is furrowed, giving his face a perpetual look of anxiety.

Music therapy assessment revealed that his compulsive behaviors interfered with his ability to manipulate rhythm instruments to such a degree that frustration and a sense of failure began to build. An area of strength was demonstrated in his ability to comprehend the words of songs and respond with appropriate body movements.

Gregory was enrolled in a special education program in a public school. His social worker was notified that his assaultive behavior was becoming more frequent and disruptive in class. The music therapist, who had established a close relationship with Gregory in an after-school music therapy group, was asked to work with him on an individual basis in an attempt to avert a "crisis." Daily individual sessions were arranged.

Using his strength—receptive language—to help him gain self-control and make his energy available for self-direction rather than self-abuse and abuse of others, a highly individualized treatment plan was designed. In working to make him aware of his behaviors and redirect his energies into productive channels, the therapist explored the idea of encouraging Gregory to express certain behaviors within the structured environment that music provides. Vigorous, rhythmic gross motor activities were stimulated by musical improvisations that vocally and instrumentally directed him to exert and assert himself in strong bodily actions. Onomatopoeic words such as *stamp, push, beat,* and *bang,* as in "Stamp your feet," "Push your arms," "Beat the drum," and "Bang the floor," gave impetus to forceful psychomotor expression that was not only acceptable but beneficial. The conga drum, which he was encouraged to beat vigorously with his hands, was used to give him a socially acceptable, musical means of ventilating feelings of frustration, anxiety, and anger. The structure of musical phrasing was used for impulse control, with Gregory and the therapist taking turns singing/chanting words, rhythmic phrases, and song phrases in call-and-response style. Manual signing for *start, stop,* and *wait* was used in combination with verbal prompts. In the relatively short period of three weeks, Gregory showed signs of facial and bodily change. He experienced many moments of bodily and emotional release. His forehead was less furrowed.

Growing out of the preceding activities was the enactment of an adapted form of the work song, "Pick a Bale of Cotton" (Langstaff & Langstaff, 1970). Played with sharp contrasts in tempo and dynamics (slow and loud, slow and fast, fast and loud, fast and soft), Gregory's responses related more and more to the movements into which the song led him. Having him deliberately and consciously pick up pieces of paper (prepared as an environment for him) and put them in a wastepaper

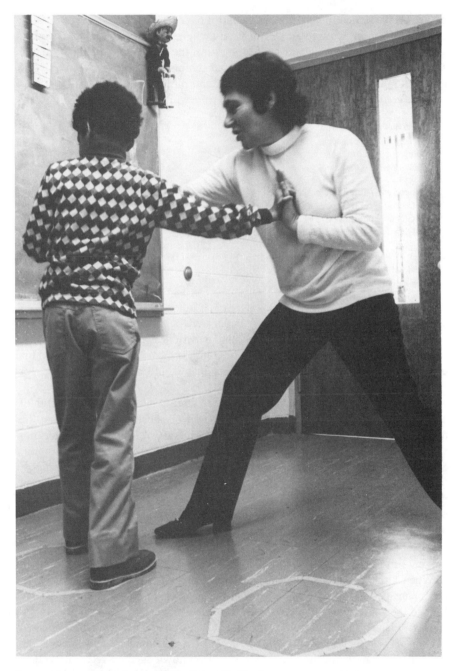

Source: Photo courtesy of photographer Robert Beckhard.

basket was designed to help him gain control over his compulsive need to "stop everything" to pick up a speck of dust. By engaging him in being consciously aware of the behavior that was controlling him, the goal was to help him gain a sense of self that obviated the need to lash out at himself and others, a sense of self that could do things that were constructive and pleasurable. The song that was selected conveyed the idea of having a good time while performing a specific task:

> Jump down, turn around,
> Pick up a piece of paper,
> Jump down, turn around,
> Pick it up from the floor.
>
> O Gregory, put it in the basket,
> O Gregory, put it there right now.
> O Gregory, put it in the basket,
> O Gregory, put it there right now.
>
> Pick up the paper,
> And put it in the basket,
> Pick up the paper,
> And put it there now.

This was repeated until all the pieces of paper were put in the basket, enhancing his opportunity to learn through the pleasurable experiences provided for him in this prepared environment. The aim was to help him achieve mastery of self and his environment by providing creative outlets that would diminish the need for destructive outlets.

Gregory was beginning to enjoy this game. Entering into the spirit of the fun of picking up paper that was deliberately scattered on the floor, he looked at the therapist with a glint in his eyes and laughed. This was full-bodied laughter, not the high-pitched, inappropriate compulsive giggling that he could not control. Singing and chanting action phrases such as "Jump down," "Turn around," "Pick up," and "Put it," gradually served to counteract the compulsive giggling that used to interrupt the flow of his movements. By slowing down the tempo and waiting for him to fill in the words (lining-out singing), he became able to absorb and assimilate motorically and cognitively what the words indicated. As sessions proceeded, deeper connections between the words and his actions took place while singing full phrases ("Pick up a piece of paper" and "Put it in the basket").

When Gregory entered the music therapy room for his twelfth session, he communicated clearly that he wanted a piece of paper by extending his hand toward the sheets that were set out for his game, assertively (not aggressively) saying "Piece of paper." Until that time his speech had been echolalic. *This was his first purposeful verbal communication.* The therapist immediately handed him a sheet of paper, answering him in words that acknowledged his request. He then proceeded happily to tear the paper and scatter it on the floor. He then placed the wastepaper basket nearby. On his own initiative he sang the words of the song as he acted them out. The therapist matched his tempo and pace until their voices and the piano accompaniment were in complete synchrony rhythmically and melodically. Gregory had incorporated—internalized—the meaning of the activity and had attained the beginnings of control of himself and his environment by being able to do *consciously* what he previously had done compulsively.

Evidence of carryover to his classroom performance and behavior was reported at a case conference shortly thereafter. He was sustaining activity for longer and longer periods of time, and his self-abusive and assaultive behaviors were diminishing in frequency and intensity. And, as a very definite outgrowth of the singing, his speech was improving in articulation and spontaneous expression.

The consensus of the interdisciplinary team was that individual sessions should continue in order to maintain and stabilize the gains that Gregory had attained.

Chris A.: *23½ years; severe mental retardation; etiologic factor: unknown prenatal influences.*

Long-Term Goals: to improve affective state and reduce bodily tension.

Modes of Therapeutic Music Activity Used: singing, rhythm instrument playing, and music-movement.

Components of Music Used: rhythm, melody, tempo, dynamics, timbre, and text of song.

Rhythm and Musical Instruments Used: resonator bells, Orff xylophone, handbell, and piano (client and therapist).

Music Materials Used: clinical music improvisation and "Angels Watching Over Me."

Nonmusic Materials Used: scarves, and crepe paper streamers.

Some Strategies and Techniques Used: humming (for relaxation), hand-over-hand assistance, lining-out singing, modeling of body movements, use of specific rhythm instruments for specific therapeutic purpose.

Chris's behavior is characterized by extreme bodily and emotional tension. Myopia and scoliosis have combined to give his body the appearance of a bent-over old man. He perseverates verbally, clenching his mouth and teeth, spurting verbiage, and grunting in ways that are symptomatic of dyskinesia. His arms and head make spasmodic movements, his hands open and close constantly in a robotlike fashion, and his hunched shoulders move in sudden thrusts.

From the findings of music therapy assessment, in-depth therapeutic intervention to effect relaxation and reduce his extreme bodily and emotional tension was strongly recommended. The interdisciplinary team agreed that individual music therapy was advisable until he was ready to benefit from group sessions. Two half-hour sessions per week were scheduled.

Work with Chris centered on evoking moods through music that would have a soothing, calming, relaxing effect. Usually it was possible to anticipate moments when his tension showed signs of escalating. If, during a music-movement activity, his body stiffened and he emitted a tight grunting sound, the therapist would instantly suggest that they hum a song together. Chris would respond immediately, the therapist easing him into a gentle hum that brought welcome relief.

In the initial stage of therapy, the method of helping him relax began with the following short-term objectives:

- to hum melody of song softly and slowly
- to hum melody of song in steady rhythmic flow
- to shake handbells slowly and gently to music
- to swing arms gently and rhythmically with therapist
- to swing arms gently and rhythmically independently

To foster self-control over his loud verbalizations and the spasmodic quality of his bodily movements, the dynamic level of vocal and instrumental musical stimuli was kept soft and the pace of activity slow. The therapist worked in close physical proximity with Chris, coexperiencing motoric activities, sometimes waving soft scarves and crepe paper streamers that had a quieting, soothing effect, while singing a lilting melody slowly and softly. The steady rhythmic flow had an integrating effect, creating a feeling of harmony within him and in relation to the therapist. When this occurred, the therapist noted a shift in his bodily stance from stiff rigidity to a softening and lightening up of his entire body.

Rhythm instruments were carefully selected for their timbre (tone color) and dynamic range. Resonator bells/tone bars were particularly suitable because of their clear resonating sound. To produce this quality of sound, it was necessary to help Chris play in as relaxed a manner as possible. This was accomplished by using a loose, hand-over-hand guiding of his arm movements to give him the kinesthetic sensation of the light touch needed. Soft humming and singing aided the process. The mellow tone of the Orff xylophone (with removable wooden bars) was also used this way. An added advantage to this instrument was that, by removing all but the lowest and highest bars, it was necessary for Chris to swing his arm from one end to the other in a slow arched movement. Again, in order to produce an even flow of sound and movement, in the beginning stages of therapy hand-over-hand assistance was necessary to help him control his arm movements. As he attained these initial objectives and was able to play on an increasingly independent basis, the therapist played rich textured accompaniments on the piano or Autoharp®, giving him strong musical support. His responses were becoming more related to the musical stimuli as he gained in self-control.

At one session, while the therapist was at the piano and Chris was shaking a handbell, he pulled his chair close to the piano. In a tense, urgent manner he called out, "Piano, piano, piano," the volume of his voice escalating with each repetition. He then "attacked" the keyboard in harsh clusters. It seemed that the excitement of playing *with* the therapist caused his arm muscles to tighten. (It was learned later that the piano had a special meaning for him. His father had played the piano when Chris, as a young child, had lived at home.) However, the therapist continued to play with her left hand while she lifted Chris' right arm back and forth with her right hand—back and forth on the keyboard with large sweeping movements. His arm was iron-heavy with tension.

Gradually the therapist felt an easing of tension and a lessening of weight in his arm. As the tempo was slowed down and the volume reduced, his arm relaxed making a flow of movement possible. They then went through the same process with his left arm. Both arms, in fact, his entire body, had relaxed perceptibly. They were sharing a musical improvisation, humming and swaying to the pulse set by the arpeggio accompaniment that supported Chris's clusters, which were now blending with the therapist's playing.

At the next session, there was a gratifying repetition of this experience. Yet, at one moment, his body was gripped by a spasm. The therapist suggested that he close his eyes as if he were sleeping. He did so while she sang a song that had been used before in such instances—a song that had special appeal for him. As he closed his eyes, he started to hum, at first in unpleasant harsh tones. The therapist led him into humming softly. Simulating sleep, Chris curled up in a comfortable position on the floor as they sang "Angels Watching Over Me" (see Figure 6–6). Humming would follow each verse.

There were sessions in which the therapist and Chris played this song in duet form at the keyboard (as described above), with Chris playing clusters that he gained the capacity to control in volume and pace through this kinesthetic approach.

Chris would return to his workshop, usually able to apply himself to tasks that required fine motor skills. A therapy aide who worked with him regularly was instructed to sing or hum *to* and *with* him whenever it became obvious that tension was mounting.

Chris's ability to perform tasks that required both gross and fine motor skills improved steadily. The physical therapist was pleased to note that his body had become generally more flexible and that he was maneuvering with much more ease, both ascending and descending stairs. She attributed this, in part, to music therapy.

Upon the recommendation of the music therapist, Chris entered a group for one session per week and continued to receive one individual session as well.

Kathy D.: *7½ years; early childhood autism; etiologic factor: unknown.*

Long-Term Goals: to awaken awareness of self and others, to reduce autistic behaviors, and to develop communication skills.

Figure 6–6 Angels Watching Over Me

Modes of Therapeutic Music Activity Used: singing, rhythm instrument playing, and music-movement.

Components of Music Used: rhythm, melody, harmony, dynamics, and text of song.

Rhythm and Musical Instruments Used: hand drum.

Music Materials Used: clinical music improvisation, "See How I'm Jumping" (adaptation), and "This Old Man."

Nonmusic Materials Used: plastic ball and pieces of colored felt.

Some Strategies and Techniques Used: Reflection, Identification, Our Contact Song, gestural prompts, modeling of movements, unmatching, and repetitions with variations of sounds and movements.

When first assessed, Kathy made no eye contact, had no speech, and rarely responded to the spoken word. Her behavior was characterized by a need for sameness, perseverative rocking, and the mannerism of wiggling the fingers of her right hand close to her eyes.

On the Vineland Social Maturity Scale (administered to her mother when Kathy was 6 years of age), Kathy obtained a Social Age (SA) of 2 years and 3 months. Though a neurological examination placed her within normal limits and her electroencephalogram (EEG) was normal, there was some suspicion of minimal brain damage.

Music therapy assessment was not possible in the formal sense. There were no *overt* responses nor any evidence of awareness of the therapist or musical stimuli.

Despite the unknowns of autism, the exploration of ways to treat the autistic child continues. Many forms of traditional therapeutic treatment have been attempted, most to little or no avail. There has been no evidence that psychotherapy has been effective in diminishing the autistic symptoms, mainly because it is based on verbal communication, a skill conspicuously lacking in the autistic child (Wing, 1974). Extreme deficit in the ability to communicate in the broadest sense, specifically, the ability to use speech for purposive communication (even when the child has speech), is the common denominator of early childhood autism. Establishing and developing means of communication—stimulating nonverbal as well as verbal contact with others—is the overriding aim of music therapy with the autistic child.

Music therapy makes available preverbal and nonverbal means of communication. Natural "organic" sounds, vocalizations, bodily movements and gestures, and behaviors are reflected and translated into musical structures through clinical improvisation. If, for instance, the child hyperventilates or becomes excessively active, the therapist explores means of making musical contact by reflecting the sounds or movements of the child. Using music as an agent of change, the music therapist helps the child move from a fragmented world into an integrated one, from *una*ware experiencing to *aware* experiencing.

It is not easy to make contact with one whose unseeing eyes look away from or through you, who does not seem to hear, who retreats by lapsing into what appear to be involuntary mannerisms or engages in self-stimulatory stereotypic behaviors. At least it is not easy to make contact that is immediately observable. The therapist must literally burrow into the child's inner world.

At Kathy's first session, she held her head aloof, her eyes looking inward. With a stiff-legged gait, she swayed forward on tiptoe, her body held rigidly, her chest thrust out, her shoulders hunched. The therapist did not exist for her, nor did the therapy aide who brought her to the music therapy room. The aide "deposited" her on a chair. At once, she folded up like a jackknife, wiggling the fingers of her right hand near her eyes, touching her tongue fleetingly with two fingers of her left hand, sniffing her fingers. The therapist sat close by, watching the here-and-now Kathy.

"Hello Kathy," when sung to her, seemed to bounce off and evaporate. It had no meaning for her. There was not a ripple of a tight muscle, not a flick of her fixed eyelids, not a stir of her aloof head. The therapist sang a variety of children's songs and improvised music, playing accompaniments on the Autoharp®, using a variety of tempi, dynamics, and harmonic progressions designed to arouse her. At the very end of the session, Kathy wiggled her fingers and grunted. The therapist grunted too, Kathy's wiggling fingers stopped in mid-air. Her eyes flickered as if in surprise.

Kathy came to her second session with a plastic ball clutched in her hand. She threw it around the room in a random, frenetic fashion, darting in all directions. The therapist again greeted Kathy by singing, "Kathy, Kathy, hello Kathy," but made an immediate switch, improvising words to the tune of a brisk Flemish folk song, "See How I'm Jumping" (Langstaff & Langstaff, 1970):

> Kathy is bouncing, bouncing, bouncing,
> Kathy is bouncing a ball,
> Kathy is bouncing, bouncing, bouncing,
> Kathy is bouncing a ball.

Kathy flung the ball haphazardly. The therapist joined her, scooped up the ball, and slowly rolled it back to her, identifying, through the words of the song, what Kathy was doing. The ball bouncing began to take on a semblance of order and direction. The therapist adjusted constantly to Kathy's activity. The words became:

> Kathy is bouncing the ball to me,
> I am bouncing the ball to Kathy.

The therapist sat on the floor when Kathy sat on the floor. With legs spread apart, feet almost touching, they rolled the ball to each other to the words:

> Kathy is rolling the ball to me,
> I am rolling the ball to Kathy.

Then retreat. Wiggling her fingers, Kathy's eyes became fixed, inward, averted. Reflecting her movements, the therapist was nonverbally expressing acceptance of Kathy and perhaps making her aware of herself. The therapist sang to the same tune:

> Kathy is wiggling, wiggling her fingers,
> Kathy is wiggling her fingers now,
> Kathy is wiggling, wiggling her fingers,
> And now she's going to S T O P! (with humor).

As the therapist sang, she wiggled her fingers also. Kathy's body relaxed.

Kathy brought her plastic ball to the next session. This ball was important to her and had become the focus of musically structured activity. At one point, Kathy was lying on the floor. As she began to wiggle her fingers, the therapist bent over her, reflecting her gestures in movement and song. Then Kathy *looked up at the therapist* and, in the exact rhythm and pitch of the song she had heard over and over during these sessions, she sang back:

> Nn-nn-nn-nn-nnnn, nn-nn-nn-nn,
> Nn-nn-nn-nn-nnnn, nn-nn-nnnnnn,
> Nn-nn-nn-nn-nnnn, nn-nn-nn-nn,
> Nn-nn-nn-nn-nnnn, nn-nn-nnnnnn.

This was Our Contact Song, the first two-way reciprocal communication initiated by Kathy, the first communication directed purposively to the therapist. They sat there, looking at each other, singing to each other. Kathy seemed to know that something special had happened. And the therapist certainly knew, identifying and reflecting in song:

> Kathy is singing, singing, singing,
> Kathy is singing a song to me,
> Kathy is singing, singing, singing,
> Nn-nn-nn-nn-nnnn, nn-nn-nn-nn,
> Nn-nn-nn-nn-nnnn, nn-nn-nnnnnn,
> Nn-nn-nn-nn-nnnn, nn-nn-nn-nn,
> Nn-nn-nn-nn-nnnn, nn-nn-nnnnnn.

After this contact was made, Kathy was open to a variety of musical experiences. When she lapsed into perseverative rocking, her body moving diagonally, her eyes and head averted, the therapist would take her hands and rock back and forth with her, structuring the movements rhythmically, improvising words to fit the action. When the therapist would sing "And now we're going to S T O P!"

(always playfully making it a game), Kathy began to gain control of her compulsive behavior.

With changes in words and tempo, Kathy and the therapist would engage in different bodily movements. They would swing their arms up and down together, slide their feet in dancelike steps, jump around the room, repeating the song with variations on a theme that expanded Kathy's repertoire of movements and redirected her energy in ways that not only freed her from entrapment in her stereotypic and perseverative behaviors but also gave her the experience of sharing and playing with another.

Many short-term objectives were interwoven into the sessions. One objective that reinforced a special education goal was to have Kathy match colors. The therapist used pieces of colored felt, two of each color, to play a game that Kathy helped invent. The therapist would place a piece of blue, red, or green felt on Kathy's lap and Kathy would find a matching piece to put on the therapist's lap. Kathy laughed for the first time when the therapist put a piece on her head instead of in her lap. So the game took on a new dimension. All through this game, the therapist chanted:

> Kathy is putting a (color) piece
> Of felt on my head,
> I am putting a (same color) piece
> Of felt on Kathy's head.

Another objective was to vary Kathy's experiences to reduce her need for sameness. A hand drum was the first rhythm instrument that was introduced. The therapist found that Kathy responded to the song, "This Old Man" (Langstaff & Langstaff, 1970). Sitting on the floor together, Kathy, now singing more spontaneously ("nn-nn-nn-nn" rhythmically and on pitch), sang with the therapist as they beat the drum to the words:

> Kathy, Kathy, she's playing one,
> Kathy's playing knick-knack on the drum,
> With a knick-knack paddy whack,
> Kathy's beating the drum,
> Kathy, Kathy is beating the drum.

Since this song seemed to be familiar to Kathy, the therapist used it in many different ways to raise her awareness of self, her body, her immediate environment. Sometimes a motor activity would evolve from the words (whether comprehended or not) as the therapist sang and identified what Kathy and the therapist were doing together. At times when the therapist sang the words "This little girl came rolling home," Kathy would be led into rolling on the floor—a developmental skill that she did not perform spontaneously or naturally. After initial resistance to the therapist's attempts to give her the kinesthetic experience (working closely with her on the floor while singing gently), Kathy grew to enjoy the movement, actually to find physical and emotional release in it.

When the therapist met with Kathy's mother, it was a truly happy meeting. Kathy's mother couldn't contain her excitement about what was happening: "I just can't believe the change. She's been singing and laughing and *sitting on my lap*! She's a different Kathy. I could hardly wait to tell you . . ."

Darryl M.: *11½ years; early infantile autism; etiologic factor: unknown.*

Long-Term Goals: to develop speech for communicative purposes and to reduce autistic behaviors.

Modes of Therapeutic Music Activity Used: singing, rhythm instrument playing, and music-movement.

Components of Music Used: rhythm, tempo, pitch, dynamics, text of song, and timbre.

Musical Instruments Used: finger cymbals, metallophone, and Autoharp.

Music Materials Used: clinical music improvisations and "Pop! Goes the Weasel."

Nonmusic Materials Used: construction paper of various colors.

Some Strategies and Techniques Used: Reflection, Identification, Our Contact Song, onomatopoeic and action words with appropriate movements, exact repetition of words of song and rhythmic patterns, repetition of music with variations, lining-out singing, call-and-response singing, use of specific rhythm instrument for specific therapeutic purposes, use of cassette tape recording as therapeutic tool.

Darryl exhibited many of the symptoms identified by Leo Kanner in 1943: aloofness, echolalic speech, pronominal reversal, ritualistic behavior, and preoccupation with inanimate objects. Except when engaged in autistic behaviors such as spinning an object (or himself), his energy level was low.

Music therapy assessment revealed that his gross motor skills were underdeveloped and his fine motor skills were well developed. Generally his body movements were limp in contrast to the strength and skill with which he handled spinnable objects; his legs and feet moved lifelessly except when spinning himself. In the initial encounters, there were no observable behaviors that directly related to musical stimuli. He touched many of the rhythm instruments without any discernible interest. The challenge would be to make contact with him that would establish two-way communication.

One-to-one sessions were scheduled for two half-hour sessions a week. At the first four sessions, in seeking to make contact with Darryl, the therapist used a variety of musical improvisations that reflected and identified his behaviors and metaphorical utterances. There was no energy flowing outward when the therapist attempted to engage him in music-movement activities. He did, however, become totally absorbed in spinning a hand cymbal on the floor or twirling a record on the record player. The therapist observed him closely, watching and waiting and exploring musical possibilities that would bring him into contact with her.

At a session several weeks later, during a moment of just sitting together in silence, the therapist heard a familiar tune coming from Darryl. He was singing, very softly and inwardly in a monotone, "All around the cobbler's bench, pop! goes the weasel" (Langstaff & Langstaff, 1970). Aha! thought the therapist. This might be a pathway. This could open up a line of communication with him. She sang along with him but he did not seem to notice.

At the next session, the therapist used a cassette tape recording of the song so that she could position herself close to him. It was while playing it that the word *pop* gave rise to a way to develop eye contact (a first objective), namely, to face each other and clap hands *at* each other. In order to do this, Darryl's eyes would have to be directed toward the therapist. It was the *pop!* that provided the impetus.

However, because Darryl showed signs of retreating from the human touch, the therapist experimented with using finger cymbals. Fascinated with objects, he accepted having them put on the middle finger of each hand. The therapist then put one on each of her middle fingers and began to sing:

All around the cobbler's bench,
The monkey chased the weasel,
The monkey thought 'twas all in fun,
POP! goes the weasel.

This first trial met with lukewarm response. The therapist then drew a chalk circle on the floor. Perhaps this would attract his attention. For the following two sessions, Darryl dragged his feet listlessly, mouthing a word of the song here and there in a barely audible parrotlike monotone.

To give an element of surprise that might arouse Darryl into a state of consciously focusing his energy, the therapist sang softly and moved slowly around the circle until the "POP!" seeking out his hands in a quick, staccato movement that matched the sound.

Darryl and the therapist "went around the cobbler's bench" many times. Gradually he began to lift his arms in anticipation of the *pop!* More and more energy came from him *toward* the therapist until one day he popped his cymbals against the therapist's, tentatively yet focused.

Once this contact was made, there were many exact repetitions of this activity. Then the therapist explored changes of hand positions—to the left, to the right, upward, downward—and variations in tempo and dynamics to expand the awareness that had been awakened. As these movements became more spontaneous, the therapist decided to try the *pop!* with their hands. After several trials, Darryl popped his hands at the therapist's. This was their first actual physical contact. It opened up a delicate but very definite line of communication that would need tender nurturing.

At his eighteenth session, on his own initiative, Darryl sought out the metal-lophone. The therapist sat by, watching and listening. Darryl started to play the song, and as he played he sang the words more clearly than ever before and on pitch. The first phrase caught the rhythmic pattern of the words, with a break here and there in the flow. As he went on, phrase by phrase, there were sections of the melody (such as the musical interval of a sixth) that presented problems for him. He stopped, sang, went back to the beginning of a phrase, and, with intense concentration, repeated the melodic line until he had played it to his satisfaction.

At the next session, he not only played the song in the key of G major, articulating the *pop!* with vigor, but followed this up by transposing the entire song into the key of F major.

The therapist witnessed a very different Darryl from the elusive, fragmented young boy that she had been working with. He had internalized this music and had brought it to expression, not as one parroting another but as one who was in tune with a self that was experiencing a sense of integration (for the first time?).

Some weeks later, a family situation caused a tremendous upheaval in Darryl. When he was brought to the music therapy room in an agonized, chaotic condition, it was this song that gradually brought order and harmony within him. The therapist sang to him as he went through a ritual (never before witnessed) of repeatedly touching three places in the room in succession and then running to the therapist who gathered him in her arms each time. He then attempted to play *his* song on the metallophone—the song he had played so fluently at the previous session. After many abortive attempts, while the therapist sat close by and sang it over and over, Darryl was able to gather his energy together. He finally played it in its entirety once again. What had become Our Contact Song provided a source of security and safety for him, a means of channeling his energies in music that was familiar to him and was a connection with another person with whom he had experienced his first give-and-take relationship.

In the course of the evolvement from echolalia to the use of speech for communicative purposes, music therapy techniques specifically designed to stimulate Darryl to sing answers to questions rather than echo words were applied through the use of improvisational singing. The process which spanned many months, began with the use of colors, initially those that were associated with articles of clothing that he and the therapist were wearing:

> Therapist: Darryl, what color is your shirt (while holding up a piece of construction paper that matched his shirt)?
> Darryl: Is your shirt (in parrotlike tones)?
> Therapist: Yes, Darryl, what color is *your* shirt (touching his shirt)?
> Darryl: Shirt red (pointing to his shirt).

The day that Darryl and the therapist took a walk out of doors marked a special milestone in his life. After walking a distance, they sat down on a bench to rest a while. Abruptly, Darryl tugged at her hand and commanded in loud, resonant tones, "Get up! Get up!" This was his first spontaneous verbal communication. The therapist stood up immediately. Darryl smiled, put his hand in hers, and they walked back, *hand in hand*.

A week later, while walking from the music therapy room to his classroom, he once again tugged the therapist's arm, this time announcing, "Want a Snicker, pleeezzz." In an instant the therapist answered, "Yes, yes, Darryl, let's buy one for you." As they turned in the direction of the candy machine, he tugged harder at her arm. She looked down at him and met eyes that were wide with excitement. He repeated even more assertively and confidently, "Buy me a Snicker, pl-eee-zzz." In a few minutes, he was happily munching on the candy bar.

Now that Darryl had used speech to communicate directly with another person, the next goal was to stimulate contact with his peers. To that end, the therapist arranged to have another child at one of the sessions each week. This sparked a relationship between Darryl and Jimmy. Darryl didn't stand alone and apart in the playground after that. He learned how to play with other children.

Juan T.: *19 years; severe mental retardation; etiologic factor: encephalopathy due to postnatal cerebral infection.*

Long-Term Goals: to improve coordination and phonation.

Modes of Therapeutic Music Activity Used: singing/chanting, instrument playing, and music-movement.

Components of Music Used: rhythm, harmony, pitch, tempo, and text of song.

Rhythm and Music Instruments Used: handbells, timpani drum, maracas, clavés, melodica, and Autoharp®.

Music Materials Used: clinical music improvisation, and "The Merry Old Land of Oz."

Nonmusic Materials Used: puppets and scarves.

Some Strategies and Techniques Used: Reflection, humming for relaxation, sequential movements (adaptation of Orff method), lining-out singing, call-and-response singing, hand-over-hand assistance, onomatopoeic and action words, and modeling of movements.

Except for a congenital twisted right foot, Juan's development was apparently normal for the first six months. At six months, a severe febrile illness diagnosed as encephalitis left him with brain damage that caused cerebral palsy of the mixed (athetoid and spastic) type, characterized by writhing movements of arms, tilted head, clonus and stretch reflex of lower extremities, and an unsteady scissor gait. He learned to walk unassisted, demonstrated good receptive language, and emitted barely audible sounds in an attempt to communicate his needs.

In the assessment process, Juan attempted to beat the timpani drum, exhibiting extreme dysrhythmic beating. He also made an attempt to sing with the therapist.

His comprehension of the words of song was indicated through gestural responses and smiles. His ability to relate to the therapist was outstanding. Because of his extreme condition, it was necessary to schedule him for individual sessions until such time as it might be possible for him to join a group.

Whether dystonia is mild or severe, cerebral palsied persons have a need to extend their muscles and to use their extremities in ways that will improve coordination. Inducement of relaxation and increase of voluntary control of movement can improve the conditions. The following music therapy techniques and activities are designed to induce relaxation and increase muscular control, motility, and coordinated movements:

- various music-movement activities in slow tempo
- humming for relaxation
- use of a variety of instruments and music-movement for gross and fine motor coordination
- singing/chanting for increase of vital capacity/breathing
- singing/chanting of rhythmic patterns
- sequential movements to music that assist voluntary control of movements and body–mind integration through rhythmic recurring patterns and repetition of movements
- use of simple wind instruments such as the flutophone, melodica, and kazoo for breath control

Treatment of cerebral palsied persons requires skilled and careful handling starting with symmetrical positioning that facilitates relaxation and slow-paced activities. For example, when offering a rhythm instrument to a right-handed person, approach the person directly in front and just to the left of the midline (to the right of the left-handed person). In this way, it is unnecessary for the person to turn his or her head—an action that would cause extension and involuntary movements. Also, each motor response should be patterned before introducing musical materials such as instruments or nonmusical materials such as hoops, balls, puppets, and scarves. Singing/chanting, playing/manipulating rhythm instruments, and music-movement must be *layered* gradually to avoid sensory overload. Each additional segment of an activity is introduced only when a previous one has been fully assimilated. Whenever possible, the music therapist should work in consultation with a physical therapist.

Juan received half-hour individual sessions three times a week. To improve Juan's coordination, general body functioning, and phonation, music therapy experiences were centered on developing a kinesthetic sense of movement in response to musical stimuli, with motoric activity and sound production reinforcing each other. Sessions began with Juan closing his eyes and taking a deep breath, after which he and the therapist would make humming sounds together on ascending and descending thirds. Done repeatedly at all sessions, control of the intake and expulsion of air became stronger, his breathing more regulated. The humming had three effects: it helped him to relax, increased his ability to produce sound, and improved the quality of his voice.

The first month of sessions was devoted to gross motor movements of the arms and hands, at first with hand-over-hand assistance and then imitatively while supported by singing/chanting of onomatopoeic action words in the pulsation of four beats (1-2-3-4):

> Clap, clap, clap, clap (with hands toward therapist's hands).
> Clap, clap, clap, clap (with hands together).
> Push, push, push, push (while pushing against the therapist).
> Push, push, push, push (while pushing against the therapist with alternate arms).
> Tap, tap, tap, tap (with alternate hands on knees).
> Swing, swing, swing, swing (while swinging arms with therapist).

As Juan gained voluntary control of these movements and the sounds he emitted increased in volume, leg and foot movements were added (in sitting position):

> Stamp, stamp, stamp, stamp (while alternating feet slowly).
> Kick, kick, kick, kick (while alternating legs slowly).

Strong full chords were played on the piano to stimulate these movements and give him constant, supportive matching at his pace. Gradually his movements became smoother and more coordinated. He was beginning to be eager to move around the room.

At the end of the second month of therapy, the movements were done in a standing position with the therapist ready to assist him whenever he wavered. Juan's enthusiasm and desire to improve became stronger with each feeling, *emotionally* and *physically*, of success. The new sensations he was experiencing gave him an awareness of the progress he was making. This awareness was expanded by the therapist's words of encouragement and acknowledgment.

The movements described above were in preparation for music-movement that was to be combined with singing the words of the song, "The Merry Old Land of Oz" (Harburg & Arlen, 1966), with which Juan had become familiar (see Figure 6–7). Preplanned sequential movements were designed to increase his ability to move with more fluidity. These movements, set to the rhythmic patterns of the words of the song, were done simultaneously with rhythmic chanting of the words. The security that Juan derived from the repetition of movements that he could anticipate had very definite results. (This adaptation of the Orff method of music education can be used with different songs and different sequences of movements devised by the therapist and client or both.) The process started with the therapist sitting opposite Juan, knees touching, using hand-over-hand assistance. He

Figure 6–7 The Merry Old Land of Oz

Music by **HAROLD ARLEN**
Words by **E.Y. HARBURG**

watched the therapist's mouth and movements closely, mouthing the words that were sung in a slow, exaggerated manner and imitating the movements (with assistance when needed):

> Ha - ha - ha! Ho - ho - ho!
> And a couple of tra - la - las,
> That's how we laugh the day away,
> In the Merry Old Land of Oz.

Each line was repeated slowly, with accompanying gross motor movements: clapping hands to Juan's left on the phrase "Ha-ha-ha!" and clapping hands to Juan's right on the phrase "Ho-ho-ho!" The process was slow yet gratifying and enjoyable as he succeeded in imitating the movements. His chanting became more rhythmic and audible upon each repetition of the four-beat pulsation of the music. He would chant only single words that he was able to produce with some ease and that were key words in the rhythmic patterns (e.g., *ha, ho, tra, la, away,* and *Oz*).

Juan's stamina and determination were remarkable. The music visibly aroused and motivated him. He never tired of repetition, for with each repetition he gained more control of his movements and phonation. At times, in his enthusiasm, he rushed to get to the next part of the song and would lose momentary control. The therapist would adjust the activity, wait, slow down, and sometimes stop completely to give him time to rest and restore his equilibrium. When this happened, Juan would smile broadly at the therapist, and she would return the smile with unspoken understanding.

He was making such excellent progress that there came a time when he transcended his condition: Momentary lessening of the motoric disfluency caused by his pathology occurred when he executed all the movements in succession without a break in sequence. *The effect on his self-image was enormous.*

Juan missed sessions for a period of two months because of an operation to correct his twisted foot. When he returned to therapy, his improved ambulation made it possible to increase work on locomotor skills and movement in space.

Simultaneous with the work on gross motor skills, fine motor skills were developing. The use of drum mallets, handbells, maracas, and clavés resulted in an improved ability to manipulate objects with pincer grasp. Blowing through the mouthpiece of a melodica while fingering the keys both increased his breathing capacity and breath control and his fine motor skills.

Maintenance of motoric gains was an ongoing process that required constant renewal. As his phonation improved, attempts at verbalization pointed the way to the next developmental step that Juan could conceivably attain—namely, the ability to use words functionally.

In the months that followed, Juan did attain some speech skills through chanting and the use of melodic patterns of ascending and descending musical intervals of thirds and fifths, a broad application of a technique called melodic intonation, which is the use of melody, rhythm, musical intervals, and tonal patterns that are imitated by the client (Rogers & Fleming, 1981; Sparks & Helm, 1973). By the end of the year, he was speaking in three-word sentences. Although it was sometimes difficult to understand, his speech was becoming more intelligible. Juan was determined to improve.

Florence D.: *27 years; moderate mental retardation; etiologic factor: encephalopathy associated with maternal toxemia of pregnancy.*

Long-Term Goals: To improve articulation and quality of voice and to stabilize affective state.

Modes of Therapeutic Music Activity Used: singing/chanting; rhythm instrument playing.

Components of Music Used: rhythm, melody, harmony, tempo, pitch, dynamics, and text of song.

Rhythm and Musical Instruments Used: piano (therapist and client).

Music Materials Used: clinical music improvisation, and "Sometimes I Feel Like a Motherless Child."

Nonmusic Materials Used: none.

Some Strategies and Techniques Used: Reflection, lining-out singing, vocal and verbal prompts, and pacing and tempo adjustment.

Florence is hemiplegic. Her posture exhibits partial range against gravity, and in recent years her gait has deteriorated, necessitating the wearing of a brace on her left leg. During music therapy assessment she was extremely responsive to musical stimuli although unable to match physically what she perceived and comprehended. Her speech was most in need of immediate remediation. The distinctive features of her speech are phonatory and articulatory in nature: Her voice is low pitched, harsh, and nasal in quality, with marked loudness and frequent breakup of words, sometimes punctuated by gasps.

Florence was scheduled for one individual half-hour session a week and one half-hour group therapy session a week.

In working with a verbal yet speech-handicapped person, the relationship between speech and music can be the pathway to enhancing the quality and fluidity of verbal expression. Speech and music have structural and expressive elements in common: rhythmic patterns, tempo and pacing, stress/accent, pitch and changes in pitch, dynamics/volume, intonation/inflection, phrasing, and prosody and cadence. And the emotional content of a song that has special meaning for a person is a source of release for pent-up feelings.

Florence came to many a session crying. She might have been home for the weekend and become upset about the separation from her family or she might have had an unpleasant incident with another resident. Emotionally labile, she expressed her feelings freely and openly.

Early in Florence's therapy, it became obvious that her swings of mood could be stabilized through singing. It was a source of immense release for her. Sad, happy, coy, self-assertive, flirtatious, Florence presented a complex mixture of moods and emotions. And she let it be known, verbally and nonverbally, what her emotional needs of the moment were. In her belabored speech she would often start a session with an announcement of what she wanted, how she felt, who had been annoying her. A conversation would go like this:

Florence: I feel very sad today (head bowed and tears streaming down her cheeks). I'm very sad.
Therapist: Yes, Florence, I see that you're feeling sad. I see that you're crying.
Florence: I was home for the weekend. I was with my father and my mother and my uncle.
Therapist: Florence, would you like to sing your favorite song?
Florence: Yes, I'd like to sing my favorite song. Play it for me. You sing it too.

With tears gushing out more profusely than ever, she sang "Sometimes I Feel Like a Motherless Child" (Johnson, 1940) in unsteady tones and slurred words:

> Sometimes I feel like a motherless child,
> Sometimes I feel like a motherless child,
> Sometimes I feel like a motherless child,
> A long way-ay from hoooo-mmmmmme,
> A long way-ay from hoome.

With each repetition, her articulation became clearer. And so the therapist and Florence sang together, the minor chords and slow pacing matching Florence's sadness and belabored speech. Over and over they would sing. At times the tempo was slowed down even more to give Florence the leeway she needed to enunciate the words clearly; at times the dynamics were changed from soft to loud, from loud to soft—sometimes in sharp contrasts, sometimes gradually—to stimulate tonal variety. When Florence felt that she had "sung herself out," she stopped, her face now transformed by a broad smile, the tears gone. Her head, which had been bowed sorrowfully, would be lifted toward the ceiling. With a deep sigh of relief she would declare: "Wheeeeeee! I feel better. Got that off my chest!"

At the session during which Florence asked to "play" the song on the piano, she used her right hand to depress clusters of keys in a rhythmic pattern that followed the words of the song. The therapist played the song, converting the combined effort into a duet. Florence was thrilled. Then Florence asked the therapist to lift her left hand to the keyboard. She wanted to use both hands. With valiant determination, she moved her left hand and produced a feeble but undeniable sound. Now her joy was boundless. She insisted on going back to her apartment to tell everyone about this new accomplishment. The therapist was overjoyed too. So they did just that. They walked through the corridors, Florence holding onto the therapist's arm but walking as upright as she possibly could as she called out in clarion tones:

> I played the piano—both hands. BOTH HANDS!
> If you don't believe me, ask her . . .

Donald L.: *24 years; mild mental retardation; etiologic factor: microcephaly.*

Long-Term Goals: to increase impulse control and awareness of self in relation to others.

Modes of Therapeutic Music Activity Used: singing and instrument playing (guitar).

Components of Music Used: rhythm, melody, harmony, and text of song.

Rhythm and Musical Instruments Used: guitar (by client) and piano (by therapist).

Music Materials Used: ''Donald's Blues'' (composed by client and therapist).
Nonmusic Materials Used: none.
Some Strategies and Techniques Used: manual signing for *start, stop, wait*,
call-and-response singing, and use of tape recorder as a therapeutic tool.

Having been institutionalized since the age of 4, there are wide discrepancies in
Donald's development and functional skills. He prints and draws in an infantile
fashion and knows the concept of money but not its relative value. Though he has
well-developed speech skills, his ideation is often distorted or confused. Yet, despite the years of psychosocial deprivation, Donald's creative energy and imagination pushed through, seeking expression. Because the proper outlets were not
always available, this expression often went awry.

During music therapy assessment, his musical abilities were found to be
outstanding. He sang entire songs on pitch and played rhythm instruments appropriately and in ways that related to the musical stimuli, beating the drums in
complete synchrony with the music. His gross and fine motor skills and dance
movements were excellent. It was in the area of adaptive behavior that he
displayed marked deficits in impulse control and age-appropriate social skills.

In addition to group music therapy sessions, which were scheduled for one-half
hour twice a week, Donald spent some of his leisure time in the music therapy
room following his workshop program. He would ask to come in and play records
or amuse himself by singing and strumming on the guitar (he had learned to play
two chords in a simplified form). The music therapy room had become his haven—
the place where he could give positive expression to his active imagination. The
therapist made the room available to him as often as possible.

One day as he sat and strummed the guitar, he became impatient and wanted
attention. The therapist was writing reports and asked him to wait five minutes,
showing him where the big hand on the clock would be at that time. He reluctantly
agreed to wait. However, in keeping with the goal to help him gain impulse
control, the therapist quickly added:

> Therapist: How about making up a song of your own?
> Donald: About what?
> Therapist: What about something you've done or some place you've gone to.
> Donald: I can't think of anything.
> Therapist: All right, Donald. I'll be with you in five minutes. Be sure to watch the clock.

Much of our work in group music therapy sessions and in these informal
encounters had been centered on increasing awareness of others and decreasing his
need for instant gratification. Because of the years of deprivation, this need was
deeply ingrained. Therefore, we dealt with behavior problems not only through
the music therapy process but we also talked about them often. Donald had, in
fact, been involved in setting his own goals and was actively participating in

bringing about changes in his own behavior. We discussed his need to control his impulsive behavior, which had gotten him in trouble on many occasions. And he asked for help in learning how to be more considerate of others, how to cooperate with others. This was fertile ground for music therapy.

When the therapist finished the report (within the allotted time!), she crossed the room to join Donald where he sat looking at the clock:

> Therapist: Any ideas?
> Donald: Nope.
> Therapist: Well, let's try to come up with something.
> Donald: Yeh, let's.
> Therapist: Remember the last time we went to José's restaurant?
> Donald: Yeh, I really love to go there. Every time we go, you teach me to read the sandwiches and everything.
> Therapist: Donald, what happened the other day when we got back? What *usually* happens when we walk together?

Donald pursed his lips, rolled his eyes upward, and thought and thought, placing his hands on his forehead (a characteristic avoidance gesture he assumed whenever he felt that he was being "put on the spot"):

> Donald: I name all the cars on the street. I know the names of all the cars.
> Therapist: Donald, I know that and I think it's great. But I was talking about something else. I think you know what I mean.
> Donald: Oh, you mean when I ran ahead of you and slammed the door in your face?
> Therapist: Hmm. Do you think we could sing about that?

After tuning the guitar so that all the strings formed an E major chord, the therapist sat down at the piano and started to play an E_7 chord in the blues idiom. Then Donald was to change to an A chord when the therapist played an A_7 chord. This would be the harmonic structure for the "Donald's Blues" song they composed together (see Figure 6–8).

Donald learned a powerful lesson from this song. He sang it many times, recorded it on a tape recorder, performed it for the staff and his group. Most important, it was the catalyst for a different behavior pattern. Not only did he become aware of and sensitive to others (in the group therapy setting and in general), but he was making headway in his ability to control his impulsive behavior.

It was a banner day, indeed, when his social worker reported that Donald would be considered for placement in a group home if his behavioral problems continued to diminish.

Donald's social skills improved over the next six months to the degree that he was accepted in a group home where he was able to lead a more self-reliant, independent life.

Figure 6–8 Donald's Blues

Words and Music by
DONALD L. and
EDITH HILLMAN BOXILL

2. I love the taste of those English muffins,
   Yes, I love the taste of those English muffins,
   Mmm, I love the taste of those English muffins,
   They're so delicious with hot choc'late.

3. When we got back from José's restaurant,
   Yes, when we got back from José's restaurant,
   When we got back from José's restaurant,
   I ran ahead and slammed the door in Edi's face.

4. And what do you think Edi said?
   Yes, what do you think Edi said?
   Mmm, what do you think Edi said?
   She said, "Donald, let's sit down and talk it over."

5. So we sat down and we talked it over,
   Yes, we sat down and we talked it over,
   Mm, we sat down and we talked it over,
   And now I won't do it NO MORE!

Angela N.: *26 years; moderate to severe mental retardation; etiologic factor: encephalopathy due to asphyxia at birth.*

Long-Term Goals: to regain functional use of left hand and ability to verbalize.

Modes of Therapeutic Music Activity Used: singing and instrument playing.

Components of Music Used: rhythm, melody, pitch, dynamics, and text of song.

Rhythm and Musical Instruments Used: Autoharp® (by client and therapist), guitar (by client and therapist), and shaker.

Music Materials Used: clinical music improvisation and "Sing."

Nonmusic Materials Used: rubber ball (with physical therapist).

Some Strategies and Techniques Used: hand-over-hand assistance, melodic intonation, call-and-response singing, and use of specific rhythm and musical instruments for specific therapeutic purposes.

When Angela first came to the institution, she was mildly hemiplegic with good function of her right hand. She walked independently with a slow, sluggish gait, spoke fairly intelligibly (often mixed with jargon), and interacted well with both peers and staff. She had a history of grand mal seizures. Several months after admission, she suffered a stroke that resulted in the loss of ambulation, severe loss of the use of her left hand and arm, and almost total loss of speech. Confined to a wheelchair, her body became slouched and inert, her head bowed in depression. Before this drastic change, she had been actively involved in a music therapy group. With great enthusiasm she would strum the Autoharp® rhythmically and quite firmly with her left hand while the therapist pressed down the chord bars. She would sing isolated words and some word phrases with relish and gusto. When she sang and played her favorite song, "Sing" (Raposo & Moss, 1971), her own delight and that of the therapy aides (who rarely saw her so energized and active), brought a most welcome liveliness to sessions.

Now, individual sessions were necessary. Intensive rehabilitative work was to be done on a daily basis. At first the therapist and a speech therapist worked alone, later to be joined by a physical therapist using a hands-on transdisciplinary approach. Angela had (in the physical therapist's words) been balking at doing exercises and had been resisting all attempts to work with her. Witnessing Angela's responses to music and her efforts to regain the ability to strum the Autoharp® and the guitar, the physical therapist was eager to formulate a treatment plan with the music therapist to rehabilitate the functional use of Angela's left hand, using music as the motivating force. In the main, the two instruments—Autoharp® and guitar—were used because they were both suitable for the specific problem and were Angela's preferred instruments. A cylindrical shaker, which was rolled back and forth on her wheelchair tray, was also used.

Because there was a possibility that Angela could regain use of her left hand (residual sensation existed after the stroke) and because she enjoyed the feeling of vibrating strings as she strummed the Autoharp® or guitar, she was assisted and encouraged to strum with her bare fingers rather than with an adapted pick attached to her hand. While she strummed, she would attempt to vocalize and form the syllables *la-la* and *da-da* in the rhythmic pattern of the melody sung by the music therapist. Whereas she had formerly approximated the tonality of a song, she now could only voice a monotonal sound. Yet even this uplifted her spirits *and* her body. She would sit up, raise her head, and make a valiant effort to sing and use the instruments as she had in the past. Movement of her arm and legs, in time with the music, was carefully guided by the physical therapist who knew that, despite Angela's limitations, if motivated by the music, she could participate in her own rehabilitation. Hand-over-hand techniques were used to activate her left hand and arm. As she regained some muscle strength and more sensation in her fingers, hand-over-hand assistance was gradually phased out. Her strumming and picking at the strings of the guitar became stronger. And as she heard more sound emanating from the instruments, she gained in confidence and well-being.

By means of a technique that both music therapists and speech therapists use to facilitate the return of speech in neurologically impaired/stroke clients, the music therapist, together with the speech therapist, applied melodic intonation. (See description of "Juan" earlier in this chapter, for explanation of *melodic intonation*.) Some speech began to return. These transdisciplinary sessions, both with the physical therapist and the speech therapist, were conducted on a daily basis, with a music therapy intern taking over some of the sessions. Over a period of five months, Angela made progress in the functional use of her left hand. She was able to grasp, hold, and lift a spoon to her mouth. Her verbalizations and gestural communication became more frequent. Three months later she was transferred to a group home for multiply handicapped people. In order to maintain and further the rehabilitative program, arrangements were made to continue the same kind of transdisciplinary work.

CONCLUSION

Perhaps to the procedurally oriented observer, moments or segments of sessions may appear to be unstructured or accidental because of the nature of the human interaction that takes place between client and therapist in humanistically oriented therapy. Apropos of this, the word *appear* is key. What may not always be obvious is that virtually everything the skilled therapist does is therapeutically purposeful, engaging clients in active participation in their own growth.

REFERENCES

Agay, D. (Compiler). *Best loved songs of American people*. New York: Doubleday, 1975.

Boxill, E.H. *Music adapted, composed, and improvised for music therapy with the developmentally handicapped*. New York: Folkways Records, 1976. (Record FX 6180, booklet included)

Ginglend, D.R., & Stiles, W.E. (Compilers). *Music activities for retarded children*. New York: Abingdon Press, 1965.

Harburg, E.Y., & Arlen, H. *Vocal selections: The Wizard of Oz*. New York: Leo Feist, 1966.

Johnson, W.J. (Ed.). *The book of American Negro spirituals*. New York: Viking Press, 1940.

"Kum ba ya" (H. Dexter, arranger). Torrance, Calif.: California Music Press, 1971. (Sheet music)

Langstaff, N., & Langstaff, J. (Compilers). *Jim along, Josie*. New York: Harcourt Brace Jovanovich, 1970.

Raposo, J., & Moss, J. *The Sesame Street song book*. New York: Simon & Schuster, 1971.

Rogers, A., & Fleming, P.L. Speech therapy for the neurologically impaired. *Music Therapy*, 1981, *1*(1), 33–38.

Sparks, A.M., & Helm, N. Melodic intonation therapy for aphasia. *Archives of Neurology*, 1973, *29*, 130–131.

"When the saints go marching in." *50 fabulous favorites*. New York: Cromwell Music, 1962.

Wing, L. *Autistic children*. Secaucus, N.J.: The Citadel Press, 1974.

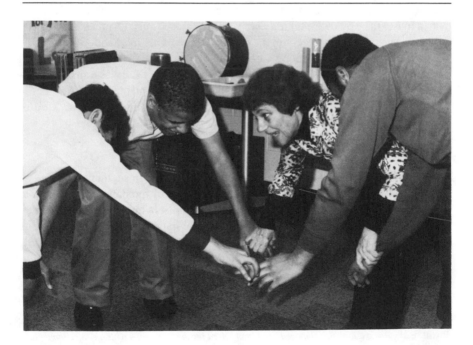

Chapter 7

Resource Materials

The best effect of any book is that it excites the reader to self-activity.

Thomas Carlyle

INTRODUCTION

Practicing music therapists must constantly seek out and test suitable music materials to meet the needs of their clients and keep their own creative juices flowing. Students training for a career in the field must begin early to accumulate a large and varied repertoire of music materials in order to enrich the therapeutic process. The resource materials assembled in this chapter, consisting of designs for therapeutic music activities, music books (see Appendix 7–A), and a discography (see Appendix 7–B), are intended not only to assist in this work but also to offer guidance for the selection of other materials that may be utilized in inventive ways to answer the special needs and problems as well as interests of this population.

DESIGNS FOR THERAPEUTIC MUSIC ACTIVITIES

The music therapy process involves creative therapeutic shaping and molding of music—whether composed, improvised, or adapted—not merely singing and playing songs and instrumental music as entertainment or for a diversionary activity. Designs for therapeutic music activities provide flow and pace to the therapy session. The designs offered in this chapter are but a few of many that have proved effective for this client population. They may be used as presented here, adapted, or be catalysts for the design of other activities. All are suitable for either individual or group therapy.

Each activity is built around a particular song or instrumental composition selected for its age-appropriateness and potential for achieving specified goals and objectives. Some use a single mode of therapeutic music activity, others combine two or all three modes. However, no matter which mode is the basis for the original conception of the design, other modes can grow organically out of the activity. These therapeutic music activities consist of the music, the functioning and age levels for which the activity is considered most appropriate, possible goals, suggested uses of the components of the music, and suggested design.

Design 1

Music

"Little Betty Martin"*—traditional (adaptation); key of G; time signature 4/4.

B   GG   ED   ED   ED
Verse A: Come, Betty Martin, tiptoe tiptoe,

B   GG   ED   BG   A
Come, Betty Martin, tiptoe fine,

B   GG   ED   ED   ED
Come, Betty Martin, tiptoe tiptoe,

B   GG   ED   EF♯ G
Come, Betty Martin, tiptoe fine.

F♯   E   D   G   A   B
Verse B: Swing your arms, swing your arms,

A   F♯   E   D   B   G   D
Swing and swing and swing your arms,

F♯   E   D   G   A   B
Swing your arms, swing your arms,

E   E   F♯ G   A   D   D
Swing and swing and swing your arms.

(*Return to Verse A*)

Functioning and Age Levels

- moderate and high functioning children
- low and moderate functioning adolescents and adults

Possible Goals

- to increase gross motor skills
- to increase locomotor skills/mobility
- to develop body awareness

---

*Langstaff, N., & Langstaff, J. (Compilers). *Jim along, Josie*. New York: Harcourt Brace Jovanovich, 1970.

- to improve comprehension
- to improve memory/recall/retention
- to improve and stimulate speech
- to increase interpersonal awareness and socialization

Suggested Uses of Components of Music

- tempo for changes of movements and improvement of mobility
- dynamics for changes in quality of movements (e.g., tiptoeing softly, stamping feet vigorously)
- text of song for improving comprehension, memory, and awareness of body parts

Suggested Design of Activity

The foundation of this music-movement activity is the circle. As is known in African cultures as well as those of American Indians, the circle is a cohesive force that transmits energy from one person to the other. There are many songs that may be used for this kind of activity. The overall structure of this song—rondo form ABACADA, etc.—lends itself to use as a circle action song. Verse A is returned to after each intervening verse in which diverse body movements (locomotor and nonlocomotor), initiated either by the therapist or the clients, are executed or worked on. Dynamic, tempo, and rhythmic changes add to the enriching experience. Percussive body sounds and vocal sounds can also be used as integral parts of particular movements or sequences of movements. Furthermore, the structure of the music can be used to stimulate memory through anticipation of the return to Verse A.

For lower-functioning clients, the actual forming of the circle—the act of holding hands in an unbroken circular chain—often poses difficulties. Some clients do not understand how to hold hands; some hold hands for an instant and then let go; some have physical disabilities that make grasping difficult or impossible (in the latter instance the therapist or assistant should hold the person's hand or wrist); some are tactile-defensive (this condition may necessitate individualized work in order to enable the person to join in group activities of this nature); and some are resistive for emotional reasons. It is, therefore, necessary that there be several assistants for this process. Once the circle is formed, the movement activity should begin. Although there may be many stops, starts, and reforming of the circle, the mobilization of the group to maintain the circle becomes an integral part of the process. The therapist and assistants will need to give gestural prompts as well as verbal prompts over and over: "Let's hold hands," "We're making a circle," "(Client), hold (client's) hand," "Yes, now we're all holding hands." The rondo structure of this song is as follows:

- The therapist and clients form a circle, singing Verse A. (The therapist may substitute the name of a client for "Betty Martin" at each return to Verse A.)
- The therapist and clients sing Verse B with appropriate actions.
- After each return to Verse A, the therapist and clients suggest actions for Verses C, D, E, F, etc., executing appropriate actions such as turning around, jumping, hopping, bending knees, dancing, etc., improvising words to suit the actions and rhythm of the music.
- The therapist and clients return to Verse A after each new verse is added.
- As the structure of the rondo form indicates, the activity ends with Verse A.

Design 2

Music

"He's Got the Whole World in His Hands"*—Gospel song; key of B♭; time signature 4/4.

F   F   F   F   D͡ B♭ F G   F

Verse: He's got the whole world in his *hands,*

F   F   F   E♭   C͡ A F G   F

He's got the whole world in his *hands,*

F   F   F   F   D͡ B♭ F G   F

He's got the whole world in his *hands,*

F   F   F   F   F E♭ C B♭

He's got the whole world in his *hands.* . . .

Verse: He's got you and me brother in his *hands.* . . .

Verse: He's got you and me sister in his *hands.* . . .

Verse: He's got the little bitty baby in his *hands.* . . .

Functioning and Age Levels

- all functioning levels and all ages

Possible Goals

- to heighten awareness of self and others
- to stimulate and improve speech/verbalization
- to improve fine and gross motor skills

---

*Ginglend, D.R., & Stiles, W.E. (Compilers). *Music activities for retarded children*. New York: Abingdon Press, 1965.

- to improve comprehension/memory
- to reduce stereotypic behaviors (hand movements)
- to improve interaction/interpersonal relations/socialization

Suggested Uses of Components of Music

- rhythm for unifying the group
- melody for sensory stimulation by means of a pleasurable musical experience of singing a familiar song
- harmony for a full textured accompaniment in gospel style
- tempo for changes in the quality of the music as the text of the song changes
- dynamics for changes of mood and quality
- text of song for comprehension, speech, and pantomiming of words

Suggested Design of Activity

Because awareness of and the ability to use the hands and fingers are critical to overall development, much emphasis is placed on developing, improving, and increasing the functions of the hands through therapeutic music activities. From strengthening grasp by manipulating rhythm instruments to playing an instrument appropriately, opportunities to develop the use of the hands are many and varied. Therefore, songs that concentrate on the hands are a valuable and necessary part of a music therapist's repertoire. This is one of many versatile songs that lends itself to broad application not only within the therapy setting itself but also as preparation for group singing at special events (social evenings, Home Talent Nite, etc.). The activity might take the following form:

- The therapist sings and plays the song in its entirety in a slow tempo to convey the gospel quality of the music and to provide the opportunity for the clients to sing as many words as they are able to sing. The clients are directed to clap their hands while singing.
- As the song is repeated, the therapist emphasizes the word *hands* each time it appears in the text.
- The therapist holds up his or her hands each time the word *hands* is sung, interjecting, "Let me see your *hands*."
- The therapist repeats this until all persons in the group hold up their hands.
- The therapist encourages verbal clients to sing the word, or an approximation of the word (lining-out singing), at the end of each line.
- The therapist encourages nonverbal clients to utter some form of vocalization along with the movement of holding up hands.

- The therapist makes changes in tempo and dynamics to convey the quality of the music as the text of song is changed, for example, singing "He's got the little bitty baby in his hands," as a lullaby.
- The therapist uses the text of song for comprehension by pantomiming "you and me" (pointing to clients and self) and "little bitty baby" (modeling the cradling of a puppet or an imaginary baby in arms).
- To vary the activity and increase the repertoire of hand movements and decrease stereotypic hand movements, the therapist either makes or asks for suggestions for different ways of moving or using the hands (e.g., shaking them, opening and shutting them, clapping them with another client).
- The therapist adds verses such as "He's got (client) in his hands."
- The therapist brings singing of song to finale with sweeping movements of the arms on phrase "He's got everybody in his *hands*."

Rhythm instruments can be played to the phrases, "We're playing (instrument) with our hands," or "I'm playing (instrument) with my hands," or "(Client) is playing (instrument) with his/her hands." This not only emphasizes the significance and importance of the hands, it also raises awareness of experiencing their function.

Music-movement can also grow organically out of either of the above activities. The clients would move out into the room, form a circle or semicircle, hold hands, and move their feet in a left-to-right, right-to-left gospel-style foot movement while singing, lifting hands individually or together with the person on either side upon the word *hands*. This activity aids speech, vocalization, memory, gross motor skills, and interaction/socialization.

Design 3

Music

"Pat-A-Pan"*—traditional French carol; key of G-minor; time signature 4/4.

> G   G   D   D C   D   B♭
> Now we'll play upon the   *drum,*
>
> A   B♭   C   A   B♭ B♭   A
> And we'll make our voices *hum,*
>
> A   B♭ A F♯ G   A   B♭
> We'll be joyous as we *play,*
>
> G   A B♭ C   D   C D C B♭ A
> *Pat-a- pat-a- pan, pat-a- pat-a- pan,*

---

*Boni, M.B. (Ed.), *Fireside book of folk songs.* New York: Simon & Schuster, 1947.

A B♭ A F♯ G A B♭
We'll be joyous as we *play*,

A B♭ C A   D A   G
On a merry Christmas *Day*.

Functioning and Age Levels

- moderate and high functioning adolescents and adults

Possible Goals

- to stimulate verbalization/speech
- to increase attending behavior
- to improve auditory perception

Suggested Uses of Components of Music

- tempo (slow) for speech articulation and inflection
- text of song for speech and auditory perception
- pitch for intonation and tonality

Suggested Design of Activity

This design illustrates the many inventive ways the therapist extracts and adapts structural elements of a particular song in order to work on objectives and goals. The song used is one of many songs that is sung for the sheer enjoyment of singing, giving a sense of accomplishment when the rhyming words are sung "correctly," with closer approximations upon each repetition. When supported by singing and lively piano, guitar, Autoharp®, or Casiotone® playing by the therapist or clients, a rhythm instrument arrangement can add to the motivation to learn and improve auditory perception further by accenting rhyming words on the instruments (as directed and modeled by the therapist).

- The therapist plays and sings the song in its entirety in a slow tempo, emphasizing the words that rhyme. The group (or individual) is directed to clap hands in a steady beat to the music.
- The therapist encourages and assists clients to sing the words that rhyme.
- At each word that rhymes, the clients clap their hands to the right and left or up and down or snap their fingers (for fine motor skills and motoric activation that reinforces verbal learning while increasing auditory perception).
- The clients swing their arms from side to side, as modeled by the therapist, matching the rhythmic flow of the music.

- The clients sing song phrases, as modeled by the therapist, matching the rhythmic flow of the words.
- The clients raise and lower their arms, singing melodic line and stressing the inflections of the words, as modeled by the therapist.
- Using lining-out technique for singing or chanting the last word of song phrases, the therapist and clients mouth words in exaggerated manner (the degree of exaggeration depends on the individual's speech development).
- The therapist and clients repeat song phrases in different tempi and on different dynamic levels.
- The therapist and clients clap melodic rhythmic patterns or play them on drums or other percussive instruments.
- The clients are directed to take turns and exchange instruments. Each one may be asked to lead the group (particularly if the person's speech is fairly clear). Every client is given the opportunity to take leadership (with the assistance of an intern or therapy aide or the therapist when needed).

Design 4

Music

"Shoo Fly"*—traditional; key of C; time signature 4/4.

                    E   C   D   EF D
    Phrase 1: Shoo fly don't bother *me,*

                    D   B   C   DE C
    Phrase 2: Shoo fly don't bother *me,*

                    E   C   D   EF D
    Phrase 3: Shoo fly don't bother *me,*

                    D   G GG F E D C
    Phrase 4: 'Cause *I* belong to somebody.

                    E E E E E
    Phrase 5: I do, I do, I do,

                    E E EE F E D
    Phrase 6: I'm not gonna tell you who

                    D DD D   D DD
    Phrase 7: *I* belong to somebody,

                    G   GF D C
    Phrase 8: Yes! indeed I do.

---

*Boxill, E.H. *Music adapted, composed, and improvised for music therapy with the developmentally handicapped.* New York: Folkways Records, 1976. (Record FX 6180, booklet included)

Functioning and Age Levels

- moderate and high-functioning children
- low to high-functioning adolescents and adults

Possible Goals

- to improve fine and gross motor skills
- to improve coordination, locomotor, and nonlocomotor skills
- to improve memory, including kinesthetic memory
- to improve speech (inflection and intonation), sound production, and gestural communication
- to increase awareness of self and others

Suggested Uses of Components of Music

- pitch for inflection and intonation
- tempo for reflecting/matching an individual's pace
- text of song for speech stimulation

Suggested Design of Activity

The overall structure of the song form lends itself to an Orff-like sequential set of movements and the onomatopoeic quality of words such as *shoo* gives impetus to sound and speech production. For improving coordination, both fine and gross motor movements, such as opening/closing fingers and moving them independently (fine motor) and raising arms and stamping feet (gross motor), are among the many possible body movements. Movements are simplified or made more complex in accordance with the functioning and age levels of the clients as well as the individual's physical condition. High-functioning clients are encouraged to work out their own sequence of movements with the assistance and support of the therapist. Because individual paces and disabilities vary, there must be a great deal of leeway in the process, that is, starting, stopping, repeating small sections, working on movements, waiting for assimilation, etc. Executing the movements sequentially may take a long period of time (many sessions). As the process evolves, however, the small objectives subsumed in the goals are cumulative, and the anticipation of movement from one action to another can have a stabilizing and integrating effect on the mind and body.

Singing/chanting and movement can be done in a humorous, joyous spirit. A sense of fun can be conveyed whether or not the words are comprehended. Funny movements can add to the playful mood of the song making the task enjoyable rather than a chore. The sequence consists of one movement for each song/word phrase, as directed or modeled by the therapist:

1. The clients sit or stand in semicircle opposite the therapist.
2. The clients and the therapist sing or chant the words of the song while executing the movements.
   - On the first phrase, the therapist and the clients rhythmically clap their hands to the right.
   - On the second phrase, the therapist and the clients rhythmically clap their hands to the left.
   - On the third phrase, the therapist and the clients rhythmically push their arms forward.
   - The therapist and the clients rhythmically point with their index fingers to their chests on the fourth phrase, "*I* belong to somebody."
   - The therapist and the clients slap their thighs and point to their chests on the fifth phrase, "I do, I do, I do."
   - The therapist and the clients rhythmically stamp their feet, snap their fingers, or shake their heads gesturally on the sixth phrase, indicating "I'm not gonna tell you who."
   - The therapist and the clients rhythmically point with their index fingers to their chests on the seventh phrase, "*I* belong to somebody."
   - On the eighth phrase, the therapist and the clients clap loudly on the word "Yes!" and fling their arms up into the air on "Indeed I do."

Design 5

Music

"Who Has a Nose?"*—to the tune of "Frère Jacques"; key of D; time signature 2/4.

D   E E F♯ D
Who has a nose?

D   E   E F♯ D
I   have a nose,

F♯   G   A
Who has toes?

F♯ G   A
I have toes,

_____

*Nelson, E.L. (Compiler). *Dancing games for children of all ages*. New York: Sterling Publishing Co., 1974.

$\overset{\frown}{AB}$ $\overset{\frown}{AG}$ F♯ D
Who has fingers?
$\overset{\frown}{AG}$ $\overset{\frown}{AG}$ F♯ D
I   have fingers,

D   A   D   D   A   D
Now we know, now we know.

Functioning and Age Levels

- low-functioning or multiply handicapped children and young adults

Possible Goals

- to increase body awareness
- to improve ability to manipulate objects (simple rhythm instruments)
- to improve eye–hand coordination/perceptual-motor skills
- to increase visual perception and imitative movements

Suggested Uses of Components of Music

- text of song for directing action of song and for call-and-response singing if client(s) can verbalize
- melody for its aesthetic appeal and possible familiarity and to stimulate vocalization
- harmony to supply a textured bassline accompaniment for the instrument playing in order to create a fulfilling music making experience

Suggested Design of Activity

- The therapist begins by singing/chanting the various parts of the body that will be included in the song, modeling by pointing to the nose, eyes, fingers, etc., on his or her own body and on each client's body.
- The therapist holds up a mirror in front of the client or, if the client is in a wheelchair, positions the person in front of a wall mirror or standing mirror. Visual aids such as pictures, drawings, and puppets (of human figures) are used for identifying body parts on which work is being done.
- While singing and moving from one client to the next, the therapist uses hand-over-hand assistance for those who are unable to or find it difficult to locate the body parts being sung about. Though there may not always be awareness of the words, experiencing the body kinesthetically may give a sense of self on some level and with each repetition may heighten awareness.

The therapist can also apply the same process to the use of simple rhythm instruments ("Who has a bell/drum/tambourine/maracas/rhythm sticks, etc.?"). These give immediate feedback and are the instruments most easily manipulated. When working on grasp with those who have not developed the ability to use their hands with intention or who have not developed palmar grasp, hand-over-hand assistance is used to stimulate the manipulation of the instrument and provide the opportunity to participate in a musical experience.

Design 6

Music

"Freedom Train"*—traditional; key of B♭; time signature 4/4.

```
                 F  F  DFDF   FG  D Bb
Verse 1: Oh what is it I see yonder coming?

                 F  F  DFC F  FG  D Bb
         Oh what is it I see yonder coming?

                 F  F  F GBb G  GF  D Bb
         Oh what is it I see yonder coming?

         Bb Bb  D   C C   Bb
         Git on board! Git on board!

                 F  D   FF    D  F F G D Bb
Verse 2: It's the freedom train I  see a-coming,

                 F  D   FF    C  F F G D Bb
         It's the freedom train I  see a-coming,

                 F  D   F G   Bb G G  F D Bb
         It's the freedom train I  see a-coming,

         Bb Bb  D   C C   Bb
         Git on board! Git on board!
```

Functioning and Age Levels

- high-functioning children

Possible Goals

- to increase awareness of environment/transportation
- to increase attention span

---

*Boxill, E.H. *Music adapted, composed, and improvised for music therapy with the developmentally handicapped.* New York: Folkways Records, 1976. (Record FX 6180, booklet included)

- to increase impulse control
- to stimulate sound production/phonation/speech (depending on functioning level and disability)
- to improve auditory perception and discrimination
- to improve perceptual-motor skills
- to improve comprehension
- to promote group unity

Suggested Uses of Components of Music

- tempo for stimulation of auditory perception, perceptual-motor skills, music-movement, and dramatization
- text of song for stimulation of vocalization/speech, comprehension, and dramatization
- dynamics for auditory perception, perceptual-motor skills
- timbre for auditory discrimination

Suggested Design of Activity

- The clients begin by emitting the train whistle sound "toot, toot," while the therapist or a client blows a train whistle or the therapist plays train whistle sounds on the piano, demonstrating the vocal sound of a whistle at the same time. (It may take repeated modeling and exaggerated mouthing on the part of the therapist to assist each one to produce the sound. Cupping hands around the mouth may aid vocalization.)
- The therapist creates a playful atmosphere and a sense of fun while calling out "All aboard! All aboard!" (verbal clients are directed to join in) and "Now get ready to start."
- The therapist begins playing the train music with a steady *ostinato* figure in the bass (alternating open fifth and perfect sixth chords repeated) to give the effect of chugging. The clients are directed to either rub their hands back and forth in the rhythm of the *ostinato* or to rub sand blocks to create the "chug-chug" or "choo-choo" sound while chanting. (Because there are varying degrees of ability to relate to the rhythmic *ostinato* figure, the therapist and assistants work closely with the clients, using the strategies of Reflection and Identification and giving hand-over-hand assistance or gestural and physical prompts.)
- As the activity evolves, other instruments that simulate train sounds or that help the clients experience group music making are added: cabasa, guiro, shakers, timpani drum, hand drum, hand cymbals. The therapist says "Now

get ready to start'' and sings/chants the following improvised words that indicate the action of the train:

> The train is starting slowly, slowly,
> Now it is getting faster, faster, faster,
> Now it is getting slower, slower, slower,
> Now it is going to STOP!

- The therapist can repeat the song any number of times, augmenting or contracting the music, using the names of familiar places or station names. Possible changes might include: ''It's the soul train I see a-coming.'' ''It's the subway train I see a-coming,'' ''It's the freight train I see a-coming.'' Other more complex dramatizations can be added, for example, going under tunnels or over bridges. Changes in dynamics can be used imaginatively to give the illusion of distance and closeness, incorporating diminuendoes and crescendoes.

Design 7

Music

''Here We Are Together''—clinical improvisation; key of G ; time signature 2/4.

    B   B B   D C B   A A A C B A
    Here we are together, here we are together,

     G G G G G A   G D
    Here we are together, today.

     B B   D C B   A A   C B A
    Singing together, singing together,

     G   G G A   G D
    Singing together, today.

Functioning and Age Levels

- all functioning and age levels

Possible Goals

- to improve socialization/group cohesion
- to improve fine and gross motor skills
- to stimulate memory
- to increase awareness and use of body parts

- to stimulate speech
- to arouse and sustain attention

Suggested Uses of Components of Music

- rhythm for group cohesion
- changes in tempo for mobility and to adjust to the functioning levels of clients
- changes in dynamics for fine and gross motor skills
- text of song for cognitive skills (comprehension, memory) and speech skills

Suggested Design of Activity

- The therapist claps hands while singing the song, adjusting the tempo to the various levels of functioning of the clients and working toward synchronicity and relatedness to the steady rhythmic pulsation of the repetitive word phrases and encouraging the clients to sing and clap together.
- The therapist adds new words to the song, such as "Here we are dancing together, marching together, walking together, running together, skipping together, snapping fingers together, holding hands together," executing appropriate movements while singing. (Other movements may be added based on the verbal or gestural cues of the clients.)
- Upon repetition of "today," the therapist and clients clap their hands together on "to" and fling their arms in the air on "day." (This motoric activity stimulates speech, sound production, and memory.)
- Rhythm instruments are then added, with the therapist and clients singing, "Here we are playing (instruments) together," etc. Upon repetition of "today," instruments can be played louder for arousing and sustaining attention.

Design 8

Music

"Haitian Song of Possession"*—original instrumental composition based on Haitian folk song (see Figure 7–1); key of F-minor; time signature 2/4.

Functioning and Age Levels

- high-functioning adolescents and adults

---

*Boxill, E.H. *Music adapted, composed, and improvised for music therapy with the developmentally handicapped.* New York: Folkways Records, 1976. (Record FX 6180, booklet included)

Figure 7–1 Haitian Song of Possession

Possible Goals

- to raise energy level of individual or group
- to provide emotional release
- to stimulate auditory perception
- to stimulate creative movement
- to establish group unity and interrelatedness

Suggested Uses of Components of Music

- rhythm for group unity
- melody for providing the flavor of the music and its emotional drive
- harmony for providing full, richly textured sounds that stimulate feelings and emotions and that, in combination with the driving rhythmic pattern, evoke physical action
- dynamics for evocation of moods and feelings expressed on instruments and by bodily movement
- tempo changes to help sustain concentration and stimulate auditory perception

Suggested Design of Activity

- Each client chooses a rhythm instrument from among Latin and African percussion instruments: conga drum, bongos, maracas, clavés, cabasa, kalimba, and "talking" slit drum. A flutophone or song flute is added to simulate a piccololike wind instrument that is indigenous to Haitian music.
- The therapist plays the music on the piano in a rhythmically hypnotic accompaniment with sound effects that are evocative of the Haitian musical idiom while chanting "Erzulie! Erzulie!"
- The clients echo (call-and-response) and chant "Erzulie! Erzulie!" before beginning the instrument playing.
- The therapist continues to play while directing the musical arrangement, cuing the clients when necessary. (The rhythmic component is dominant and serves to propel the clients into a cohesive integrated whole. The driving melody adds impetus to the musical expression as it gains in momentum and power. The effect is exhilarating and the energy generated is transmitted from the therapist to client, from client to client, from client to therapist.
- With the musical support of the therapist, each client takes a turn playing freely or in the rhythmic pattern of the melody. (This provides a sense of self-esteem.)

- Upon the directive of the therapist, the entire group matches the tempo or dynamic level at which the client is playing, providing further acknowledgment of each individual.
- The therapist devises ways of making the members of the group aware of each other by saying, "Let's do it (client's) way," "Let's play softly now," "Let's play louder." (With clients who have a high level of auditory perception, the therapist uses the music directly as a stimulus to guide these changes.)
- The final cadence, with all playing together, is brought to a dramatically expressive finale.

A natural outgrowth of the use of this music is a music-movement activity such as dramatic dance movements that provide emotional release. The steps would either be demonstrated by the therapist or initiated spontaneously by the clients in response to the music. The movement may be structured as a circle dance or freewheeling.

Design 9

Music

"Thursday Night Is Disco"—original song by clients; key of F; time signature 2/2.

```
                F   F A A  F    F
        Verse:  Let's put on our best clothes,

                 F    FF F F  D F
                We're going to the disco,

                 F    F   A A A   F
                That's where everyone goes,

                 F   A F    F
                On Thursday night.

                F  C Bb  A G
        Chorus: It's disco tonight,

                 F   C Bb  A G
                It's disco tonight,

                 F   C Bb  A G
                It's disco tonight,

                 F    F
                All right!
```

Functioning and Age Levels

- high-functioning children
- moderate and high-functioning adolescents and adults

Possible Goals

- to enhance socialization
- to stimulate creativity
- to enhance self-esteem

Suggested Uses of Components of Music

- rhythm as an energizer and for evoking the spirit of the disco beat
- dynamics for promoting a variety of psychomotor responses
- harmony to create the effect of the disco idiom
- text of song for stimulating the imagination to contribute to words to the song, dramatization, and social singing

Suggested Design of Activity

The preceding song is an example of the kind of song that can be composed by the clients themselves. The therapist may offer ideas or themes stemming from subjects in which the clients have expressed interest. This particular song was composed because of the clients' interest in the monthly Disco Nite held at their institution. (High-functioning clients serve as disc jockeys at these affairs.) The process might take the following form:

- In order to start the song off, the therapist or a client might initiate the first line, either chanting or singing words and melody.
- The clients then sing/chant the words of the therapist or the client in call-and-response style.
- The therapist then encourages everyone to add a word or words or an idea, which the therapist shapes into song form.
- As the clients continue to compose the song in this manner, the therapist may wish to use a tape recorder to facilitate the process, playing the song back for the clients after each addition. (This constant playback and repetition gives the clients the opportunity to hear their voices and receive acknowledgment as they contribute to the making of the song. The words and melody can be played over and over, aiding learning of the song and promoting a sense of

pride in their accomplishment as the song evolves and becomes a complete whole.)

- In this particular song, the therapist and clients sing the song accompanied by rhythm instruments in verse-chorus form, with the group singing the words of the verse, keeping the beat while each person plays a solo (chorus) on specific instruments such as timpani drum, standing cymbal, conga drum or snare drum set when available.

- Those clients who wish may sing solos, using a microphone or simulating the use of one to add to the effect of a disco combo and solo singer.

- Clients then move into the room, with or without instruments, and dance either singly or with partners with the support of the therapist's playing and singing. This may provide an opportunity for clients to learn specific disco dance steps they can try out at an actual Disco Nite.

Design 10

Music

"Mary Wore a Red Dress"*—American folk song; key of D; time signature 2/4.

D E G A B B̂D A ÂB G ĜE
Mary wore a *red* dress, *red* dress, *red* dress,

D E G A B B̂D A A B G
Mary wore a *red* dress, all day long.

Functioning and Age Levels

- moderate and high-functioning children
- low functioning adolescents

Possible Goals

- to increase color recognition
- to heighten awareness of self
- to improve visual perception
- to learn articles of clothing

---

*Langstaff, N., & Langstaff, J. (Compilers). *Jim along, Josie*. New York: Harcourt Brace Jovanovich, 1970.

Suggested Uses of Components of Music

- text of song for comprehension

Suggested Design of Activity

This song illustrates the simplicity and repetitiveness so typical of folk songs, which make them especially suitable for working on cognitive skills (in this instance, color recognition).

- The therapist selects a client to sing about, adapting the words to the structure of the song: "(Client) is wearing a (color and article of clothing, repeated three times)," etc.
- The therapist holds up one or several flash cards, puppets, articles of clothing, or pieces of cloth that are the color being sung about while improvising a chant, "What color is this (or this, or this, or this, etc.)?"
- The therapist or client sings back, "It is (color)."
- Either therapist or client sings entire song, "(Client) is wearing a (color and article of clothing)," or "I am wearing a (color and article of clothing)," etc.
- The therapist extends this activity to include everyone in the room (interns, therapy aides, teacher, therapist, even observers) and to various objects and articles in the room, including any instruments such as red temple blocks or yellow maracas or a blue conga drum.

The therapist or the clients can make a game of this activity.

Design 11

Music

"Angel Band"*—traditional; key of F; time signature 4/4.

```
             C   D   F   C   D   F
Verse:   There was one, there were two,

             C   D   F  AA  AG
         There were three little angels,

             C   D   F   C   D   F
         There were four, there were five,

             C   D   F AA  AG
         There were six little angels,
```

---

*Ginglend, D.R., & Stiles, W.E. (Compilers). *Music activities for retarded children*. New York: Abingdon Press, 1965.

```
    C    D    FF    C    D    F
There were seven, there were eight,

    C    D    F    AA    AG
There were nine little angels,

    A  CC    AF    D    C    F
Ten little angels  in that band.

    A    AG    A    G    F
Chorus:  Oh wasn't that a band,

    A A    A͡G F    G G    G͡F G    A A    A͡G F
Sunday morning, Sunday morning, Sunday morning,

    A    AG    A    G    F
Oh wasn't that a band,

    A A    A͡G F    G G    A͡G F    F
Sunday morning, Sunday morning, Soon!
```

Functioning and Age Levels

- moderate and high-functioning children and adolescents
- low-functioning adults

Possible Goals

- to increase understanding of numeration and number concepts
- to learn days of week/time of day
- to increase awareness of each other
- to promote musical relatedness and expressivity

Suggested Uses of Components of Music

- changes in tempo to reflect the pace of the individual
- changes in dynamics for auditory perception, to give variety to musical expressivity upon each repetition, and to provide contrast between the verse in which each individual plays alone in succession and the chorus in which all play together spiritedly

Suggested Design of Activity

The lively quality of this song makes the interweaving of goals (number concepts, days of week, time of day) a joyous experience.

- The clients (4 to 6 in a regular therapy group and up to 12 in a supplemental therapy group) sit in a semicircle.

- Each client then selects or is given a rhythm instrument and the therapist kneels in front of each person, singing and assisting him or her to play in succession.

- The therapist adapts the verse and chorus of the song as follows: "There is *one*, there are *two*, there are *three* little children (or boys and girls) . . . in this band" and "Oh isn't this a band, Tuesday *afternoon* (Wednesday *evening*, etc.), Tuesday *afternoon*, Tuesday *afternoon*, Oh isn't this a band, Tuesday *afternoon*, Tuesday *afternoon*," exaggerating italicized words to foster development of speech skills, imitative singing, understanding of number concepts and days of week. (A further adaptation of the verse would be "(Client) is playing (instrument)," repeated for each client, ending with the last line, "Everyone is playing in this band," followed by the chorus.)

- The therapist asks clients to play the instruments the appropriate number of times when the number is sung, to fill in the days of the week or time of day either spontaneously, when asked, "What day is today?" or to sing them imitatively, when the therapist sings, "Today is Tuesday (Wednesday, etc.)."

- Clients sing and play the rhythm instruments together on the chorus in a cohesive, musically integrated fashion.

Design 12

Music

"Rookoobay"—adaptation of a Trinadadian calypso song; key of D-minor; time signature 4/4.

	D A G F E D
Verse:	Come sing with me,
	G G G G A B♭ G
	Sing and play the maracas,
	G A G F E D
	Come sing with me,
	G G E F C♯ D
	And play the conga too,
	A G F E
	Yeh, yeh, yeh, yeh.
	D D A
Chorus:	Roo-koo-bay,
	D D A G
	Roo-koo-bay,
	A A D
	Roo-koo-bay.

Functioning and Age Levels

- moderate and high-functioning adolescents and adults

Possible Goals

- to increase attention span
- to raise energy level
- to promote interaction/interpersonal relations
- to provide emotional release and musical expression
- to improve speech prosody

Suggested Uses of Components of Music

- rhythm for perceptual-motor skills, arousal of energy level, and intrapersonal and interpersonal integration
- dynamics for affective adjustment and changes of mood
- tempo for increasing attending behavior and changes in energy level
- harmony for rich musical texture and flavor of the musical idiom to stimulate emotional responses and musical expression
- pitch for improvement of prosody of speech and auditory perception of tonality

Suggested Design of Activity

"Rookoobay," which seems to be a simple chant, can be transformed into a richly textured musical and physical experience that can be expanded and amplified by changes of mood and emotions. The basic rhythmic pattern, when projected vigorously, has the potential for arousal physically and emotionally. Throughout, the therapist plays full chordal progressions in various registers, at various dynamic levels, tempi, and with varying accompaniments.

- The therapist begins this activity by playing a vigorous steady beat in open fifths on the keyboard, singing the song as written. Clients are encouraged to pick up the beat, clapping hands in the dynamic level stimulated by the music or as suggested or modeled by the therapist.
- After the beat is established (in as related a way as the level of the clients will allow), the therapist begins to chant "Roo-koo-bay" rhythmically. Clients are encouraged to take up the chant as rhythmically as possible, with the therapist constantly making adjustments until there is a sense of synchrony between clients and therapist.

- The therapist and clients continue to sing/chant in different tempi and on various dynamic levels.
- As singing continues, rhythm instruments, mainly Latin percussion instruments such as conga drums, bongos, cowbell, guiro, maracas, cabasa, clavés, and tambourine (a wooden Orff xylophone can be added to enhance variety of timbres), are distributed.
- The therapist sings the entire song to each client, substituting the client's name for "Come" and the name of the instrument the client is playing for "maracas" and "conga."
- The therapist and clients sing chorus together.
- Accompanied by the therapist, the entire group plays together, first keeping a steady pulse on the instruments, then—functioning level permitting—beating the rhythmic pattern of the chant.
- The therapist and clients play instruments and chant "Roo-koo-bay" in call-and-response form. (Roo-koo-bay, essentially nonsense syllables for the clients, can become a playful interchange between the therapist and the clients or between client and client.)
- The therapist directs pairs of clients in instrumental dialogues using various combinations of instruments, identifying the instruments by name.

A music-movement activity may emerge by having the clients form a circle using small instruments while moving rhythmically and chanting. Some may want to dance in a circle formation, creating their own foot movements.

Appendix 7–A

Music Books

The music books listed here encompass music of many styles, idioms, origins, and subject matter.

American Folk Songs for Children (Ruth Crawford Seeger). Doubleday & Company, Inc., 1948.

American Rock & Roll: The Big Hits of the Late 50's and Early 60's (Vol. 4). Creative Concepts/Dover Publications, Inc., undated.

Beatlemania. ATV Music Publications, 1980.

Best of the 80's (so far) Continues. Cherry Lane Music Co., 1983.

The Best of Jazz. Hansen House, undated.

The Best Singing Games (Edgar S. Bley). Sterling Publishing Co., Inc., 1957.

The Book of American Negro Spirituals (James Weldon Johnson). The Vail-Ballou Press, Inc., 1937.

Children Discover Music and Dance (Emma D. Sheehy). Henry Holt and Company, Inc., 1959.

Children's Playsongs with Resonator Bells. Theodore Presser Company, 1968.

Country: The Top 50 of 1982. Columbia Publications, undated.

Creative Rhythmic Movement for Children (Gladys Andrews). Prentice-Hall, Inc., 1954.

Dancing Games for Children of All Ages. Sterling Publishing Co., Inc., 1974.

Easy Listening Favorites. Hal Leonard Publishing Corporation, undated.

Echoes of Africa in Folk Songs of the Americas (Beatrice Landeck). David McKay Company, Inc., 1961.

An English Songbook. Anchor Books, Doubleday & Company, Inc., 1963.

The First Book of Children's Play-Songs (Paul Nordoff and Clive Robbins). Theodore Presser Company, 1962.

Folk Dances of the United States and Mexico. The Ronald Press Company, 1948.

The Folk Song Book I (David Goldberger). Consolidated Music Publishers, Inc., 1963.

Folk Song USA (John A. Lomax and Alan Lomax). Duell, Sloan and Pearce, 1947.

The Folk Songs of North America (Alan Lomax). Doubleday & Company, Inc., 1959.

Folk Songs of the Caribbean. Bantam Books, 1958.

Fun for Four Drums (Paul Nordoff and Clive Robbins). Theodore Presser Company, 1968.

Fun with the Classics. Magnus Organ Company, 1958.

Good Old Standards (Vol. 2). United Artists Music, undated.

Great Songs Through the Years: The Golden Oldies. Columbia Pictures Publications, undated.

I'd Like to Teach the World to Sing. Charles Hansen Educational Music & Books, 1974.

The Incredible 88 Super Hits. Bradley Publications, undated.

Jim Along, Josie: A Collection of Folk Songs and Singing Games for Young Children. Harcourt Brace Jovanovich, Inc., 1970.

Making Music Your Own (Vol. 3). Silver Burdett Company, 1964.

More Songs to Grow On (Beatrice Landeck). Edward B. Marks Music Corporation/William Sloane Associates, Inc., 1954.

Music Activities for Retarded Children (David R. Ginglend and Winifred E. Stiles). Abingdon Press, 1965.

Music for Early Childhood (Osbourne McConathy). Silver Burdett Company, 1952.

Music Time (Evelyn Hunt). The Viking Press, 1958.

The New Very Best of Pop & Rock. Charles Hansen Music & Books, Inc., undated.

150 American Folk Songs to Sing, Read and Play. Boosey & Hawkes, 1975.

106 Great Songs of the 20th Century. The Big 3 Music Corporation, undated.

1000 Jumbo: The Magic Song Book. Charles Hansen Music & Books, Inc., undated.

Orff-Schulwerk: Music for Children (Carl Orff and Gunild Keetman). Schott & Co. Ltd., 1956.

Primitive Song. Mentor Books, 1963.

Rhythms Today! Silver Burdett Company, 1965.

Sally Go Round the Sun (Edith Fowke). Doubleday & Company, Inc., undated.

The Second Book of Children's Play-Songs (Paul Nordoff and Clive Robbins). Theodore Presser Company, 1968.

The Sesame Street Song Book. Simon & Schuster, 1971.

Sing and Learn. John Day Co., 1965.

Songs for All Seasons and Rhymes without Reasons. Edward B. Marks Music Corporation, 1968.

Songs in Action. McGraw-Hill, 1974.

Songs My True Love Sings (Beatrice Landeck). Edward B. Marks Music Corporation, 1946.

Songs of the Caribbean. Peer International Corporation, 1964.

Songs to Grow On (Beatrice Landeck). Edward B. Marks Music Corporation/William Sloane Associates, Inc., 1950.

Spirituals for Children to Sing and Play (Paul Nordoff and Clive Robbins). Theodore Presser Company, 1971.

Thirty Negro Spirituals (Hall Johnson). G. Schirmer, Inc., 1949.

Timeless Standards. Columbia Pictures Publications, 1983.

Top Hits of 1983 (Vol. 1). Warner Brothers Publications, Inc., undated.

A Treasury of American Folklore (foreword by Carl Sandburg). Crown Publishers, 1944.

A Treasury of American Song (Elie Siegmeister). Consolidated Music Publishers, Inc., 1943

A Treasury of Folk Songs. Bantam Books, 1951.

World's Best Loved Songs of the 60's. Columbia Pictures Publications, 1983.

World's Best Loved Songs of the 70's. Columbia Pictures Publications, 1983.

World's Greatest Golden Oldies. Hansen House, undated.

World's Greatest Hits of the Christmas Season. Charles Hansen Educational Music & Books, 1973.

Your All-Time Favorite Songs. Shapiro, Bernstein & Co., Inc., undated.

Appendix 7–B

Discography

The records listed here are divided into the following categories: (a) folk, traditional, and ethnic; (b) records for special needs; (c) action songs, games, and dances; (d) holiday and seasonal music; (e) contemporary; and (f) ragtime, jazz, rock, and disco. As mentioned earlier, live music is basic to the approach to music therapy presented in this book. Therefore, these recordings are intended primarily as resources rather than for actual use in sessions. The organic process of therapy demands constant adjustment of the music to the here-and-now needs of the client.

FOLK, TRADITIONAL, AND ETHNIC

Abiyoyo and Other Story Songs for Children (Pete Seeger). Folkways Records FTS 31500.
African Musical Instruments. Folkways Records 8460.
African Songs and Rhythms for Children: Orff-Schulwerk. Folkways Records 7844.
Afrikana Children's Folk Songs. Folkways Records 7201.
American Favorite Ballads (Pete Seeger). Folkways Records FA 2321.
American Folk Songs. Folkways Records 2005.
American Folk Songs for Children (Pete Seeger). Folkways Records FC 7601.
American Negro Folk & Work Song Rhythms (Ella Jenkins). Folkways Records FC 7654.
Ancient Echoes. Halpern Sounds HS 783.
Animal Folk Songs: Birds, Beasts, Bugs & Fishes (Pete Seeger). Folkways Records FC 7610.
The Artistry of Greece. Prestige/International Records LP 13080.
Brazilian Songs for Children. Peripole Records PR 8005.
Camp Songs (Pete Seeger and Erik Darling). Folkways Records FC 7028.
Children's Songs. Folkways Records FC 7036.
Creole Songs of Haiti. Folkways Records 6833.
Drums of Haiti (Harold Courlander). Folkways Records FE 4403.
English Folk Songs. Folkways Records 6917.
Folk Song Carnival (Hap Palmer). Activity Records AR 524.

Folk Songs and Ballads of the British Isles. Folkways Records 8719.

Folk Songs for Young People (Pete Seeger). Folkways Records FC 7532.

Folk Songs from Czechoslovakia. Folkways Records 6919.

French Folk Songs. Folkways Records 6832.

Greensleeves and Other Songs of the British Isles (Kenneth McKellar). London International TW 91389.

Hawaiian Chant, Hula, and Music. Folkways Records 8750.

Hebrew Folk Songs. Folkways Records FW 6928.

Hi Neighbor (Songs and Dances of Brazil, Israel, China, Japan, Turkey). CMS UNICEF 2.

Hungarian Folk Songs. Folkways Records 4000.

Irish Jigs, Reels, and Hornpipes. Folkways Records 6819.

Italian Folk Songs and Dances. Folkways Records 6915.

Jamaica Calypso Rock. Folkways Records 31308.

Jump Up Calypso (Harry Belafonte). RCA Victor LPM 2388.

Jungle Calypso (Duke of Iron). Stinson Records 10.

Kenya Folk Songs. Folkways Records 8503.

Leadbelly: Take This Hammer. Folkways Records 31019.

Little Calypsos. Peripole Records PP 9085.

Mahalia Jackson: The World's Greatest Gospel Singer. Columbia CL 644.

Melodies and Rhythms of Arabic Music. Folkways Records FW 8451.

More Songs to Grow On (Beatrice Landeck). Folkways Records FC 7676.

Mountain So Fair: Folk Songs of Israel. Folkways Records 31305.

The Musical Heritage of America (Tom Glazer). CMS Records CMS 650/4L.

Negro Folk Songs for Young People (Leadbelly). Folkways Records 7533.

Odetta at Town Hall. Vanguard Stereolab BSD 2109.

Russian Folk Songs. Folkways Records 6820.

Sing a Spiritual with Me (Tennessee Ernie Ford). Capitol STAO 1434.

Sea Song Favorites. Folkways Records SFX 2 (cassette).

Seasons for Singing (Ella Jenkins). Folkways Records FC 7656.

Simplified Folk Songs (Hap Palmer). Activity Records AR 518.

Songs and Dances of Brazil. Folkways Records 6953.

Songs and Dances of Greece. Folkways Records 6814.

Songs and Dances of Haiti (Harold Courlander). Folkways Records FE 4432.

Songs and Dances of Spain. Westminster WP 12005.

Songs of Mexico. Folkways Records 6815 (Vol. 1), 6853 (Vol. 2).

Songs to Grow On (Woody Guthrie). Folkways Records FC 7005 and FT 531502.

Songs to Grow On: School Days (Pete Seeger, Charity Bailey, Leadbelly, Adelaide Van Way, Cisco Houston). Folkways Records FC 7020.

Sounds of Animals. Folkways Records 6124.

Spirituals. Folkways Records 31042.

This Land is My Land. Folkways Records FC 7027.

Traditional Chilean Songs. Folkways Records 8748.

Two-Way Trip: Scottish and English Folk Songs. Folkways Records 8755.
Work and Dance Songs of Kenya. Folkways Records 8715.
World Tour with Folk Songs. Folkways Records 2405.
You'll Never Walk Alone (Mahalia Jackson). Harmony Records HS 11279.

RECORDS FOR SPECIAL NEEDS

Activities for Individualization in Movement and Music. Activity Records AR 49.
Auditory Training with Use of Rhythm Band Instruments. Developmental Learning Materials DLM 138.
Body-Space Perception through Music. Think-Stallman Productions Ltd./Stallman Educational Systems Inc. TSR 2810.
Call-and-Response (Ella Jenkins). Scholastic Records SC 7638.
Coordination Skills: Rhythmic Eye-Hand and Patterned Movement Activities. Activity Records KEA 6050.
Creative Movement and Rhythmic Exploration (Hap Palmer). Activity Records AR 533.
Daily Living Skills. Kimbo Records KIM 8057.
Developmental Motor Skills for Self-Awareness. Kimbo Records KIM 9075.
The Development of Body Awareness and Position in Space (Dorothy B. Carr and Bryant J. Cratty). Activity Records AR 605 (guide included).
Discovery through Movement Exploration. Activity Records AR 534.
Dynamic Balancing Activities (Dorothy B. Carr and Bryant J. Cratty). Activity Records AR 658 (guide included).
Early Childhood, Rhythms—Songs—Skills: Signs—Shapes—Colors—Houses—Feelings— Sounds— Nursery Rhymes. Kimbo Records LP 7011 (Series 12).
Early Early Childhood Songs (Ella Jenkins). Scholastic Records SC 7630.
Finger Play and Hand Exercises. Kimbo Records KIM 7051.
Fun Activities for Fine Motor Skills. Kimbo Records LP 9076.
Innovative Rhythmic and Tonal Textures for Developing Creative Motor Skills Activities. Folkways Records FC 7535.
Learning Basic Awareness through Music. Stallman-Susser Educational Systems LPED 121A.
Learning Basic Skills through Music (Hap Palmer). Activity Records AR 514.
Learning Basic Skills through Music: Vocabulary (Hap Palmer). Activity Records AR 521.
Listening and Moving (Dorothy B. Carr and Bryant J. Cratty). Activity Records LP 606–7.
Mod Marches (Hap Palmer). Activity Records AR 527.
More Learning as We Play (Winifred E. Stiles and David R. Ginglend). Folkways Records FC 7658.
More Music Times & Stories (Charity Bailey). Folkways Records FC 7528.
Music, Adapted, Composed, and Improvised for Music Therapy with the Developmentally Handicapped (Edith Hillman Boxill). Folkways Records FX 6180 (booklet included).
Music Time (Charity Bailey). Folkways Records 7307.
Perceptual Motor Development (Dorothy B. Carr and Bryant J. Cratty). Activity Records AR 605–607, 655–658 (10 LP records with guides).

Play Your Instruments and Make a Pretty Sound (Ella Jenkins). Folkways Records FC 7665.
Sensorimotor Training in the Classroom. Activity Records LP 532.
Sesame Street. Columbia CR 21530.
Special Music for Special People. Kimbo Records EA 85.
This is Rhythm (Ella Jenkins). Scholastic Records SC 7652.
You'll Sing a Song & I'll Sing a Song (Ella Jenkins). Folkways Records FC 7664.

ACTION SONGS, GAMES, AND DANCES

Action Songs & Rounds. Activity Records LP 508.
Activity and Game Songs (Tom Glazer). CMS Records CMS 657 (Vol. 1), CMS 658 (Vol. 2).
American Indian Dances. Folkways Records 6510.
American Play Parties (Pete Seeger). Folkways Records FC 7604.
Around the World in Dance. Activity Records AR 542.
Children's Dances Using Rhythm Instruments. Activity Records KR 9078.
Circle Dances for Today. Kimbo Records KEA 1146.
Counting Games and Rhythms for the Little Ones (Ella Jenkins) Scholastic Records SC 7679.
Dances of the World's Peoples. Folkways Records 6501 (Vol. 1), 6502 (Vol. 2), 6503 (Vol. 3).
Honor Your Partner. Activity Records 23.
Latin American Children's Game Songs of Mexico and Puerto Rico. Folkways Records 7851.
Let's Square Dance. RCA Victor LE 3000, 3001, 3002, and 3003.
Popular and Folk Tunes for Dancing and Rhythmic Movement. Hoctor Dance Records HLP 4074.
Rhythm Activities. RCA/Children's Record Guild 1004 and 1019.
Rhythm and Game Songs for the Little Ones (Ella Jenkins). Scholastic Records SC 7680.
Simplified Folk Dance Favorites for Exceptional Children. Activity Records EALP 602.
Singing Action Games. Activity Records HYP 507.
Singing Games. Activity Records LP 510.
Song & Play-Time (Peter Seeger). Folkways Records FC 7526.
Square Dances (Piute Pete). Folkways Records 2001.

HOLIDAY AND SEASONAL MUSIC

Carols and Holiday Songs. Peripole Records PP 9384.
Early Childhood, Rhythms—Songs—Skills: Christmas Fantasy. Kimbo Records LP 7005.
Holiday Action Songs. Activity Records K 3080.
Holiday Songs for All Occasions (Christmas, Hanukkah, Easter, Halloween). Kimbo Records KIM 0805.
The Little Drummer Boy: A Christmas Festival. Springboard International Records MLP 1201.
The Phil Spector Christmas Album. Apple Records C10398.
Traditional Christmas Carols (Peter Seeger). Folkways Records FAS 32311.

CONTEMPORARY

The Beatles: Revolver. Capitol Records ST 2576.
The Beatles: Yellow Submarine. Capitol Records SW 153.
Blessed Are . . . (Joan Baez). Vanguard VSD 6570/1.
Carpenters: Now & Then. A&M SP 3519.
Colors of the Day: The Best of Judy Collins. Elektra EKS 75030.
The Freewheelin' Bob Dylan. Columbia CS 8786.
Godspell. Arista Records 4001.
John Denver's Greatest Hits. RCA CPL1-0374.
Johnny Mathis' All-Time Greatest Hits. Columbia PG 31345.
Kismet. RCA LSO 1112.
The Manhattan Transfer. Atlantic SD 18133.
Oklahoma. Columbia OS 2610.
Paul Simon in Concert: Live Rhymin'. Columbia PC 32855.
Peter, Paul, and Mary. Warner Bros. WS 1449.
Poems, Prayers & Promises (John Denver). RCA Victor LSP 4499.
The Sound of Music. RCA LSOD 20005.
The Wizard of Oz. MGM S3996 ST.

RAGTIME, JAZZ, ROCK, AND DISCO

Afro American Jazz Rhythms. Kimbo Records KIM 8040.
Art Blakey and the Jazz Messengers. Blue Note Records 4003.
Children's Disco. Kimbo Records KIM 1220.
Disco. RCA PD-11213.
Disco Dances and Games. Kimbo Records KIM 9069.
Disco Party. Adam VIII Ltd. A-8021.
Disco Single. RCA YD-12299.
The Golden Age of Rock N' Roll. Kama Sutra Records, Inc. KSBS 2073.
Panorama Disco. RCA PD-12244.
Rock's Danceable Side. K-Tel International PTU 2860.
Scott Joplin: The Red Back Book (The New England Conservatory Ragtime Ensemble). Angel S 36060.
Soul Train Super Tracks. Adam VIII Ltd. A22-4052.

Chapter 8

Organizing a Music Therapy Program

An enriched music therapy program expands beyond the portals of the music therapy room.

INTRODUCTION

Group and individual therapy sessions are at the core of a multifaceted music therapy program. From this core, a full and enriching program can be built that offers clients many benefits that are unique to music therapy. In essence, such a program provides, through the universal modality of music, means of communication, learning, and expressivity (musical and nonmusical) and opportunities for socialization and gratifying use of leisure time. It can truly be described as music therapy for living, music therapy that helps clients lead the most normal and productive lives possible. The concept of milieu therapy (Jones, 1953) may be said to be embodied in such a program.

Inasmuch as a music therapy program is planned in accordance with the structure and overall treatment philosophy of the particular center, it is the responsibility of the music therapist to be fully acquainted with the policies and procedures, administrative hierarchy, nature of the client population served, services and therapies offered, and duties of professional and paraprofessional staff. Of utmost importance is knowledge of the treatment philosophy, that is, whether it patterns itself on a medical or nonmedical model; whether it uses interdisciplinary or transdisciplinary approaches to treatment; and whether music therapy is viewed as an integral part of the total treatment program.

AN ORGANIZATIONAL PLAN

The following organizational plan is discussed with reference to the environment in which the program should be carried out; the formation and scheduling of

group and individual therapy sessions, supplemental group therapy sessions, and therapeutically oriented musical events; staffing; the internship program; in-service training for allied professionals and other staff; and equipment and materials needed to set up a program. Because transdisciplinary approaches to treatment are relatively new, a separate discussion on aspects of these approaches and their relevance to the practice of music therapy is included at the end of this chapter. The music therapist may adopt features of transdisciplinary treatment whether or not it is the treatment approach used by a particular center.

Environment

When we talk about environment, we refer to a totality that encompasses attitudes as well as physical surroundings. Creating this environment involves the selection of a room that is cheerful, well ventilated, and soundproof (if possible), one that is spacious enough to allow for multidimensional therapeutic music activities and accessibility of appropriate equipment to implement the work. Because the lives of developmentally disabled persons often lack stability, purpose, productivity, or opportunities for self-direction, such an environment must foster emotional security in an aesthetic, structured setting—in other words, a setting that stimulates the senses and feelings, that offers opportunities to gain mastery over oneself and one's environment. Such a prepared, safe environment offers healthy parameters for action, yet freedom within which to explore, to learn, and to grow in awareness and sense of self.

Formation and Scheduling of Therapy Sessions

Group and Individual Therapy Sessions

Group music therapy sessions, preferably consisting of no more than four to six clients, are scheduled for a minimum of two half-hour sessions per week per group. Whenever possible, the group is selected for homogeneity. Although the members may be at similar levels developmentally, their specific problems and conditions will of course vary. Whatever the makeup of the group, whether homogeneous or divergent, the challenge for the therapist is to create an interrelated group, yet address the needs of each person, interweaving individual objectives and goals with group goals. In a center that has a daily in-house special education program, groups can be formed in whole or in part from classrooms. Based on the number of music therapy staff available, clients who work in sheltered workshops or attend other outside programs are referred for regular group or individual therapy sessions or are scheduled for supplemental group therapy sessions in late afternoons, evenings, or on weekends. Obviously, in a large center, group sessions are the predominant form of therapy.

Individual therapy sessions are scheduled for at least two half-hour sessions a week. Because the one-to-one process is necessarily more in-depth and intensive than group therapy, selection is primarily based on assessment of the nature and severity of the client's disabilities and problems. Other considerations and bases for selection are a client's inability to tolerate a group setting and referral by other professional staff or the interdisciplinary treatment team because of special problems and needs.

In some instances, the interdisciplinary treatment team recommends that a client receive both one-to-one and group therapy. However, some clients may be confused by having, at times, undivided attention and, at other times, having to share the therapist with others. Therefore, at the discretion of the music therapist, it may be necessary for those who cannot tolerate a change of situation to receive one-to-one therapy only until such time as he or she is able to enter a group setting. On the other hand, another client, in need of both kinds of sessions, may be comfortable in both settings and can profit by the combination.

Supplemental Group Therapy Sessions

Supplemental group therapy sessions for clients who attend outside programs are an important component of late afternoon, evening, and weekend programming. They can be viewed as supplemental inasmuch as formal assessments and treatment plans are not involved and treatment is less in-depth than that of regular group and individual therapy sessions. Such sessions therefore address the needs and interests of the group in an informal setting. In residential treatment facilities, each group, consisting of 8 to 10, can be drawn from a specific residential unit. Continuity is maintained by logging the materials used.

Therapeutically Oriented Musical Events

A multifaceted music therapy program may encompass dimensions other than group and individual therapy sessions that constitute its core. In order to augment or extend the program, the therapist may wish to consider including therapeutically oriented musical events that are a natural outgrowth of the therapy process inasmuch as they emanate directly from the music activities, ideas, and dramatizations that take place in therapy sessions. These events may take the form of spontaneous group or solo renditions of songs and rhythm instrument arrangements supported by the therapist. Others, planned around a theme or holiday celebration, may consist of playlets, pantomimes, and piano duets with the therapist. Their underlying purpose is to enable the clients to have additional experiences of success through musical expression and to demonstrate the normalizing effects of the therapy process. They not only offer the therapist an opportunity to extend the music therapy program beyond the walls of the therapy room; they also add a new dimension to the lives of clients. For the lowest- to the highest-functioning clients, opportunities are provided to "live" their gains, to share with others, to enhance their self-worth, to expand awareness of the world about them, and to receive appreciation from their peers and staff. These events also afford parents and other family members a means of sharing enjoyable musical experiences and witnessing the benefits of the therapy.

Programs for a therapeutically oriented event planned around a special theme and one planned around a holiday celebration appear in Exhibits 8–1 and 8–2.

Staffing

In a large center, the music therapy department comprises a director of music therapy who heads a staff of music therapists, interns, and music therapy assistants or therapy aides who are trained to assist music therapists.

Music therapy assistants or therapy aides specifically trained to augment staffing for the music therapy program are needed to assist in regular group therapy sessions as well as supplemental group therapy sessions. This is *especially* important for therapy with clients having severe behavior disorders, the multiply handicapped, and for large, therapeutically oriented musical events. Candidates for the position of music therapy assistant or therapy aide should be given in-service training in the basics of the music therapy process and ways of assisting that will contribute to the program.

Exhibit 8–1 Program for a Therapeutically Oriented Event Planned around a Special Theme

HOME TALENT NITE
Songs and Dances of Many Nations

ENTRANCE THEME SONG .... All Clients
  "When Everyone Comes Marching In"
  (to the tune of "When the Saints Go Marching In")

SINGING .... All Clients
  "Ev'rybody Loves Home Talent Nite"
  (to the tune of "Ev'rybody")
  "Jamaica Farewell"
  "This Little Light of Mine"
  "Zinga Za!"

RHYTHM INSTRUMENT PLAYING ...., Singers/Instrumentalists
  "Guantanamera"
    (sung and accompanied by conga drum, bongo drums, clavés, cabasa, castanet with
    handle, maracas, tambourine)

PIANO DUETS WITH THERAPIST
  "La Cucaracha" .... Margarita D.
  "Russian Melody" .... Philip S.
  (transposed into four different keys)
  "Hora" .... Raymond P.

SONG SOLOS
  "This Land Is Your Land" .... Pablo R.
  "Wade in the Water" .... Brenda N.
  "Ave Maria" .... Rolanda Y.

MUSIC-MOVEMENT .... *Dancers:* Shirley B., Robert C., Ramona D., Michael M.,
  "Haitian Song of Possession" and   Harry R., Laurette S., Joyce T., Ronald Y.
    "Mexican Hat Dance"   *Combo:* George B., Ellis D., Linda E.,
    with dancers and Latin percussion   Angel N., Jimmy V.
    combo (maracas, clavés, bongo
    drums, tambourine, conga drum)

EXIT THEME SONG .... All Clients
  "When Everybody Goes Marching Out"
  (to the tune of "When the Saints Go Marching In")

Exhibit 8–2 Program for a Therapeutically Oriented Event Planned around a Holiday Celebration

HOME TALENT NITE
Christmas Song Fest

ENTRANCE THEME SONG . . . . All Clients
"When Everyone Comes Marching In"
(to the tune of "When the Saints Go Marching In")

SINGING . . . . All Clients
"Ev'rybody Loves Christmas Day"
(to the tune of "Ev'rybody")
"Silent Night"
"Deck the Halls"
"Rudolf, the Red Nosed Reindeer"
"We Wish You a Merry Christmas"

RHYTHM INSTRUMENT PLAYING
"Jingle Bells"
(sung and accompanied by hand bells, triangles,
    sleighbells) . . . . Marla K., Ricky D., Pamela R.
"Deck the Halls"
(sung and accompanied by six single resonator
    bells) . . . . Mary C., Torre R., Larry M., Kenny A., Juan D.
"Pat-a-Pan"
(sung and accompanied by timpani drum, standing cymbal, conga drum,
    bongo drums, maracas) . . . . . . Steven T., Andre C., Ronnie L., Stella M., Elsie B.

THE CHRISTMAS DREAM
An Original Play in Pantomime to "Silent Night" and "White Christmas"
Narrator . . . . Therapist
Mary . . . . Sarah L.
Snow Mountains . . . . Barbara J., Evelyn P.
Snow Gatherers . . . . Rita A., Florence M., Santa P.
Solo of "White Christmas" . . . . Angel G.
Record Player Operator . . . . Gloria T.

SONG SOLOS
"Jingle Bell Rock"
(with conga drum) . . . . Ernest K.
"The Lord's Prayer" . . . . Laura B., Henry C.

FINALE . . . . All Clients
"The Little Drummer Boy"   *Instrumentalists:* Andre B., Wilson D.,
(sung and accompanied by timpani drum,   Lewis N., Maria R.
    conga drum, bongo drums, temple blocks)

EXIT THEME SONG . . . . All Clients
"When Everybody Goes Marching Out"
(to the tune of "When the Saints Go Marching In")

The following are the duties of the director of music therapy and the music therapist and the criteria for the selection of music therapy assistants or therapy aides.

Duties of the Director of Music Therapy

- designs and implements a comprehensive music therapy program
- interviews and makes recommendations for hiring music therapy staff
- administers music therapy assessments or supervises assessments administered by other music therapists on staff
- formulates treatment plan for each client on case load
- conducts individual and group therapy sessions
- conducts supplemental group therapy sessions in late afternoons and on evenings and weekends for clients who attend programs outside the institution
- as part of the extended music therapy program, conducts therapeutically oriented musical events
- writes or supervises the writing of all music therapy progress reports and evaluation summaries
- trains and supervises music therapy students and music therapy interns
- attends all case conferences and other meetings of the interdisciplinary treatment team for all clients on personal case load
- provides in-service training for professional and paraprofessional staff
- acts as a resource for nonmusic therapy staff with regard to in-house social events and as a consultant for determining the appropriateness of in-house and community musical programs attended by clients
- selects, orders, and maintains music therapy supplies and equipment

Duties of the Music Therapist

- administers music therapy assessments for all clients on case load
- formulates treatment plans for all clients on case load
- conducts or assists in both individual and group therapy sessions
- conducts or assists in supplemental group therapy sessions as assigned
- participates in therapeutically oriented musical events as assigned
- writes progress and other required reports for each client on case load
- attends case conferences and other meetings of the interdisciplinary treatment team for all clients on case load

Criteria for Selection of Music Therapy Assistants

- availability for regular assignment
- capacity and willingness to be actively involved in facilitating the music therapy process
- evidence of responsiveness to the therapist's verbal and nonverbal cues/ directives during sessions
- possession of a pleasant singing voice and the ability to sing on pitch

Internship Program

An internship program with a college or university benefits the center in many ways. It makes an important contribution to the therapeutic programming and adds substantially to its prestige while providing a training ground for the profession. In addition, as an intern develops the ability, under supervision, to assume responsibility for treatment of clients, there is a possibility for serving a greater number of clients. As a requirement of the college or university music therapy program at which the intern is enrolled, the intern is trained to conduct group and individual therapy sessions and is evaluated through on-site observation by the academic supervisor of a college or university, if affiliated with the AAMT, two times each semester (see Chapter 1). The duties of the intern are as follows:

- Assists in group and individual therapy sessions preliminary to conducting them independently
- Conducts group and individual therapy sessions as assigned under supervision
- Participates in therapeutically oriented musical events as assigned
- Writes music therapy progress reports for all clients assigned
- Writes a daily log of individual and group music therapy sessions in which he or she is involved
- Attends case conferences for all clients assigned

In-Service Training

In-service seminars for administrative staff, professionals of other treatment disciplines, and interested paraprofessional staff are necessary to further understanding and knowledge about the field of music therapy, its use as a primary treatment modality for mentally retarded and other developmentally disabled persons, and the interdisciplinary nature of the discipline. Such training should consist, at a minimum, of an introduction to music therapy methodology, the overall treatment objectives, and strategies and techniques used.

Equipment and Materials

The administrator of the center at which the music therapist is employed must be apprised of the necessity for providing specific kinds of equipment and musical instruments that are essential for the practice of music therapy. Provision for their replacement and repair, including tuning of the piano, and the need for an ongoing expense account for such materials as records, music books, and nonmusic materials should be included in the planning. Also, it is essential to emphasize that instruments be of professional quality both with regard to sound and durability. (Rhythm instruments that come in all-purpose packaged sets are usually flimsy, toylike, and unsatisfactory musically.) Even to the untrained or unperceptive ear, the quality of sound produced can have a deep impact emotionally and physically. The better the quality of sound, the greater the response and influence are likely to be. Also, because of the prevalence of destructive behaviors among developmentally disabled persons, careful selection of instruments for long, hard use is important. This is why it is essential to instill in clients a healthy respect for the instruments and why an adequate budget for repairs and replacements is an absolute necessity.

Although music therapists have individual preferences, the following equipment and materials, music and nonmusic, are considered essential for the practice of music therapy:

1. piano
2. guitar
3. Autoharp®/miniharp
4. Casiotone®
5. rhythm instruments (percussion, melodic bar, wind)
   - *percussion instruments*
     timpani
     hand drums (tambour, tom-tom, barrel tub, hand snare with handle)
     snare drums
     "talking" slit drum
     Latin percussion instruments (conga drum, bongo drums, cabasa, claves, cowbell with beater, maracas, shaker, guiro, castanets with handles)
     cymbals (finger, hand, standing)
     tambourine (wooden and aluminum)
     triangle
     temple blocks (set of five on stand)
     bells (handbells, sleighbells, wristbells, Swiss-tuned bells, jingle bell sprays)
     rhythm sticks
     sand blocks

- *melodic bar instruments*
  resonator bells/educator tone bars (diatonic and chromatic sets)
  standing tone bars
  xylophone
  metallophone (Orff instrument with removable bars)
- *wind instruments*
  song flute/flutophone/recorder
  melodica
  horn
  train whistle
  bird whistle
  kazoo

6. various kinds of mallets, drum sticks, and beaters

   - wood-tipped mallets (for wood blocks)
   - rubber-tipped mallets (for xylophone, metallophone)
   - soft felt and lamb's wool mallets (for timpani drum and tom-tom)
   - multiheaded mallets (with two, three, or four heads) in wood with a wide, flat handle

7. brushes (for snare drums and standing cymbal)
8. record player and records
9. cassette tape recorder and tapes
10. music books
11. microphone
12. nonmusic materials such as flash cards, pictures, photographs, mirrors, scarves, crepe paper (for streamers), puppets, hoops, balls, toy animals, crayons, and paper

Annotated List of Instruments

The following instruments are considered especially useful in working on the multitude of sensorimotor, perceptual-motor, behavioral, physical, social, and affective problems common to this population.

1. *Timpani drum:* The timpani drum (from the Orff instrumentarium) ranges from 10 to 20 inches in diameter and stands on adjustable legs. It is played with a felt mallet and produces a resonant reverberating sound that provides excellent feedback at all levels of functioning. A large drumhead can serve as a central focus for group participation with clients seated in a circle around the drum, either taking turns or beating it simultaneously. For example, with a group that might not be ready developmentally to play different instruments together in response to music, this basic instrument

would be introduced as a first experience in instrument playing and used for auditory perception, attending behavior, imitative skills, interactional skills, etc. Because of the intimacy of the experience of the therapist and clients gathered around the drum together, it is an especially effective instrument for generating group stability and security.

2. *Conga drum:* The conga drum is about 20 inches high with an 8-inch skin head and is made of heavy wood or plexiglass. It can be played with the hands, fingers, or various kinds of felt mallets. Its size, substantial construction, timbre, and professional quality make it a particular preference for high-functioning adults as well as practical for low-functioning adults. Also, because it is used in professional combos and orchestras, it is a source of self-esteem for clients who have had exposure to this kind of drum.

3. *"Talking" slit drum:* An adaptation of an ancient African instrument, the "talking" slit drum has a hollow wood resonating chamber with built-in tynes of different pitch and is played with a rubber-tipped mallet. Its mellow tones have a soothing effect that can give a sense of calm to the client. The tonal variations produce a path to auditory perception and stimulate communication through musical dialogues and group participation.

4. *Barrel/tub drum:* The barrel drum is made of lacquered heavy wood with a heavy skin head. It is played with a felt mallet, hands, or drumsticks. Its durability and convenient size (it fits into the crook of the elbow and rests snugly against the body) can provide a sense of security through tactile contact and auditory stimulation through its full-bodied tone.

5. *Bongo drums:* Bongo drums are two drums of slightly different sizes that are bolted together. When played with alternating hands, they can evoke duple (1–2) pulsation that is a natural body rhythm and lends itself to work on coordination and numeration (concept of the numbers 1 and 2).

6. *Hand drum:* The hand drum is 6 inches in diameter with a wooden handle and is played with a small rubber mallet or the hand. It is useful for clients of all functioning levels, especially for those whose palmar grasp needs strengthening.

7. *Tambour:* The tambour is a shallow hand drum, single- or double-headed, ranging from 10 to 16 inches in diameter. The single-head, 10- to 12-inch sizes are recommended for comfortable handling by the client. Its portability makes it convenient for working on locomotor skills and other music-movement activities.

8. *Steel drum:* Originating in Trinidad, the steel drum is hand hammered into tones of the musical scale. The size that is most appropriate for use in music therapy is 11½ inches in diameter and 3 inches deep. It is equipped with two mallets and a sling that fits around the neck, which makes it especially useful for developing perceptual-motor skills with clients who cannot grasp

or hold an instrument. Its timbre and tonal variety have sensory appeal that provide the client with instant musical gratification.

9. *Clavés:* Clavés are percussion sticks used to mark rhythm in Latin American music. They are made from fine seasoned hardwood and, when struck together, they produce a sharp, hollow click. Exceptionally sturdy, they are very useful with persons of all ages and functioning levels. For refining perceptual-motor and musical skills, one clavé is held between the thumb and four fingers of one hand and struck with the other.

10. *Tambourine:* The tambourine is a framed drum with jingling metal discs attached to the rim, which is made either of wood or aluminum. It also comes without a skin head. The aluminum tambourine is particularly useful for clients who have difficulty grasping or holding an object.

11. *Temple blocks:* Chinese in origin, temple blocks are wooden bulbs or blocks (Orff version) of varying sizes and tones. They come singly or in sets of three, four, and five that are mounted on an aluminum rod attached to a stand. They are useful for auditory discrimination, coordination, and for working on numeration and number concepts.

12. *Rhythm sticks:* Rhythm sticks are smooth or fluted 12-inch sticks that are struck together to produce a sharp click. Fluted sticks produce a soft, gourdlike effect when rubbed or scraped. A pair is recommended for each member of the group for working, for example, on imitative movements that involve directionality (when tapped up, down, to right, left). They are lightweight and therefore relatively easy to handle and are usually brightly colored (red or blue), providing visual stimulation.

13. *Cabasa:* The cabasa is a wooden cylinder or gourd whose outer surface is strung with beads. It is played by moving the beads back and forth when held in one hand and resting against the other, producing a chugging sound. It can also be shaken like a maraca. It is excellent for tactile stimulation and auditory discrimination.

14. *Maracas:* Maracas come in pairs of hollow gourds (or gourdlike bulbs) partially filled with dried seeds or pebbles. They are easily manipulated by low-functioning persons and are useful on many levels, from developing the ability to grasp to keeping a steady rhythmic beat while alternating hands in duple pulsation.

15. *Guiro:* African in origin, the guiro is a large, hollow gourd with a long ridged stem. The sound is produced by rubbing a wooden or metal scraper back and forth over the ridges. The manmade guiro is substantially constructed of heavy wood and is usually colorfully decorated, making it an exceptionally stimulating instrument tactually and visually.

16. *Kalimba/sansa/thumb piano:* African in origin, the kalimba is a plucked instrument consisting of metal strips/tynes attached to the bridge of a board or box resonator. It has a delicate, soothing timbre and is played by holding

it in both hands and plucking it with the thumbs. It is especially useful for working on fine motor skills.

17. *Handle castanets/clappers:* Handle castanets are a pair of hardwood clappers attached to a flat center piece. A "roll" is produced by shaking the handle back and forth. They can also be played by holding them in one hand and striking them against the palm of the other hand. Profoundly retarded and multiply handicapped persons can manipulate this instrument without assistance, thus providing a means of active participation on an elementary level.

18. *Handbells:* Handbells are of varying sizes and kinds such as clusters of sleighbells, jingle bell sprays, and Swiss-tuned bells with handles. A low-functioning group, using handbells, can participate in creating varied musical sounds and effects when supported by structured musical stimuli by the therapist. A high-functioning group can use all these bells for specific musical effects and the Swiss-tuned bells for melodic purposes. The very act of shaking bells can have a salutary effect on the emotions. This is true also of the effect that the timbre of bells can have both physiologically and emotionally.

19. *Resonator bells:* Resonator bells, also called educator tone bars, are categorized as a melodic percussion instrument. Made of aluminum tone bars mounted on wooden or plastic resonator boxes, they produce sounds of definite musical pitches and come in diatonic and chromatic sets of 8, 20, or 25 tone bars beginning on middle C. Separately tuned, they are played with hard rubber or Neoprone® mallets, supplied with each bar, or several can be played at one time with multiheaded mallets (producing chords). The soft, vibrant, melodious tone of resonator bells is especially pleasant and may be soothing, having effects similar to those described in the preceding item. The bells are played as a diatonic or chromatic set in ways like a xylophone or singly by an individual, alone or together with other members of the group who would also be playing them singly. Any number of the bells can be selected from the entire set for a variety of arrangements of tonal relationships that will blend musically with the music being used, thus ensuring a successful musical experience. Therapeutic uses of resonator bells range from the emotional gratification derived from an aesthetic experience to developing specific skills such as eye–hand coordination by holding the bell in one hand and striking it with the mallet (or placing one or more on a table) to developing advanced musical expressivity (ability to play melodic lines, melodic rhythm patterns, intervals, etc.). As with other bar or keyboard instruments, these sets can be used for numeration, auditory discrimination, and directionality. Exceptionally versatile for work with all age groups at all levels of functioning, they are a *must* for all music therapy programs.

20. *Cowbell:* The cowbell is made of lacquered copper and is held by a wide handle. When struck with a hard rubber mallet, it produces a dull, metallic tone. Its size and substantial construction make it an excellent instrument for developing eye–hand coordination.

21. *Finger cymbals:* Finger cymbals come in a set of two pairs with elastic slings and are attached to the index finger and thumb. They are useful for making gentle contact with a client (with the therapist and client each wearing a pair) by clashing them toward each other and for fine motor coordination.

22. *Hand cymbals:* Hand cymbals, 5 to 8 inches in diameter, are held with thong holders, plastic straps, or wooden knobs. A crash effect is obtained by clashing them together slightly off center and a gong effect by striking them with a felt mallet. They can be a means of arousal or, when used by two persons together, a means of interaction.

23. *Standing cymbal:* The standing cymbal is 8 to 22 inches in diameter and is mounted on a stand. It can be played with a brush or with a lambskin or felt mallet. It is effective for clients on varying levels of functioning for visual as well as auditory perception. Its timbre can serve many musical purposes as well as therapeutic purposes such as arousal, eye–hand coordination, and self-esteem (because of its familiarity as an orchestral/professional instrument).

24. *Standing tone bars:* Standing tone bars are metal or wooden bars mounted on a wooden box (resonator) that stands 15 inches off the floor. Those commonly selected are tuned to C, F, and G. Their full vibratory quality and resonance make them an excellent source of sensory stimulation for the hearing impaired and their large size and surface make them especially useful for the multiply handicapped, visually impaired, and clients who have deficits in eye–hand coordination.

25. *Xylophone:* The xylophone is a melodic percussion instrument mounted on a solid one-piece wood frame. There are two kinds: (a) diatonic single-row, 8- and 12-note models and (b) chromatic two-row, 20- and 25-note models arranged in piano keyboard order. The xylophone is easily manipulated by a wide range of clients and can be used to produce random sounds or play highly structured melodies.

26. *Orff xylophone:* The Orff xylophone is a melodic percussion instrument that has removable wooden bars mounted on an enclosed resonator box. It comes in three registers (soprano, alto, and bass) in diatonic (16 bar) and chromatic (22 bar) models. An important feature is that any number of bars can be selected to blend with the tonality of music being played by the therapist, thus assuring the client's successful music making.

27. *Orff metallophone:* The Orff metallophone is a melodic percussion instrument that has removable heavy-gauged aluminum bars mounted on an

enclosed resonator box. It comes in three registers, as does the xylophone, and any number of bars can be selected to blend with the tonality of music being played by the therapist, thus assuring the client's successful music making. In addition, the Orff xylophone and metallophone can be used for work on numeration by varying the number of bars to be played. (Multi-headed mallets are useful for striking two, three, or four resonator bells or bars of a xylophone/metallophone to produce chords and intervals. They are easier to grasp than single-headed mallets and are, therefore, recommended for use with the multiply handicapped person or any person whose grasp is deficient.)

28. *Soprano melodica:* The melodica is a wind instrument with simulated piano keys, either 25 chromatic keys (C′ to C‴—two octaves) or 20 chromatic keys (C′ to G″). It is excellent for developing fine motor skills, breath control, oral musculature, and phonation.

29. *Song flute/flutophone/recorder:* The song flute, flutophone, and recorder are wind instruments characterized by a cylindrical tube, a whistle, and eight finger holes; they are held vertically. The song flute and flutophone are made of plastic and have raised finger holes that provide tactile stimulation. The recorder can be made either of plastic or pear wood. Tones are produced by covering the holes. On the most primitive level, these instruments can be used to develop phonation, oral musculature, and breath control. High-functioning clients can learn to play simple melodies on them or use them freely in musical improvisation.

30. *Autoharp®:* The Autoharp® is a stringed push-button chording and strumming instrument that has valuable therapeutic uses for our work. It can be used in many ways by the therapist (as a basic and versatile musical instrument for accompanying singing, rhythm instrument playing, and music-movement), by the therapist and client together, and by the client independently. The most commonly used model has 15 chord bars: E♭, D, F_7, G-min, B♭, A_7, C_7, D-min, F, E_7, G_7, A-min, C, D_7, G. The sound is produced by pressing the chord bars and strumming the strings with the fingers or a pick (plastic or felt). The instrument is both musically gratifying and stimulating tactually. It is especially useful for sensory stimulation for the hearing impaired and deaf who can experience the vibrations of the strings by having the instrument placed close to the ears and other parts of the body.

31. *Miniharp:* The miniharp is a five-chord Autoharp® (C, F, B♭, G_7, C_7). It is useful for a variety of clients because of the limited number of chord bars to be depressed. It is especially useful for younger clients because of its small size. With a strap attached, it can be manipulated with more ease than the full-sized Autoharp®. It fulfills purposes similar to those described in the preceding item.

32. *Casiotone®:* The Casiotone® electronic keyboard is a portable keyboard that produces different instrumental effects and timbres plus automatic rhythm accompaniments at the touch of various buttons. It comes in various sizes and can be used by both the therapist and the client. An added advantage is that it can run on batteries and thus is highly portable and accessible for use in many situations.

33. *Omnichord®:* The Omnichord® is a small, lightweight, guitar-shaped electronic musical instrument with features usually found in much larger instruments. Its design is such that instantaneous harplike effects can be produced by merely sliding the ball(s) of the finger(s) across it or by lightly touching a touchplate (sonic strings). Among its varied features are a full electronic section and a chordal section consisting of 27 major, minor, and 7th chords (both produced by depressing buttons). This instrument is exceptionally useful for the therapist and clients of all functioning levels, including the multiply handicapped, for it is a rich source of sensory stimulation, a means of developing coordination skills, and highly conducive to creative musical exploration and discovery. As an accompaniment instrument, it is very accessible to high-functioning clients.

A TRANSDISCIPLINARY APPROACH TO TREATMENT

In recent years, a new concept in interdisciplinary services has been introduced. The term *transdisciplinary** best describes this new concept, which requires an intellectual as well as an emotional acceptance that disciplines cannot be insular in their perspective and that they must work together in a concerted effort to deal with human problems (Haynes, Patterson, D'Wolf, Hutchison, Lowry, Schilling, & Siepp, 1976). Transdisciplinary approaches are, in the main, an outgrowth of the need to implement more effective means to deal with severely, profoundly, and multiply handicapped persons. Various models are being explored, some of which have been described in the literature.**

Requisites for this approach are preparation and competency in one's own discipline and a commitment to working together with other providers of services that manifests itself in a willingness to learn about other disciplines and to view

---

*Originally, the term *cross modality* was used to designate this concept. Subsequently, the term *transdisciplinary* emerged as a more accurate and appropriate term to characterize the work and purpose of this method. Another term associated with the transdisciplinary approach is *synthesizer*, namely, an interventionist who seeks appropriate information or techniques from professionals of various disciplines, applies such information or techniques to develop effective intervention strategies, and implements such strategies to remediate problems or to facilitate the acquisition of new skills.

**See Hart, 1977; Haynes et al., 1976; Hutchison, 1974; Hutchison & Haynes, in press; Lyon & Lyon, 1980; McCormick & Goldman, 1979; Miller, 1980; Sirvis, 1978.

familiar subjects with fresh outlooks that lead to the adoption of new ideas unilaterally and collectively. By working together in areas of shared function to develop jointly planned programs for individuals and groups and by pooling and exchanging information and skills across traditional disciplinary boundaries, professionals gain knowledge and understanding of other disciplines and enlarge the common core of knowledge and competency in each team member. According to McCormick and Goldman (1979): "In the transdisciplinary approach . . . the respective disciplines are responsible for initial assessments in their area. In addition, they are expected to contribute to the development of a comprehensive individualized treatment program" (p. 154). It must be emphasized that the client–therapist relationship need *never* be sacrificed when using a transdisciplinary approach to treatment.

It has been indicated in Chapter 2 that the nature of music as used in music therapy with this client population is interdisciplinary. Therefore, music therapy is ideally suited to selective transdisciplinary applications that take the form of cotherapy or hands-on therapy conducted conjointly by the music therapist and two or more members of an interdisciplinary team who are working with individuals or groups on goals determined by the team (Boxill, 1982). The value of this kind of cotherapy is evident in treatment of the developmentally disabled at all levels of functioning for it has been found that any number of clients are more receptive to physical, occupational, and speech therapy when functional music is the energizing force in the treatment process. Indeed, frequently a "chore" requiring stamina and effort becomes a pleasurable experience when music is used to stimulate and motivate activity and learning. Added value is derived through the various therapists who, by consultation and demonstration, supply strategies and techniques unique to their discipline. This kind of cross-modal interaction can contribute illuminating and fruitful insights into ways of working on psychobiological problems. (Several of the process-oriented descriptions of treatment in Chapter 6 indicate the effectiveness of conjoint or cotherapy with other disciplines.)

Even if the transdisciplinary approach has not been instituted in a center, the experimental and creative music therapist will seek out this approach whenever and wherever it would enhance the effects of therapy. Hands-on conjoint therapy sessions with a speech therapist or a psychologist, for instance, can add dimension and benefit to the therapy process that no amount of routine conferring and consultation will bring about.

The following discussion touches on reasons why music therapy, in combination with any one or more of the following allied disciplines, can be used to create the synergistic effect of this approach.

Speech Therapy. There is a natural union between speech and music that makes the interdisciplinary and transdisciplinary approaches to speech and music therapies exceptionally effective. The components of music that pertain to speech—melody, rhythm, tempo, dynamics, pitch, and text of song—can be used directly to stimulate random vocalization, preverbalization, and verbalization. Auditory perception, articulation, prosody, and quality of voice are improved through the therapeutic music activities of singing/chanting, the playing of simple wind instruments (for respiration and phonation), and motoric activities. The speech impairments of this client population cover a wide range: dysarthria, apraxia, articulatory errors, and omissions, to name a few. Many speech impairments can be dealt with in music therapy rather than traditional speech therapy (as speech and hearing pathologists have stated), inasmuch as music can trigger verbal or vocal responses that may be the beginning of speech. Working together on a transdisciplinary basis is an invaluable contribution to this domain.

Special Education. With regard to special education, the extent of the transdisciplinary approach is virtually limitless. For example, functional academic and cognitive skills that can be reinforced and stimulated through the use of music are: (a) auditory perception and discrimination that can enhance all areas of learning through varied uses of instruments; (b) memory/recall/retention through the repetition of songs and the structure of music; (c) color and object identification by means of many music therapy activities that use the text of songs and rhythmic chanting; and (d) comprehension through the stimulation of mental processes involved in all modes of therapeutic music activities—singing/chanting, instrument playing, and music-movement.

Physical Therapy. Music can provide support that develops rhythmic, harmonious motor functioning. Through the functional use of music the following areas worked on in physical therapy can be improved: gross motor skills, eye–hand coordination, perceptual-motor skills, mobility, agility, balance (dynamic and static), posture, gait, and physical coordination. Action songs and words are especially useful in increasing bodily control and motivating both locomotor and nonlocomotor movements.

Occupational Therapy. In conjunction with the occupational therapist, the inventive music therapist experiments with and finds ways to develop fine motor skills through the use of instruments and music-movement activities. Many a mentally retarded individual has difficulty in grasping or using the fingers to manipulate small objects. When offered a mallet, rhythm sticks, or a flutophone, such clients can often be motivated to manipulate a variety of instruments in response to musical stimuli. Singing songs that indicate fine motor activity is especially beneficial.

Psychology. The affective life of the client is dealt with from moment to moment in music therapy. Because of the nonverbal, nonthreatening nature of the modality, feelings may be expressed in a safe environment through singing a song that has a particular quality or by beating a drum or moving to music in innumerable ways. The music therapist, either in conjunction with or consultation with the psychologist, can, for example, work to increase impulse control or attention span or emotional release through the use of music therapy techniques, selected instruments, and all modes of therapeutic music activities.

Creative Arts Therapies. With reference to creative arts therapies (music, dance, art, and drama), it is important to note that the interface of the first three— music, dance, and art therapies—is their nonverbal nature. This makes them particularly significant tools for the development and habilitation of people in whom deficits in oral communication are prevalent. We find that the different media, when used in combination with music for therapeutic purposes, offer opportunities for action/expression, from scribbling in the tempo of a vigorous march to creative dancing in the style of a Spanish dance to dramatizations inspired by words of a song. In response to music projected by the therapist, doing and learning takes place, one form of expression enhancing the other. When we combine music therapy with dance therapy, the synthesis of the structure of music with bodily expression brings about mind–body integration and serves to galvanize groups. In combining music therapy with art therapy, the use of color and shapes stimulated by musical stimuli can be the catalyst for new connections between the motoric and cognitive systems, giving added dimension and meaning to learning. When music therapy and drama therapy are combined, depending on the functioning level of the persons involved, music can stimulate and complement activities from imaginative play to pantomime to psychodrama.

CONCLUSION

Organizing a comprehensive music therapy program requires that the therapist be ready to meet the needs of the specific setting and client population. In working closely with administrators whose understanding, commitment, and cooperation are essential, the music therapist can offer innovative ideas and approaches for treatment as well as ensure that the music therapy program is an integral component of the total treatment regimen. This kind of mutual effort and careful planning entered into by both the administrator and the music therapist facilitates the successful practice of this therapy as a primary treatment modality.

REFERENCES

Boxill, E.H. *Creative arts therapies for the developmentally handicapped: A transdisciplinary approach.* Keynote address delivered at the meeting entitled "Arts and the person who is handicapped: A transdisciplinary approach," of the Western Carolina Center Foundation and the Division of Arts of the Department of Public Instruction for the State of North Carolina, Morganton, N.C., February 19–20, 1982.

Bricker, D. Educational synthesizer. In A. Thomas (Ed.), *Hey, don't forget about me: Education's investment in the severely, profoundly, and multiply handicapped.* Reston, Va.: Council for Exceptional Children, 1976.

Hart, V. The use of many disciplines with the severely and profoundly handicapped. In E. Sontag, J. Smith, and N. Certo (Eds.), *Educational programming for the severely and profoundly handicapped.* Reston, Va.: Council for Exceptional Children, 1977.

Haynes, U., Patterson, G., D'Wolf, N., Hutchison, D., Lowry, M., Schilling, M., & Siepp, J.M. *Staff development handbook: A resource for the transdisciplinary process.* New York: United Cerebral Palsy Associations, Inc., 1976.

Hutchison, D. *A model for transdisciplinary staff development: A monograph* (Tech. Rep. 8). New York: United Cerebral Palsy Associations, Inc., 1974.

Hutchison, D., & Haynes, U. *Transdisciplinary: A team approach to the delivery of services to the developmentally disabled.* Thorofare, N.J.: Charles B. Slack, in press.

Jones, M. *The therapeutic community.* New York: Basic Books, 1953.

Lyon, S., & Lyon, G. Team functioning and staff development: A role release approach to providing integrated educational services for severely handicapped students. *Journal of the Association for the Severely Handicapped,* 1980, *5*(3), 250–253.

McCormick, L., & Goldman, R. The transdisciplinary model: Implications for service delivery and personnel preparation for the severely and profoundly handicapped. *American Association for the Education of Severely and Profoundly Handicapped Review,* 1979, *4*(2), 152–161.

Miller, M.B. *Project Tide: 6-Phase Planning Model.* New York: Author, 1980.

Sirvis, B. Developing IEP's for physically handicapped students: A transdisciplinary viewpoint. *Teaching Exceptional Children,* 1978, *10*, 78–82.

Epilogue and Concluding Notes

Making a difference in the lives of developmentally disabled persons through music therapy is at once deeply moving and challenging. Working with my many clients is a constant source of revelation—about them, individually and collectively, and about myself. Witnessing the slightest gain can be a peak experience. Sharing the moment of struggle to make that leap forward can be a thrill. Looking for a key to one person's betterment can be a consuming exploration.

In the context of *A Continuum of Awareness,* I offer an approach to the practice of music therapy that is intended to enable you to reach out for means of empowering persons who are developmentally disabled to actualize their true humanness as fully as possible. Through this approach to a treatment modality that can be a primary force in their lives, possibilities become realities. In the creative humanistic process, there is no place for preconception or prejudgment—no place for taking anything for granted. For there is no end to our searchings, no limit to our pursuits, no end to our conviction that there are new paths to take.

If your hearts and minds are open, if your vistas and horizons are broadened, if your searchings and pursuits make a difference in the lives of the developmentally disabled through music therapy, then this book will have fulfilled its purpose.

A CONTINUUM OF AWARENESS

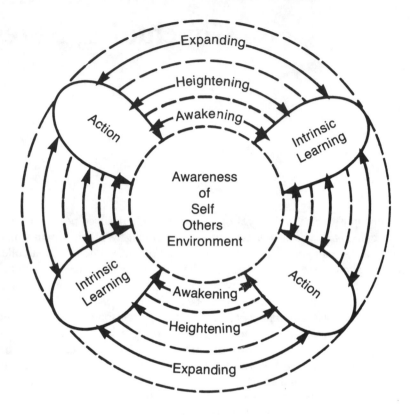

Glossary

MUSICAL TERMS

accelerando—gradual increase in tempo.

a tempo—back to the original tempo.

beat—regular pulsation/basic unit of music; temporal unit of a musical composition.

blues—style of jazz, both vocal and instrumental.

call-and-response—song or chant in which a solo voice is answered by an individual or group or a single voice by imitation.

chromatic scale—having 12 tones to the octave.

crescendo—gradual increase in volume.

decibel—unit used for measuring the relative loudness of sounds.

decrescendo—gradual decrease in volume.

diatonic scale—major or minor scale having 8 tones to the octave that follows a fixed pattern of intervals without chromatic deviation.

dynamics—variation and contrast in degree of volume or intensity of sound.

folk song—a song of unknown authorship that has been handed down orally for many generations.

glissando—sliding of tones up or down a keyboard, bars of a xylophone, or strings of a stringed instrument.

harmony—combination of simultaneous musical notes in a chord.

interval—difference in pitch between two notes (e.g., a third, a fifth).

intonation—degree of adherence to pitch.

melody—horizontal succession or arrangement of musical tones organized as an aesthetic whole to express a coherent musical idea.

meter—organizing force of rhythm; regularity of accents or beats in given units of time denoted by measures or bars; grouping of beats and accents as found in each measure (e.g., duple meter [2/4], triple meter [3/4]).

musical form—includes all the elements and relationships that distinguish music from a haphazard combination of sounds (even the simplest melody shows relationships of pitch (intervals) and time values (rhythm)); the scheme of organization that determines the basic structure of a composition.

musical idiom—typical style, form, or character indigenous to a specific region, historical period, nation, or kind of music (folk, pop, classical, rock, etc.).

musical style—represents the total effect of a composition in a given historical period (in analyzing a piece of music for style, one examines the handling of fundamentals—melody, rhythm, harmony, etc.—in relation to the interior of the music or the mood it seeks to evoke).

note value—duration of a note (e.g., quarter, half, whole).

ostinato—musical figure repeated at the same pitch throughout a composition.

pentatonic scale—scale consisting of five different tones as distinguished from the familiar diatonic (e.g., F♯, G♯, A♯, C♯, D♯).

phrase—melodic idea punctuated by a cadence.

pitch—highness or lowness of sound; the property of a sound and especially a musical sound is determined by the frequency of the sound waves producing it, i.e., a definite number of vibrations per second.

pulse—rhythmic beat or impulse.

rhythm—arrangement of successive sounds according to their relative duration; a flow of movement characterized by a regularly recurring element such as a beat or accent that is interspersed with periods of relaxation (from the Greek *rhythmos*, measured motion).

rhythmic pattern—arrangement of notes of different values.

ritardando—gradual slowing down of tempo.

rondo form—musical form in which there is repeated return to the opening theme or refrain following contrasting sections (e.g., ABACADA).

spiritual—religious song often based on a biblical story.

tempo—rate of speed of a musical piece.

texture—relationship of the vertical and horizontal elements in music.

timbre—quality of tone or tone color distinctive of a particular singing voice or musical instrument.

tonality—key relationship (e.g., C major tonality); accuracy of pitch.

TERMS PERTINENT TO DEVELOPMENTAL DISABILITIES

AAMD—American Association on Mental Deficiency.

acuity—sharpness or clearness of the senses, especially hearing and vision.

adaptive behavior—defined as the effectiveness with which or degree to which the individual meets the standards of personal independence and social responsibility expected of his or her age and cultural group.

affect—generalized feeling tone, usually distinguished from emotion in being more persistent and pervasive; *inappropriate affect:* affect that is clearly discordant with the situation; *labile affect:* affect that is characterized by rapid and abrupt shifts.

ambulation—walking.

anomaly—that which is grossly irregular or deviates from the typical (does not necessarily indicate a diseased or damaged state).

anorexia—loss of appetite.

anorexia nervosa—condition in which the person loses appetite and becomes severely emaciated in the absence of a known lesion.

anoxia—lack of oxygen (if prolonged, may cause irreversible brain damage).

anxiety—fearful apprehension.

aphasia—loss or impairment of the ability to use language because of damage to the brain; *expressive aphasia* (motor): inability to speak or write words; *receptive aphasia* (sensory): inability to comprehend speech or the written word.

aphonia—loss or absence of voice as a result of the failure of vocal chords to vibrate properly.

apraxia—inability to perform coordinated and purposeful movements as a result of lesions in the cerebral cortex.

arrhythmia—lack of rhythm.

articulation—in speech, the enunciation of words and phrases.

asymmetry—decreased similarity of corresponding parts of an opposite side of the body.

ataxia—failure of muscular coordination.

athetosis—form of cerebral palsy in which the person is subject to involuntary, uncontrollable writhing movements of the body, face, and extremities that results in strange movement patterns that are present, to some extent, whenever the person is awake and may increase when voluntary movement is attempted (usually due to a central brain lesion).

atonia—decreased muscle tone.

atypical—different from the average or ordinary.

audiology—the study of the entire field of hearing (includes the anatomy and function of the ear, impairment of hearing, and the education or reeducation of the person with hearing loss).

audiometry—measurement of hearing level.

auditory discrimination—ability to discriminate between sounds of different frequency and intensity; ability to distinguish one sound from another.

auditory memory span—ability to recall verbal items after hearing them presented.

auditory perception—mental awareness of sound.

auditory sequencing—ability to recall information previously heard in correct order or sequence.

aura—sensations experienced by an epileptic just before a seizure (can be visual aura in which subject may see stars or colors, or auditory in which subject may hear voices or bells).

autism—as defined by the National Society of Autistic Children, a condition that is characterized by disorders of behavior and communication. Four criteria are: (a) onset before the age of 30 months, (b) impaired social development that is out of keeping with the child's intellectual level, (c) delayed and deviant language development that is also out of keeping with the child's intellectual level, and (d) insistence on sameness or resistance to change.

autoerotism—self-directed erotic behavior.

autonomic nervous system—part of the nervous system that is not the central nervous system (involves peripheral motor nerves to the viscera and includes both the sympathetic and parasympathetic systems).

autonomy—freedom to decide for oneself; independence.

babbling—stage in speech development during which the child carries on vocal play with its random, repetitive production of different speech sounds (begins around three to four months).

basal age—lowest mental age score secured on a psychological test.

behavior—any act, response, or movement of a person in response to internal or external stimulation.

body image—picture or mental representation one has of one's own body, derived from internal sensation, postural changes, and contact with outside objects and people.

brain—portion of the central nervous system that constitutes the organ of thought and neural coordination (includes all the higher nervous centers receiving stimuli from the sense organs, interpreting and correlating them to formulate the motor impulses).

brain-damaged or brain-injured—may denote definite neurological evidence of structural damage, the manifestations of which would be abnormal at any age (as in cerebral palsy) or describe behavior (hyperactive, distractible, impulsive, short attention span), that is thought by the observer to be related to central nervous system damage or dysfunction, with or without definite neurologic findings.

brain lesion—localized brain tissue damage; any destructive process of the brain.

bulimia—excessive appetite; morbid hunger.

central nervous system (CNS)—that part of the nervous system anatomy composed of the brain, brain stem, spinal cord, and peripheral nerves.

cephalocaudal progression—progression of physical maturation and development in the first year of life that follows a distribution from head (cephalo) and gradually progresses down the body sequentially to include upper trunk, arms, lower trunk, legs, and, finally, toes (caudal).

cerebellar ataxia—muscular incoordination due to injury to or lack of development of that part of the brain concerned with gross muscular movement.

cerebellum—part of the brain lying behind and above the medulla involved in muscle coordination and the maintenance of body equilibrium.

cerebral dominance—dominance of one side of the brain over the other as manifested by motoric laterality (dominance and laterality are not well established until a child is about 12 years old).

cerebral dysfunction—condition characterized by distractibility, clumsiness, and hyperactivity and a short attention span (the ability to reproduce simple geometric figures or other tasks requiring perceptual-motor ability is usually poor, but memory for isolated events is likely to be amazingly good). Also see *brain-damaged or brain-injured*.

cerebral hypoplasia—incomplete or arrested development of the brain.

cerebral palsy—physical disability affecting motor functions due to non-progressive lesion of the brain occurring at or before birth or during developmental years; impairment of the coordination of muscle action with an inability to maintain posture and balance to perform normal movements and skills. There may be associated neurological abnormalities such as sensory deficits, speech problems, sensory integration deficits, intellectual impairment, seizure disorders, and emotional disturbance. Statistics indicate that approximately 30 percent of people diagnosed as cerebral palsied are mentally retarded. The view that all conditions caused by cerebral palsy are irreversible, and that a person's intellectual development is fixed, has changed. It is now recognized that development is modifiable, and effects of trauma to the central nervous system can, in many cases, be ameliorated.

cerebrum—main part of the brain, occupying the upper and forepart of the cranial vault; the organ of voluntary control, conscious sensation, and learning processes.

characteristic—typical of person, entity, or circumstance.

chromosomal anomaly—abnormality of human chromosomes in which part of a chromosome is missing.

chromosome—carrier of genetic determinates transmitting hereditary characteristics.

chronological age (CA)—actual number of years one has lived.

clonus—rhythmic, rapid alternation of contraction and relaxation of a muscle.

closure—completion of a behavior, mental process, or other process.

cognition—process of knowing and becoming aware of objects, thoughts, and perceptions; understanding or reasoning.

compulsion—repetitive behavior performed in a stereotypic fashion; an activity not connected in a realistic way and clearly excessive.

congenital—existing at or before birth.

coordination—smooth, harmonious, and synchronized functioning of related muscle groups in the execution of complex movements.

cultural-familial retardation—mild retardation of unknown origin associated with history of retardation in other family members and with psychosocial deprivation.

decoding—intake of symbols through auditory and/or visual pathways.

development—sequence of growth, usually from simple to more complex; interaction between maturational processes and environmental influences.

developmental disability—a severe chronic disability of a person that: (a) is attributable to a mental or physical impairment or combination of mental and physical impairments; (b) is manifested before the person attains the age of 22; (c) is likely to continue indefinitely; (d) results in substantial functional limitations in three or more of the following areas of major life activity: self-care, receptive and expressive language, learning, mobility, self-direction, capacity for independent living, and economic sufficiency; and (e) reflects the person's need for a combination and sequence of special interdisciplinary, generic care, treatment, or other services that are of life-long or extended duration and are individually planned and coordinated.

differential diagnosis—diagnosis aimed at distinguishing a given case or disorder from other disorders presenting similar symptomatology.

diplegia—weakness, paralysis, or spastic involvement of lower extremities bilaterally.

distal—away from the center; peripheral; farther from the reference point.

distractibility—inability to maintain a normal attention span because of the impingement of irrelevant stimuli; uninhibited response to external stimuli.

Down syndrome (trisomy 21)—form of congenital mental deficiency due to a chromosomal abnormality with a number of physical characteristics, such as epicanthal folds, microcephaly, hypotonia, flat bridge of nose, and fissured tongue that is usually large and protruding.

dysarthria—disorder of articulation due to impairment of the part of the central nervous system that directly controls the muscles of speech (includes slurred, halting, and indistinct speech).

dysfunction—abnormality of function or operation of an organ, part, or system.

dyskinesia—repetitive involuntary mouth movements such as licking, chewing, sucking, and smacking (tardive dyskinesia).

dyslalia—speech impairment due to tongue or other speech organ abnormalities.

dysphonia—difficulty in uttering articulate sounds.

dysrhythmia—abnormality of brain wave rhythm as indicated by the electroencephalograph; abnormality of speech rhythm, usually characterized by defective stress breath control and intonation and abnormality of other bodily rhythms.

dysrhythmic speech—abnormal articulation due to disorder of the oral speech mechanism or to neurological abnormalities; abnormality of speech rhythm usually characterized by defective breath control, intonation and abnormality of other bodily rhythms.

dystonia—involuntary contraction of muscle groups.

echolalia—automatic echoing of another's speech without meaning or purpose (tends to be persistent and usually uttered in a parrotlike fashion); an aspect of early, normal speech and language development but abnormal in later stages of development and if it is the only form of expressive speech.

elective mutism—refusal to speak.

empathy—recognition of the nature and significance of another's behavior; denotes a deep understanding derived from cognitive and affective as well as intellectual experience corresponding to another's.

encephalitis—inflammation of the brain or its covering.

encephalopathy—brain damage; any dysfunction of the brain.

encoding—output of verbal symbols through motor (speech, gestural, and/or written) pathways.

endogenous retardation—retardation due to brain damage.

epilepsy—convulsive disorder due to spontaneous, uncontrolled firing of neurons in the brain, usually controlled through medication; *grand mal seizure:* condition characterized by generalized, involuntary motor activity of episodic nature that may last from 1 to 20 minutes, usually less than 5 minutes; *petit mal seizure:* condition characterized by brief, episodic loss of awareness that usually lasts only a few seconds and is accompanied by unusual eye, head, and arm movements; *psychomotor seizure:* condition characterized by rapid onset of mental confusion or daze accompanied by repetitions and poorly coordinated and purposeless movements or actions, sometimes followed by incoherent speech.

etiology—cause of a disease or disorder as determined by medical diagnosis.

exogenous retardation—retardation due to environmental factors.

eye–hand coordination—integration of the visual and tactual systems leading to a point at which the hand becomes the tool to serve the visual mechanism.

figure–ground discrimination—ability to sort out one aspect of the visual or auditory field (features, figures, characteristics) while perceiving it in relation to the rest of the field.

fine motor development—use of generally small muscle groups for specific precise movements such as those involved in manipulation of objects, grasping, and releasing.

flaccid—weak or lax.

functional retardation—retardation without evidence of organic defect.

gait—manner of walking.

genetic—inherited; caused by genes.

gross motor development—use of large muscle groups for specific crude movements involved in rolling over, walking, climbing, and running.

habilitation—acquisition of functions and skills not previously attained.

handedness—refers to hand dominance.

hemiplegia—weakness, paralysis, or spastic involvement limited to one side of the body.

hydrocephalus—condition characterized by an abnormal accumulation of fluid within the brain that frequently causes an enlargement of the skull.

hyperactivity—excessive activity without purpose.

hyperkinesis—excessive muscular activity and involuntary movements.

hypernasality—voice quality characterized by excessive nasal resonance.

hypertonicity—increased muscle tone of two clinical types: spasticity and rigidity.

hypoactivity—abnormally low level of activity; lethargy.

hyponasality—voice quality characterized by inadequate nasal resonance.

hypotonicity—muscle tone so flaccid that there is inability to maintain tension or resistance to stretch, leading to discoordination, paucity of movement, and lack of postural stability.

idiopathic—of unknown etiology.

jargon—unintelligible babble; simulated speech; sequencing of sounds with the rhythm, rate, and inflection of adult speech although few, if any, words are distinguishable. It normally begins in the 10- to 15-month-old child and decreases as more words are used.

kinesthesis—muscle sense; sensory awareness of one's body movements.

lability—state of being unstable or changeable; wide fluctuations in mood and affect.

laterality—sensorimotor awareness of the two sides of the body and their differences (sometimes refers to the tendency to use one side preferentially, such as the right hand, foot, ear, eye, in voluntary motor acts).

locomotion—movement from one place to another (may involve rolling over in early development and proceeds to activities such as crawling, walking, or skipping as development progresses).

maturation—organic processes or structural changes occurring within an individual's body that are relatively independent of external environmental conditions, experiences, or practice.

mental age (MA)—assessed level of mental development in relation to chronological age norms through the use of standardized tests (either the Stanford-Binet Intelligence Test or the Wechsler Intelligence Scale for Children [WISC]).

mental retardation—refers to significantly subaverage general intellectual functioning existing concurrently with deficits in adaptive behavior and manifested during the developmental period; the four levels of retardation (which, according to the *Manual of Terminology and Classification in Mental Retardation* of the AAMD, are not absolute or static and do not necessarily dictate the particular service needed but may be helpful as one criterion in planning) are mild, moderate, severe, and profound: *mild retardation:* designates persons who test between 67 and 52 points on the Stanford-Binet and Cattell intelligence tests and between 69 and 55 on the Wechsler Scales; roughly equivalent to the educational term *educable*; *moderate retardation*: designates persons who test between 51 and 36 on the Stanford-Binet and Cattell and between 54 and 40 on the Wechsler Scales; includes those individuals who are likely to fall into the educational category of *trainable*; *severe retardation*: designates persons who test between 35 and 20 on the Stanford-Binet and Cattell and between 39 and 25 on the Wechsler Scales; includes individuals sometimes known as *dependent retarded*; *profound retardation*: designates persons who test 19 and below on the Stanford-Binet and Cattell and 24 and below on the Wechsler scales; includes those individuals sometimes called *life support level*.

microcephaly—abnormal smallness of the head.

mixed dominance—term suggesting that right or left dominance (preference) has not been established.

monoplegia—weakness, paralysis, or spastic involvement of only one extremity.

motor cortex—area in front of the Rolandic fissure on either side of the brain where motor fibers project and emanate.

motor development—process of gradual acquisition of skills that incorporate bodily movement, gross and fine motor skills (progressive maturation of the nervous system underlies the sequential development of these motor skills; adult level of maturation is reached in mid-teens).

multiply handicapped—having more than one condition that seriously interferes with functioning and learning.

nasality—quality of speech sound in which the vibrating breath stream is diverted into the nasal cavity.

neonatal—pertaining to period of time after birth up to one month.

neurological impairment—includes a group of higher brain dysfunctions, determined before the completion of nervous system development, that have a substantial impact upon the complete, usual, and adaptive use and maturation of language, cognition, memory, attention, fine motor function, and/or organically determined social behavior and other nervous system or neuromuscular disorders with similar deficits in adaptive behavior. In practice, this category encompasses cerebral palsy, epilepsy, and substantial mental retardation, spina bifida, Tourette syndrome, and neurofibromatosis, among other conditions (some research studies have implicated neurological contributions to autistic behavior).

nystagmus—involuntary rapid oscillating eye movements.

palmar grasp—grasp involving the palm of the hand.

paraplegia—weakness, paralysis, or spastic involvement of the legs and lower portion of the body.

paresis—weakness; partial paralysis.

partially sighted—given the best possible correction, a visual acuity between 20/200 and 20/70 in the better eye.

perceptual disorder—inability to recognize objects, relations, or qualities involving the interpretation and integration of sensory stimuli.

perceptual-motor—deriving meaning from sensory stimuli and integrating the sensory with the motor processes so that there is a purposeful response.

perseveration—compulsive repetition of movements, vocalizations, and verbalizations recurring without apparent external stimulus.

phenylketonuria (PKU)—disorder transmitted by a recessive gene, characterized by an abnormal accumulation of phenylalanine and a deficiency in tyrosine, resulting in a number of functional abnormalities.

phobia—persistent and irrational fear of a specific object, activity, or situation that results in avoidance of dreaded situations.

phonation—voice production.

pincer grasp—grasp involving the tips of the thumb and index finger.

President's Commission on Mental Retardation (formerly President's Panel on Mental Retardation)—appointed by President John F. Kennedy in October 1961 to prepare a national plan regarding mental retardation and composed of professionals working in the field of mental retardation in the United States.

proximodistal progression—development of fine motor skills advancing from muscle groups close to the body (proximal) and progressing to those muscle groups located farther away (distal).

psychomotor—observable, voluntary, conscious movement (as distinguished from involuntary reflex movement).

psychomotor agitation—excessive motor activity associated with a feeling of inner tension lasting from a few minutes to several hours and characterized by chewing, smacking of lips, confusion, and engaging in purposeless activity such as rubbing arms and legs (person may experience anger, rage, and fear).

psychomotor retardation—visible, generalized slowing down of physical reactions, movements, and speech.

psychosis—any mental disorder characterized by a severe disturbance of normal intellectual and social functioning and by a lack of contact with reality.

quadriplegia—weakness, paralysis, or spastic involvement affecting all four limbs.

rehabilitation—restoration of a person to a valued status, role, and reputation, and not merely restoration to adequate physical or mental functioning; reacquisition of skills lost as a result of damage.

rigidity—tenseness, immovability, inability to bend or be bent; in psychiatry, refers to one who is excessively resistant to change.

schemata—organized patterns of perception and/or behavior.

scissor gait—pattern of walking caused by loss of muscle tone of the adductors of the hips resulting in the legs being held close together.

scoliosis—lateral (sideways) curvature of the spine.

seizure—convulsion (in epilepsy characterized by severe abnormal electrical discharge in the brain).

sensorimotor—relationship between sensation and movement.

sensory cortex—refers to the area immediately behind the Rolandic fissure on either side of the brain.

sensory overload—more sensory stimulation than an individual can successfully process at one time.

sensory perception—process of organizing and interpreting raw data coming into the brain through the five senses.

socialization—learning process that guides the growth of our social personalities and makes us reasonably acceptable and effective members of our society.

soft signs—clinical evidence of an inability to perform certain perceptual-motor tasks in an age-appropriate manner.

spastic diplegia—form of cerebral palsy characterized by muscular stiffness and weakness in both arms and legs.

spastic hemiplegia—form of cerebral palsy characterized by muscular stiffness and weakness of an arm and leg on the same side of the body.

spastic quadriplegia—form of cerebral palsy characterized by muscular stiffness and weakness of all four limbs.

spasticity—hypertension of muscles causing stiff and awkward movements resulting from upper motoneuron lesion.

spina bifida—birth defect in which there has been incomplete formation of the spinal cord, usually resulting in paralysis of the lower body.

stereotypy—same verbal or motoric response to different external stimuli.

strabismus—condition characterized by imbalance in eye position resulting in deviation of one or both eyes.

symbiotic—denoting an excessive interdependency between two persons.

symptom—manifestation of a condition.

syndrome—cluster of symptoms that are characteristic of a given disease or condition.

synergy—combined and correlated force; united action of separate substances that in combination produce an effect greater than the sum of its component parts.

trisomy—condition characterized by the presence of a chromosome in triplicate instead of duplicate.

visual discrimination—adeptness at perceiving likenesses and differences.

visual-motor—term generally encompassing the visual-receptive and motor-expressive areas plus intersensory integration.

visual-motor coordination—ability to coordinate vision with the movements of the body or parts of the body.

vocalization—sounds produced by movements of lips, tongue, or vocal apparatus.

Suggested Readings

CHAPTER 1

Adorno, T. *Introduction to the sociology of music*. New York: Seabury Press, 1976.

Bauer, M., & Peyser, E.R. *Music through the ages*. New York: Putnam, 1946.

Benedict, R. *Patterns of culture*. New York: Penguin Books, 1946.

Bernstein, L. *The infinite variety of music*. New York: Simon & Schuster, 1966.

Bowra, C.M. *Primitive song*. New York: Mentor Books, 1963.

Capurso, A., Fisichelli, V.R., Gilman, L., Gutheil, E.A., Wright, J.T., & Paperte, F. *Music and your emotions*. New York: Liveright Publishing Corporation, 1952.

Dubos, R. *Man adapting*. New Haven, Conn.: Yale University Press, 1965.

Farnsworth, P.R. *The psychology of tone and music*. Worcester, Mass.: Clark University, 1964.

Fenster, C.A. Vocal communications of emotional meaning among adults and children. *Dissertation Abstracts*, 1967, *28*(4-B), 1964–1965.

Hobbs, N. Helping disturbed children: Psychological and ecological strategies. In H. Dupont (Ed.), *Educating emotionally disturbed children*. New York: Holt, Rinehart & Winston, 1969.

Institute for Therapeutic Research. *Music psychology index*. Lawrence, Kans.: Author, 1976.

Josef, K. *Musik als Hilfe in der Erziehumg geistig Behinderter*. Berlin: Marhold, 1967.

Kohut, H. *Observations on the psychological functions of music*. Paper presented at the meeting of the American Psychoanalytic Association, Chicago, May 1956.

May, R. *The courage to create*. New York: Bantam Books, 1976.

Merriam, A.P. *The anthropology of music*. Evanston, Ill.: Northwestern University Press, 1964.

Meyer, L.B. *Emotion and meaning in music*. Chicago: University of Chicago Press, 1957.

Montagu, A. *Man: His first million years*. New York: Mentor Books, 1958.

Mursell, J. *The psychology of music*. New York: Norton, 1937.

Nocera, S. *Reaching the special learner through music*. Morristown, N.J.: Silver Burdett, 1979.

Pesso, A. *Movement in psychotherapy*. New York: New York University Press, 1969.

Rossi, N., & Rafferty, S. *Music through the centuries*. Boston: B. Humphries, 1963.

Sahakian, W.S. (Ed.). *Psychopathology today: Experimentation, theory, and research*. Itasca, Ill.: F.E. Peacock, 1970.

Sinnott, E.W. *The biology of the spirit*. New York: Viking Press, 1955.

Smith, H.W. *Man and his gods.* Boston: Little, Brown and Company, 1952.

Szasz, T.S. *The myth of mental illness.* New York: Harper & Row, 1974.

Terzian, A.S. *A psychoanalytic review of music.* Paper presented at the meeting of the Philadelphia Association of Psychoanalysis, Philadelphia, October 1961.

Thibaut, J.W., & Kelley, H.H. *The social psychology of groups.* New York: John Wiley and Sons, 1959.

Van de Wall, W. *Music in institutions.* New York: Russell Sage Foundation, 1936.

Van de Wall, W. *Music in hospitals.* New York: Russell Sage Foundation, 1946.

Von Hagen, V.W. *The ancient sun kingdoms of the Americas.* Cleveland: World Publishing, 1961.

Washington State Library, Institutional Library Services Division. *Music the healer: A bibliography.* Olympia, Wash.: Author, 1970.

Wheeler, B. The relationship between music therapy and theories of psychotherapy. *Music Therapy,* 1981, *1*(1), 9–16.

Wolfe, D.E., Burns, S., & Wichmann, K. *Analysis of music therapy group procedures.* Minneapolis, Minn.: Golden Valley Health Center, 1975.

CHAPTER 2

Alley, G.P., & Carr, D. Effects of systematic sensory-motor training on sensory-motor, visual perception, and concept formation of mentally retarded children. *Perceptual Motor Skills,* 1968, *27,* 451–456.

Begab, M.J., Haywood, H.C., & Garber, H.L. (Eds.). *Psychosocial influences in retarded performance* (Vol. 1). Baltimore: University Park Press, 1981.

Blakeslee, T.R. *Thr right brain: A new understanding of the unconscious mind and its creative powers.* Garden City, N.Y.: Doubleday and Company, 1980.

Bonny, I., and Savary, L.M. *Music and your mind.* New York: Harper & Row, 1973.

Davitz, J.R. *The language of emotion.* New York: Academic Press, 1969.

Deutsch, F. *Body, mind and the sensory gateways.* New York: Basic Books, 1962.

Dobzhansky, T. *Mankind evolving.* New Haven, Conn.: Yale University Press, 1962.

Furst, C. *Origins of the mind: Origins of the mind–brain connections.* Englewood Cliffs, N.J.: Prentice-Hall, 1979.

Menolascino, F. *Beyond the limits.* Seattle: Special Child Publications, 1974.

Meyerowitz, J.H. Self-derogation in young retardates and special class placement. *Child Development,* 1962, *33*(2), 443–451.

Pribram, K.H. *Languages of the brain: Experimental paradoxes and principles in neuropsychology.* Englewood Cliffs, N.J.: Prentice-Hall, 1971.

Radocy, R.E. *Psychological foundations of musical behavior.* Springfield, Ill.: Charles C Thomas, 1979.

Robins, F., & Robins, J. *Educational rhythmics for mentally and physically handicapped children.* New York: Association Press, 1968.

Schultz, D.P. *Sensory restriction: Effects on behavior.* New York: Academic Press, 1965.

Seashore, C.E. *The psychology of music.* New York: Dover Publications, 1967.

Shrift, D.C. The galvanic skin response to two contrasting types of music. In E.T. Gaston (Ed.), *Music therapy 1956.* Lawrence, Kans.: Allen Press, 1957.

Straus, E.W. *The primary world of senses.* New York: Free Press, 1963.

Tobach, E., Aronson, L.R., & Shaw, E. (Eds.). *The biopsychology of development*. New York: Academic Press, 1971.

Von Buddenbrock, W. *The senses*. Ann Arbor, Mich.: University of Michigan Press, 1958.

Walters, L. How music produces its effects on the brain and mind. In E. Podolsky (Ed.), *Music therapy*. New York: Philosophical Libraries, 1954.

Weigl, V. About rhythm and its effects on kinetic impulses. *Bulletin of the National Association for Music Therapy*, 1961, *5*, 81–89.

Weigl, V. Music for the retarded. *Music Journal*, 1969, *1*, 56–70.

CHAPTER 3

American Psychiatric Association. *Diagnostic and statistical manual of mental disorders (third edition)* (DSM-III). Washington, D.C., 1980.

Antrobus, J.S. (Ed.). *Cognition and affect*. Boston: Little, Brown and Company, 1970.

Asmus, E.P., & Gilbert, J.P. A client-oriented model of therapeutic intervention. *Journal of Music Therapy*, 1981, *18*(1), 41–51.

Bayley, N. Mental growth during the first three years. In R.G. Baker, J.S. Kounin, & H.F. Wright (Eds.), *Child behavior and development*. New York: McGraw-Hill, 1943.

Bayley, N. *Bayley Scales of Infant Development: Birth to two years*. New York: Psychological Corporation, 1969.

Bockelheide, V. *Some techniques of assessing certain basic music listening skills of eight and nine year olds*. Unpublished doctoral dissertation, Stanford University, 1960.

Bruner, J. The course of cognitive growth. *American Psychologist*, 1964, *19*, 1–15.

Cairns, R.B. *Social development*. San Francisco: W.H. Freeman, 1979.

Cantor, G.M., and Girardeau, F.L. Rhythmic discrimination ability in mongoloid and normal children. *American Journal of Mental Deficiency*, 1959, *63*, 621–625.

Carroll, J.B. Language development in children. In S. Saporta (Ed.), *Psycholinguistics*. New York: Holt, Rinehart & Winston, 1961.

Cicourel, A.V. Oral and non-oral representations of communicative and social competence. In M.J. Begab and S.A. Richardson (Eds.), *The mentally retarded and society: A social science perspective*. Baltimore: University Park Press, 1976.

Congdon, D.M. The Adaptive Behavior Scale modified for the profoundly retarded. *Mental Retardation*, 1973, *11*(1), 20–21.

Crawford, J.L., McMahon, D.J., Conklin, G.S., Giordano, D., Alexander, M.J., & Kadyszewski, P. Assessing skilled functioning of mentally retarded persons. *Mental Retardation*, 1980, *18*(5), 235–239.

Darley, F.L. *Diagnosis and appraisal of communication disorders*. Englewood Cliffs, N.J.: Prentice-Hall, 1964.

Dileo, C. The relationship of diagnostic and social factors in singing ranges of institutionalized mentally retarded persons. *Journal of Music Therapy*, 1976, *13*, 17–28.

Ellis, N.R. (Ed.). *Handbook of mental deficiency: Psychological theory and research* (2nd ed.). Hillsdale, N.J.: Lawrence Erlbaum Associates, 1979.

Frances, R.J., & Rarick, G.L. Motor characteristics of the mentally retarded. *American Journal of Mental Deficiency*, 1959, *63*, 792–811.

Frostig, M. *Movement education: Theory and practice*. Chicago: Follett Educational Corporation, 1970.

Gesell, A., & Ilg, F.L. *Infant and child in the culture of today.* New York: Harper & Row, 1974.

Gesell, A., & Ilg, F.L. *Developmental diagnosis: Normal and abnormal child development.* New York: Harper & Row, 1975.

Ginsburg, H., & Opper, S. *Piaget's theory of intellectual development: An introduction.* Englewood Cliffs, N.J.: Prentice-Hall, 1969.

Harrow, A.J. *A taxonomy of the psychomotor domain.* New York: David McKay Company, 1972.

Harvat, R.W. *Physical education for children with perceptual-motor learning disabilities.* Columbus, Ohio: Charles E. Merrill, 1971.

Hilgard, E.R. *Theories of learning.* New York: Appleton-Century-Crofts, 1948.

Illingworth, R.S. *The development of the infant and young child: Normal and abnormal* (5th ed.). Edinburgh: Churchill-Livingstone, 1972.

Johnson, J.M. Evaluating patients in music therapy. *Journal of Music Therapy,* 1968, *3,* 108–110.

Kephart, N. *The slow learner in the classroom.* Columbus, Ohio: Charles E. Merrill, 1960.

Kluckholm, C. *Mirror for man.* New York: McGraw-Hill, 1949.

Lehman, P.R. *Tests and measurements in music.* Englewood Cliffs, N.J.: Prentice-Hall, 1968.

McGraw, M.B. *The neuromuscular maturation of the human infant.* New York: Columbia University Press, 1943.

Mithang, D., Mar, D., Stewart, J., & McCalmon, D. Assessing prevocational competencies of profoundly, severely, and moderately retarded persons. *Journal of the Association for Severely Handicapped* (JASH), 1980, *5*(6), 227–284.

Mosston, M. *Developmental movement.* Columbus, Ohio: Charles E. Merrill, 1965.

North, M. *Personality assessment through movement.* London: MacDonald and Evans, 1972.

Pflederer, M. The responses of children to musical tastes embodying Piaget's principle of conversation. *Journal of Research in Music Education,* 1964, *12,* 251–268.

Roach, E.G., & Kephart, N.G. *The Purdue perceptual-motor survey.* Columbus, Ohio: Charles E. Merrill, 1966.

Rosenzweig, L.E., & Long, J. *Understanding and teaching the dependent retarded child.* Darien, Conn.: Educational Publishing Corporation, 1960.

Sarason, S. *Psychological problems in mental deficiency.* New York: Basic Books, 1958.

Sarason, S., & Doris, J. *Psychological problems of mental deficiency* (4th ed.). New York: Harper & Row, 1969.

Schreiber, F.R. *Your child's speech.* New York: Hash-Marc/Ballantine Books, 1973.

Switsky, H., Rotatori, A.F., Miller, T., & Freagon, S. The developmental model and its implications for assessment and instruction for the severely/profoundly handicapped. *Mental Retardation,* 1979, *17*(4), 167–170.

CHAPTER 4

Apprey, Z.R., & Apprey, M. *Applied music therapy: Collected papers on a technique and a point of view.* Independence, Mo.: Institute of Music Therapy and Humanistic Psychology, The International University, 1975.

Bentov, I. Sound waves and vibration. In I. Bentov (Ed.), *Stalking the wild pendulum: On the mechanism of consciousness.* New York: Bantam Books, 1981.

Bonny, H.L. *Listening with a new consciousness.* New York: Harper & Row, 1973.

Buhler, C. Basic theoretical concepts of humanistic psychology. *American Psychologist,* 1971, *26*(4), 378–386.

Cotler, S.B., & Guerra, J.J. *Assertion training: A humanistic-behavioral guide to self-dignity.* Champaign, Ill.: Research Press, 1976.

Grossman, R.D. Enhancing the self. *Exceptional Children,* 1971, *38*(3), 248–254.

Jung, C.G. [*The undiscovered self.*] (R.F.C. Hull, trans.). New York: New American Library, 1959.

Kneller, G.F. *The art and science of creativity.* New York: Holt, Rinehart & Winston, 1965.

Koffka, K. *Principles of gestalt psychology.* New York: Harcourt, Brace & World, 1935.

Laing, R.D. *Self and others.* New York: Penguin Books, 1980.

Langer, S.K. *Feeling and form.* New York: Charles Scribner's Sons, 1953.

Lowenfeld, V. *Creative and mental growth* (5th ed.). New York: Macmillan, 1970.

May, R. The emergence of existential psychology. In R. May (Ed.), *Existential psychology* (2nd ed.). New York: Random House, 1969.

May, R., Angel, E., & Ellenberger, H.F. (Eds.). *Existence: A new dimension in psychiatry and psychology.* New York: Simon & Schuster, 1958.

McGeoch, J.A., & Irion, A.L. *The psychology of human learning.* New York: McKay, 1952.

Montagu, A. (Ed.). *Culture and human development: Insights into growing human.* Englewood Cliffs, N.J.: Prentice-Hall, 1974.

Murphy, G. *Human potentialities.* New York: Basic Books, 1958.

Ornstein, R. *The psychology of consciousness.* New York: Viking Press, 1973.

Ornstein, R. (Ed.). *The nature of human consciousness: A book of readings.* New York: Viking Press, 1974.

Reymert, M. (Ed.). *Feelings and emotions.* Worcester, Mass.: Clark University Press, 1928.

Schutz, W. *Joy: Expanding human awareness.* New York: Grove Press, 1967.

Shulman, L.S., & Keislar, E.R. *Learning by discovery: A critical appraisal.* Chicago: Rand McNally, 1966.

Stevens, J.O. (Ed.). *Gestalt is.* New York: Bantam Books, 1977.

Woodworth, R.S. *Dynamics of behavior.* New York: Holt, Rinehart & Winston, 1958.

Young, P.T. *Motivation and emotions.* New York: Wiley, 1961.

CHAPTER 5

Cratty, B.J., & Martin, M.M. *Perceptual-motor efficiency in children.* Philadelphia: Lea & Febiger, 1969.

Dobbs, J. *The slow learner and music.* London: Oxford University Press, 1966.

Evans, R.A. Word recall and associative clustering in mental retardates. *American Journal of Mental Deficiency,* 1970, *74,* 765–770.

Fleishman, E.A., & Rich, S. Role of kinesthetic and spatial-visual abilities in perceptual-motor learning. *Journal of Experimental Psychology,* 1963, *66,* 6–11.

Gagné, R.M. *The conditions of learning* (2nd ed.). New York: Holt, Rinehart & Winston, 1970.

Gaston, E.T. Dynamic music factors in mood change. *Music Education Journal,* 1951, *37,* 42–44.

Gilliland, E.G. Music therapy. In H.A. Pattison (Ed.), *The handicapped and their rehabilitation.* Springfield, Ill.: Charles C Thomas, 1957.

Grinker, R.R. The physiology of emotions. In A. Simon, C. Herbert, & R. Straus (Eds.), *The physiology of emotions.* Springfield, Ill.: Charles C Thomas, 1961.

Hood, M.V., & Schultz, E.J. *Learning music through rhythm.* Westport, Conn.: Greenwood Press, 1972.

Hunt, A. *Listen, let's make music*. London: Bedford Square Press, 1976.

Isern, B. The influence of music upon the memory of mentally retarded children. In E.H. Schneider (Ed.), *Music therapy: 1958*. Lawrence, Kans.: Allen Press, 1959.

Jaques-Dalcroze, E. *The eurhythmics of Jaques-Dalcroze*. Boston: Small Maynard and Company, 1913.

Jorgensen, J., & Parnell, M.K. Modifying social behaviors of mentally retarded children in music activities. *Journal of Music Therapy*, 1970, *7*(3), 83–87.

Kanner, L. *Child psychiatry* (3rd ed.). Springfield, Ill.: Charles C Thomas, 1957.

Kratter, F.E. Music therapy for the mentally retarded. *American Journal of Psychiatry*, 1959, *115*, 737–738.

Kronvall, E.L., & Diehl, C.F. The relationship of auditory discrimination to articulatory defects of children with no known organic impairment. *Journal of Speech and Hearing Disorders*, 1954, *19*, 335–338.

Lathom, W. Music therapy as a means of changing the adaptive behavior level of retarded children. *Journal of Music Therapy*, 1964, *1*(4), 132–134.

Lawton, E.B. *Activities of daily living for physical rehabilitation*. New York: McGraw-Hill, 1963.

Lienhard, M.E. Factors relevant to the rhythmic perception of a group of mentally retarded children. *Journal of Music Therapy*, 1976, *13*(2), 58–65.

Lindamood, C.A., & Lindamood, P.C. *Auditory discrimination in depth*. New York: Teaching Resources, 1969.

Litton, W.M. *Working with groups: Group process and individual growth* (2nd ed.). New York: Wiley, 1967.

Loven, M.A. Value of music therapy for mentally retarded children. *Journal of Music Therapy*, 1956, *6*, 105–171.

Luft, J. *Group processes: An introduction to group dynamics*. Palo Alto, Calif.: National Press, 1966.

Maloney, M.P., Ball, T.S., & Edgar, C.L. An analysis of the generalizability of sensory-motor training. *American Journal of Mental Deficiency*, 1970, *74*, 458–469.

Masterson, J.F. *Treatment of the borderline adolescent: A developmental approach*. New York: Wiley, 1972.

Menolascino, F.J. Emotional disturbance and mental retardation. *American Journal of Mental Deficiency*, 1965, *70*, 248–256.

Menolascino, F.J. Emotional disturbances in mentally retarded children. *American Journal of Psychiatry*, 1969, *126*, 168–176.

Menolascino, F.J. (Ed.). *Psychiatric approaches to mental retardation*. New York: Basic Books, 1970.

Metzler, R.K. The use of music as a reinforcer to increase imitative behavior in severely and profoundly retarded female residents. *Journal of Music Therapy*, 1974, *11*(2), 97–110.

Michel, D.E. *Music therapy: An introduction to therapy and special education through music*. Springfield, Ill.: Charles C Thomas, 1976.

Milman, D.S., & Goldman, G.D. (Eds.). *Therapists at work: A demonstration of theory and techniques*. Dubuque, Iowa: Kendall/Hunt Publishing Company, 1979.

Moustakas, C.F. *Psychotherapy with children: The living relationship*. New York: Ballantine Books, 1959.

Palmer, M.F., Nordoff, P., & Robbins, C. *Effects of a new type of music therapy upon children with neurological disorders*. Paper presented at the annual meeting of the American Speech and Hearing Association, Wichita, Kansas, 1962.

Penfield, W., & Roberts, L. *Speech and brain mechanisms*. Princeton, N.J.: Princeton University Press, 1959.

Provonost, W. The speech behavior and language comprehension of autistic children. *Journal of Chronic Diseases,* 1961, *13,* 228–236.

Purvis, J., & Samet, S. (Eds.). *Music in developmental therapy: A curriculum guide*. Baltimore: University Park Press, 1976.

Redl, F., & Wineman, D. *Controls from within: Techniques for the treatment of the aggressive child*. New York: Free Press, 1952.

Reik, T. *Listening with the third ear*. New York: Farrar, Strauss, 1949.

Robbins, C., & Robbins, C. *Music for the hearing impaired: A resource manual and curriculum guide*. St. Louis: Magnamusic-Baton, 1980.

Ruud, E. *Music therapy and its relationship to current treatment theories*. St. Louis: Magnamusic-Baton, 1980.

Schopler, E. Toward reducing behavior problems in autistic children. In L. Wing (Ed.), *Early childhood autism: Clinical, educational and social aspects*. Oxford: Pergamon Press, 1976.

Schulberg, C.H. *The music therapy sourcebook*. New York: Human Sciences Press, 1981.

Sherwin, A.C. Reactions to music of autistic children. *American Journal of Psychiatry,* 1953, *109,* 823–832.

Steele, A.L., & Jorgensen, H.A. Music therapy: An effective solution to problems in related disciplines. *Journal of Music Therapy,* 1971, *8*(4), 131–145.

Stein, J. Problem cases in individual music therapy. *Bulletin of the National Association for Music Therapy,* 1963, *12,* 9–20.

Stevens, E.A. Some effects of tempo changes on stereotyped rocking movements of low-level mentally retarded subjects. *American Journal of Mental Deficiency,* 1971, *76,* 76–81.

Stevens, E.A., & Clark, F. Music therapy in the treatment of autistic children. *Journal of Music Therapy,* 1969, *6*(4), 98–104.

Webb, R.C. Sensory-motor training of the profoundly retarded. *American Journal of Mental Deficiency,* 1969, *74,* 283–295.

Weigl, V. This rhythmic approach to music therapy. *Journal of Music Therapy,* 1962, *12,* 71–80.

Wing, L. Social, behavioral and cognitive characteristics: An epidemiological approach. In M. Rutter & E. Schopler (Eds.), *Autism: A reappraisal of concept and treatment*. New York: Plenum Press, 1979.

Winsor, C.B. *The creative process*. New York: Bank Street College of Education, 1976.

Wolf, M.M., & Anderson, R.M. *The multiply handicapped child*. Springfield, Ill.: Charles C Thomas, 1969.

Wolpow, R.I. The independent effects of contingent social and academic approval upon the musical on-task and performance behaviors of profoundly retarded adults. *Journal of Music Therapy,* 1976, *13*(1), 29–38.

CHAPTER 6

Alvin, J. The response of severely retarded children to music. *American Journal of Mental Deficiency,* 1959, *63,* 988–996.

Bailey, P. *They can make music*. London: Oxford University Press, 1973.

Barclay, P. Dalcroze eurhythmics with mentally handicapped children. *Teaching and Training,* 1965, *3*(3), 72–76.

Barker, S. *The revolutionary way to use your body for total energy: The Alexander technique*. New York: Bantam Books, 1978.

Barsch, R.H. *Achieving perceptual-motor efficiency: A space-oriented approach to learning*. Seattle: Seattle Sequin School, 1967.

Beisler, J.M. & Tsai, L.Y. A pragmatic approach to increase expressive language skills. *Journal of Autism and Developmental Disorders*, 1983, *3*(13), 287–289.

Berlin, C.I. On: Melodic intonation therapy for aphasia by R.W. Sparks and A.L. Holland. *Journal of Speech and Hearing Disorders*, 1976, *49*, 298–300.

Bion, W.R. Group dynamics: A re-view. *International Journal of Psychoanalysis*, 1952, *33*, 101–121.

Bion, W.R. *Experiences in groups*. London: Tavistock Publications, 1961.

Bevans, J. The exceptional child and Orff. *Education of the Visually Handicapped*, 1969, *4*, 116–120.

Boxill, E.H., & Bruscia, K. *Clinical practice and research in music therapy for the developmentally disabled*. Paper presented at the 102nd annual meeting of the American Association on Mental Deficiency, Denver, May 1978.

Braley, W.T., Konicki, G., & Leedy, C. *Daily sensorimotor training activities*. Freeport, N.Y.: Educational Activities, 1968.

Bruner, J.S. *The process of education*. New York: Vintage Books, 1963.

Bruscia, K.E. Auditory short-term memory and attentional control of mentally retarded persons. *American Journal of Mental Deficiency*, 1981, *85*(4), 435–437.

Carabo-Cone, M. *A sensory-motor approach to music learning*. New York: MCA Music, 1969.

Chadwick, D.R. Speech disorders and music. *Instrumentalist*, 1976, *31*(1), 28–30.

Chaney, C.M., & Kephart, N.C. *Motoric aids to perceptual training*. Columbus, Ohio: Charles E. Merrill, 1968.

Chess, S. Emotional problems in mentally retarded. In F.J. Menolascino (Ed.), *Psychiatric approaches to mental retardation*. New York: Basic Books, 1970.

Cotten, P.D. (Ed.). *A handbook on the theory and practice of music for educable mentally retarded children and youth*. Jackson, Miss.: State of Mississippi Department of Education, 1968.

Crews, K. *Music and perceptual-motor development*. Englewood Cliffs, N.J.: Prentice-Hall, 1974.

Dudas, V.C. Utilization of music therapy in the treatment of cerebral palsy. *Journal of Music Therapy*, 1964, *1*(2), 49–56.

Ellis, N.R. Memory processes in retardates and normals. In N.R. Ellis (Ed.), *International review of research on mental retardation* (Vol. 4). New York: Academic Press, 1970.

Ferguson, N. Orff with the perceptually handicapped child. *The Orff Echo*, 1970, *2*, 1–11.

Flavell, J.H. *The developmental psychology of Jean Piaget*. Princeton, N.J.: Van Nostrand Company, 1963.

Galloway, H.F., Jr., & Bean, M.F. The effects of action songs on the development of body-image and body-part identification in hearing-impaired preschool children. *Journal of Music Therapy*, 1974, *11*, 125–135.

Gardner, H. *The arts and human development*. New York: John Wiley and Sons, 1973.

Gardner, W.I. *Learning and behavior characteristics of exceptional children and youth*. Boston: Allyn & Bacon, 1977.

Ghiselin, B. *The creative process*. New York: Mentor Books, 1955.

Haywood, H.C. Experiential factors in intellectual development: The concept of dynamic intelligence. In J. Zubin & G. Jervis (Eds.), *Psychopathology of mental development*. New York: Grune & Stratton, 1967.

Hollander, F.M., & Juhrs, P.D. Orff-Schulwerk: An effective treatment tool with autistic children. *Journal of Music Therapy*, 1974, *11*(1), 1–12.

Howery, B.I. Music therapy for mentally retarded children and adults. In E.T. Gaston (Ed.), *Music in therapy*. New York: Macmillan Company, 1968.

Humphrey, T. The effect of music ear training upon the auditory discrimination abilities of trainable mentally retarded adolescents. *Journal of Music Therapy*, 1980, *17*(2), 99–108.

Kahn, J.V. Relationship of Piaget's sensorimotor period to language acquisition of profoundly retarded children. *American Journal of Mental Deficiency*, 1975, *79*, 640–643.

Keyes, L.E. *Toning: The creative power of the voice*. Marina del Rey, Calif.: De Vorss & Co., 1973.

Lowen, A. *The betrayal of the body*. New York: Collier Books, 1967.

Luckey, R.E., Carpenter, C., & Steiner, J.E. Severely retarded adults' response to rhythm band instruments. *American Journal of Mental Deficiency*, 1967, *71*, 616–619.

Maccheroni, A.M. [*Developing the musical senses: Montessori approach*] (R. Brienza, trans.). Cincinnati, Ohio: World Library Publications, 1966.

McLaughlin, T. *Music and communication*. New York: St. Martin's Press, 1971.

Metzler, R.K. The use of music as a reinforcer to increase imitative behavior in severely and profoundly retarded female residents. *Journal of Music Therapy*, 1974, *11*(2), 97–110.

Nash, G. *Creative approach to child development with music, language, and movement*. New York: Alfred Publishing Company, 1974.

Plach, T. *The creative use of music in group therapy*. Springfield, Ill.: Charles C Thomas, 1980.

Priestly, M. *Music therapy in action*. London: Constable, 1975.

Rambusch, N.M. *Learning how to learn: An American approach to Montessori*. Baltimore: Helicon Press, 1962.

Richards, L.D., & Lee, K.A. Group process in social habilitation of the retarded. *Social Casework*, 1972, *53*, 30–37.

Riordan, J.T. *They can sing too: Rhythm for the deaf*. Leavenworth, Kans.: Jenrich Associates, 1971.

Roskam, K. Music therapy as an aid for increasing auditory awareness and improving reading skill. *Journal of Music Therapy*, 1979, *16*(1), 31–42.

Sears, W.W. Processes in music therapy. In E.T. Gaston (Ed.), *Music in therapy*. New York: Macmillan, 1968.

Seeyle, W.S., & Thomas, J.E. Is mobility feasible with multiply handicapped blind children? *Exceptional Children*, 1966, *32*, 613–617.

Slavson, S.R. *Analytic group psychotherapy with children, adolescents, and adults*. New York: Columbia University Press, 1950.

Stein, J. Music therapy treatment techniques. *American Journal of Orthopsychiatry*, 1963, *33*, 521–528.

Stephens, W.E., & Ludy, I.E. Action-concept learning in retarded children using photographic slides, motion picture sequences, and live demonstration. *American Journal of Mental Deficiency*, 1975, *80*, 277–280.

Storr, A. *The dynamics of creation*. New York: Atheneum, 1972.

Werry, J.S. Developmental hyperactivity. *Pediatric Clinics of North America*, 1968, *15*(3), 581–599.

Wohlwill, J. *The study of behavioral development*. New York: Academic Press, 1973.

Wolfgart, H. *Orff-Schulwerk und therapie*. Berlin: Marhold, 1975.

Wood, M.M. (Ed.). *Developmental therapy sourcebook*. Baltimore: University Park Press, 1981.

CHAPTER 8

Acuff, C.F. *A many faceted music program for the mentally retarded.* Paper presented at the 91st annual meeting of the American Association of Mental Deficiency, Denver, Colorado, May 15–20, 1967.

Christoplos, F. A multi-disciplinary paradigm. *Journal of Learning Disabilities*, 1970, *3*, 47–48.

Crawford, J. Art for the mentally retarded: Directed or creative. In E. Ulman & P. Dachinger (Eds.), *Art therapy in theory and practice.* New York: Schocken Books, 1975.

Crocker, D.B. Using music in a speech therapy program. In E.A. Schneider (Ed.), *Music Therapy 1958.* Lawrence, Kans.: Allen Press, 1959.

Ducanis, A.J., & Golin, A.K. *The interdisciplinary team: A handbook.* Rockville, Md.: Aspen Systems Corporation, 1979.

Espenak, L. Dance therapy: A new nonverbal treatment modality for the developmentally disabled. In J.M. Levy, P.H. Levy, N. Liebman, T.A. Dern, R. Rae, & T.-R. Ames (Eds.), *From the 60s into the 80s: An international assessment of attitudes and services for the developmentally disabled—papers from a conference organized by the Young Adult Institute & Workshop, Inc. in support of the International Year of Disabled Persons, April 6–10, 1981.* New York: Young Adult Institute & Workshop, Inc., 1982.

Flanagan, P.J., Baker, G.R., & LaFollette, L.G. *An orientation to mental retardation: A programmed text.* Springfield, Ill.: Charles C Thomas, 1973.

Flynn, R.J., & Nitsch, K.E. (Eds.). *Normalization, social integration, and community services.* Austin, TX: PRO-ED, 1980.

Goodnow, C.C. The use of dance in therapy with retarded children. *Journal of Music Therapy*, 1968, *5*(4), 97–102.

Gray, V., & Percival, R. *Music, movement and mime for children.* Oxford: Oxford University Press, 1962.

Harbert, W. *Opening doors through music.* Springfield, Ill.: Charles C Thomas, 1974.

Jones, M. *Social psychiatry.* New York: Penguin Books, 1969.

Knight, D., Pope, L., Ludwig, A., & Strazulla, M. The role of varied therapies in the rehabilitation of the retarded child. *American Journal of Mental Deficiency*, 1957, *61*, 508–515.

Kramer, E. *Childhood and art therapy.* New York: Schocken Books, 1979.

Kugel, R.B., & Wolfensberger, W. (Eds.). *Changing patterns in residential services for the mentally retarded.* Washington, D.C.: President's Committee on Mental Retardation, 1969.

Maloney, M.P., & Ward, R.P. *Mental retardation and modern society.* New York: Oxford University Press, 1979.

Moreno, J.J. Musical psychodrama: A new direction in music therapy. *Journal of Music Therapy*, 1980, *17*(1), 34–42.

Murphy, M.M. A large scale music therapy program for institutionalized low grade and middle grade defectives. *American Journal of Mental Deficiency*, 1958, *63*, 268–273.

Nirje, B. The normalization principle and its human management implications. In R.B. Kugel & W. Wolfensberger (Eds.), *Changing patterns in residential services for the mentally retarded.* Washington, D.C.: President's Committee on Mental Retardation, 1969.

Ross, J. Music therapy for urban institutions. *Music Journal*, 1970, *28*(10), 15–18.

Schattner, R. *Creative dramatics for handicapped children.* New York: John Day, 1967.

Shaw, A., & Stevens, C. (Eds.). *Drama, theatre, and the handicapped.* New York: American Theatre Association, 1979.

Spero, R., & Weiner, C. Creative arts therapy: Its application in special education programs. *Children Today*, 1973, *2*(4), 8–18.

Sternat, J., Messina, R., Nietupski, J., Lyon, S., & Brown, L. Occupational and physical therapy services for severely handicapped students. In E. Sontag, J. Smith, & N. Certo (Eds.), *Educational programming for the severely and profoundly handicapped*. Reston, Va.: Council for Exceptional Children, 1977.

Stone, N.D. Effecting interdisciplinary coordination in clinical services to the mentally retarded. *American Journal of Orthopsychiatry*, 1970, *40*(5), 835–839.

Valletutti, P.J., & Christoplos, F. (Eds.). *Interdisciplinary approaches to human services*. Baltimore: University Park Press, 1977.

Williams, G.H., & Wood, M.M. *Developmental art therapy.* Austin, TX: PRO-ED, 1977.

Williamson, G. The individualized education program: An interdisciplinary endeavor. In B. Sirvis, J.W. Baken, & G. Williamson (Eds.), *Unique aspects of the individualized educational program for the physically handicapped, homebound, and hospitalized*. Reston, Va.: Council for Exceptional Children, 1978.

Wolfensberger, W. *Normalization*. Toronto: National Institute on Mental Retardation, 1972.

Wolfensberger, W. *The principle of normalization in human services*. Toronto: National Institute on Mental Retardation, 1972.

Wolfgram, B.J. Music therapy for retarded adults with psychotic overlay: A day treatment approach. *Journal of Music Therapy*, 1978, *15*(4), 199–207.

Wolinsky, G.F. *Current theory and practices of professional team concepts*. Paper presented at the annual meeting of the Council for Exceptional Children, Los Angeles, April 1960.

Wolinsky, G.F. Interdisciplinary action on special education. *Exceptional Children*, 1961, *28*(11), 151–158.

Ethical and Clinical Standards of the Profession

There are underlying principles of professional practice and standards for professional conduct that the qualified music therapist agrees to follow upon being granted registration or certification. The following ethical and clinical standards are in accordance with the codes of ethical practice of the national organizations of a number of health professions:

1. *General Professional Ethics*

   - The music therapist performs only those functions for which he or she is qualified.
   - Research conducted by the music therapist shall be in accordance with the regulations governing the employing agency.
   - The music therapist shall actively maintain and improve his or her professional competence.

2. *Clinical Relations*

   - The music therapist shall respect and protect the legal and personal rights of the client.
   - The music therapist shall continually assess the appropriateness and attainability of treatment goals.
   - The music therapist shall use every available resource needed to effect established treatment goals, including referrals to other specialists when indicated.
   - The music therapist shall inform clients (where practicable) as to the purpose and nature of an evaluative or therapeutic procedure and (when applicable) communicate to clients their freedom of choice with regard to participation.

259

- The music therapist has the responsibility to carry out the therapeutic contract established with the client or with the institution (whichever obtains).
- The music therapist shall maintain objectivity in all matters concerning the welfare of the client.

3. *Relation to Other Personnel*

- The music therapist shall function with discretion and integrity in relations with other personnel and shall cooperate with them as may be appropriate.
- The music therapist shall have a working knowledge of the function of his or her colleagues and shall offer them instruction in the aims and practices of music therapy.

4. *Relation to Employing Agency*

- The music therapist shall abide by the policies of confidentiality governing the institution.
- The music therapist shall render service ethically and shall honor the property, integrity, and reputation of the employing agency.

Suppliers of Instruments and Other Equipment

The suppliers listed here are located in various areas of the United States and offer a full range of instruments and related equipment suitable and necessary for a music therapy program.

Supplier	Equipment Available
Childcraft Educational Corp. 20 Kilmer Road Edison, New Jersey 08817	Rhythm instruments
Children's Book and Music Center 5373 West Pico Boulevard Los Angeles, California 90019	Music therapy books, films, music, music books, records
Creative Playthings Princeton, New Jersey 08540	Rhythm instruments, nonmusic materials
Hohner Company, Inc. Andrews Road Hicksville, New York 11802	Orff instrumentarium by Sonor; rhythm instruments, song flutes, recorders (wood and plastic), Latin percussion instruments
Hohner Company, Inc. 545 Busse Road Elk Grove Village, Illinois 60007	(Same as above)
Hohner Company, Inc. 760 San Antonio Road Palo Alto, California 94303	(Same as above)
Hohner Company, Inc. 400 North Grove Richardson, Texas 75081	(Same as above)

Supplier	*Equipment Available*
Kitching Educational Division of Ludwig Industrials 1728 North Damen Drive Chicago, Illinois 60647	Drum sets (bass, snare), temple blocks, xylophones, tambourines, bells, and other percussion instruments, flutes and recorders
Latin Percussion 454 Commercial Avenue Palisades Park, New Jersey 07650	Latin percussion instruments
Malmark, Inc. 100 Doyle Street Doylestown, Pennsylvania 18901	Handbells
Mandile Wood Drums Hart Road Conway, Massachusetts 01341	Gato drums
Musik Innovations Box One Allison Park, Pennsylvania 15101	Orff instrumentarium by Sonor, resonator bells
Magnamusic-Baton, Inc. 10370 Page Industrial Boulevard St. Louis, Missouri 63132	Orff instrumentarium by Studio 49; music, therapy books, records, art and dance
Oscar Schmidt-International, Inc. Garden State Road Union, New Jersey 07083	Autoharps
Oscar Schmidt 1415 Waukegan Road North Brook, Illinois 60062	Autoharps
Rhythm Band, Inc. Post Office Box 126 Fort Worth, Texas 76101	Autoharps, cymbals, tone bells, gongs, recorders, "talking" slit drums, maracas, bongos, congas
Scientific Music Industries A Division of The Gabriel Co., Inc. 525 North Noble Chicago, Illinois 60622	Educator tone bars/resonator bells
Universal Musical Instruments Company 732 Broadway New York, New York 10003	All rhythm instruments, Omnichords, Casiotones, Autoharps, Pianos, Guitars
The World of Peripole, Inc. Browns Mills, New Jersey 08015	Resonator bells, Orff instrumentarium by Bergerault, rhythm instruments, records, music books

Index

About the Author

EDITH HILLMAN BOXILL, C.M.T., holds a master's degree in music therapy and a bachelor's degree in music. Currently the Director of Music Therapy at the Manhattan Borough Developmental Services Office of the State of New York Office of Mental Retardation and Developmental Disabilities in New York City and Adjunct Assistant Professor of Music Therapy at New York University, she is widely recognized as an authority on music therapy for the developmentally disabled. Among her many commitments in the field of music therapy, she has served as a member of the Board of Directors and as Chairperson of the Task Force on State Affairs of the American Association for Music Therapy, as Chairperson of the Creative Arts Therapies Special Interest Group of the American Association on Mental Deficiency, and as Legislative Chairperson of the New York State Creative Arts Therapies Coalition.

Professor Boxill is an author, lecturer, and consultant, who has been featured on television and national radio programs. Her articles in professional journals enjoy a broad audience and her Folkways record album on music therapy with the developmentally disabled is a unique contribution to the field.